POWER AND CULTURE

Ernst W. Gohlert

POWER AND CULTURE

THE STRUGGLE AGAINST POVERTY IN THAILAND

WHITE LOTUS
Bangkok   Cheney
1991

The publication of this book has been subsidized by Eastern Washington University; Cheney, WA, 99004; USA

White Lotus Co., Ltd.
26 Soi Attakarn Prasit
GPO Box 1141
Bangkok 10501

Published 1991. First edition

Printed in Thailand

Typeset by MCCO Graphics

90-071354

Library of Congress Cataloging in Publication Data

ISBN 974 8495-46-9   (White Lotus Co., Ltd; Bangkok)
ISBN 974 8495-46-7 pbk.   (White Lotus Co., Ltd.; Bangkok)
ISBN 1-879 155-00-1   (White Lotus Co., Ltd.; Cheney)
ISBN 1-879 155-01-x pbk   (White Lotus Co., Ltd.; Cheney)

CONTENTS

POWER AND CULTURE

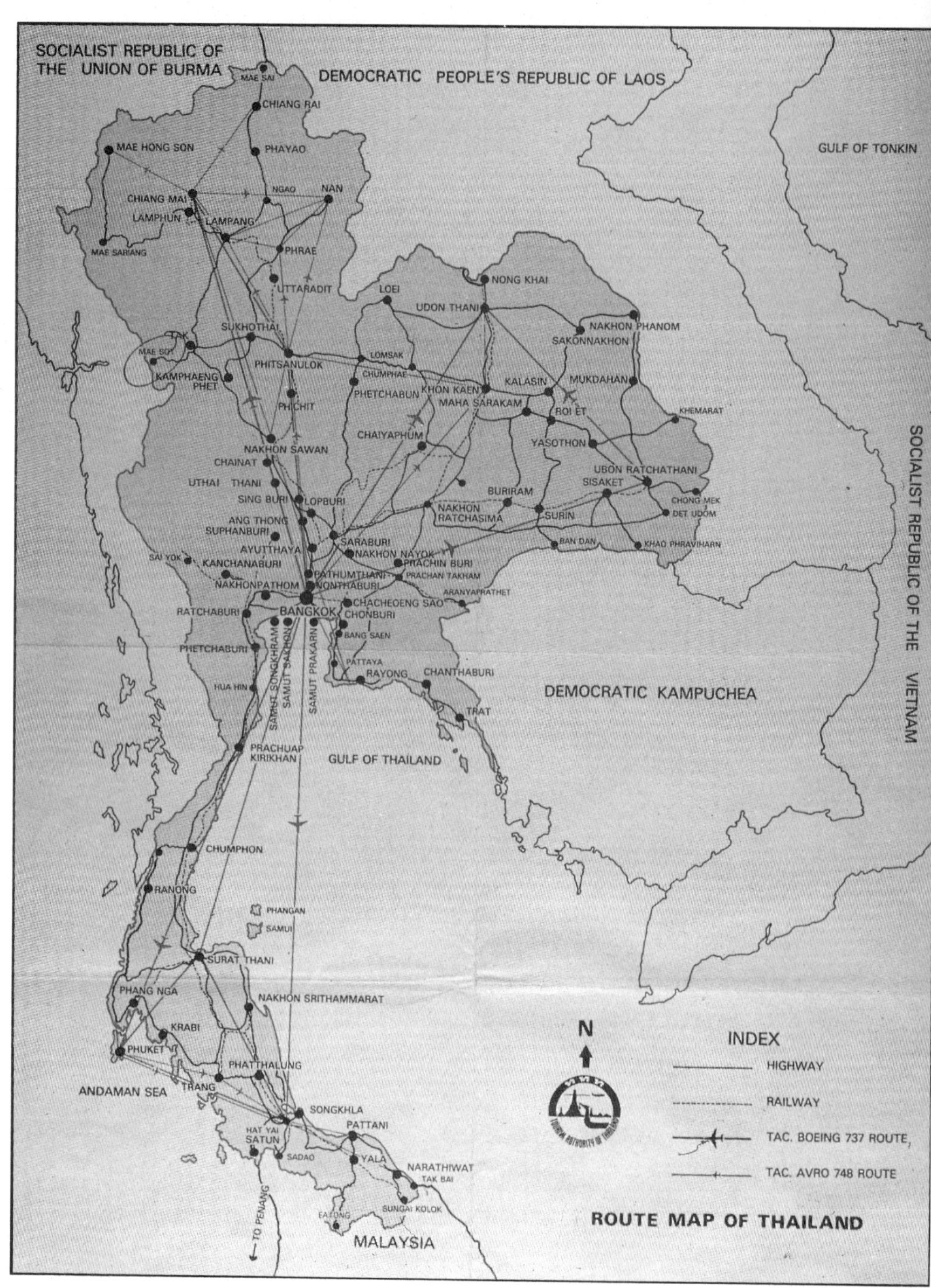

ROUTE MAP OF THAILAND

PREFACE

Power and poverty, as a rule, do not go together. People with power seldom are poor but the poor are always the underdogs, unless they know how to use their latent resources. To address the complexities of poverty and its manifestations—be it hunger, disease, lack of education, inadequate housing, crime or sheer desperation—therefore means to think and act in terms of power: calculating its origins, use and distribution.

The struggle against poverty in Thailand, as elsewhere, takes place on different fronts. The Thai government maintains that the plight of the villagers (more than 70% of the population) is unacceptable, and that the benefits of Thai society must be distributed more equitably. Its development programs are supported by foreign governments and international organizations, providing Thailand for the past three decades with development assistance ranging from foreign aid, technical assistance, trade agreements and international loans to joint venture capital.

Thailand's private sector is also part of the struggle. The business community and the non-profit organizations are helping to alleviate poverty. For example, business cooperates with the government, attempting to serve both its own and society's interests. Business advocates economic growth and expansion, calling for more jobs, more goods and more trade.

From the social fabric of society—motivated by different ideas and values—emerged another set of responses to the ills of society. These non-governmental and non-profit organizations (also referred to as private voluntary organizations or PVOs) work in agriculture, health, nutrition, education, community development and many related fields. They include religious groups, humanitarian agencies, academics, student organizations and social activists.

Yet, after several decades, untold development programs and billions of Baht, poverty in Thailand remains a desperate reality for more people than ever before. The poor are caught up in vicious cycles resulting from political and economic decisions plus unpredictable environmental conditions. The rural poor continue to migrate to urban slums, seeking work, food and shelter for themselves and their families.

This tragic state of affairs was allowed to develop by marginal efforts and outright failures in development programs throughout the world. In reaction, critical examination of the development enterprise and a general soul searching are now built into the profession. Project evaluation and development consulting has become a growth industry. Governments, international organizations and, to a lesser degree, private development agencies underwrite the continued employment of development experts by requiring studies of practically all facets of the development process.

POWER AND CULTURE

Unfortunately, lessons learned generally tend to be ignored by vested bureaucratic interests. Furthermore, conservative development approaches and strategies are not readily displaced by innovative concepts and proposals for revised priorities. Consequently, the status quo—the "business as usual" mentality—with the inevitable institutionalization and bureaucratization of development, remains intact.

After more than fifteen years of university teaching, including research on international development for the past five years with particular emphasis on the role of non-governmental development organizations, I welcome this opportunity to present the results of my study on NGOs. The analyses are based in part on data from selected NGO projects. I have studied a cross-section of some twenty foreign and indigenous NGOs, all of which are actively engaged in various facets of rural development in Thailand. (See Appendix)

Over a span of three years, interviews were conducted not only with NGO staff and field workers, but also with government officials and academics. In addition, I collected primary data during field trips involving extended stays in NGO project villages. And a survey of the Thai development literature in English translation yielded access to Thai perspectives on development.

The following chapters thus offer an interpretation of the nature and future direction of the development process in Thailand, highlighting the role of private development agencies—their strengths and shortcomings—compared to other organizational entities.

Conceptually, the analysis of Thailand's development community—which includes government, international, private and other agencies—centers on the idea of "comparative advantage." This is the claim frequently made by and on behalf of non-governmental organizations: that development funds are more effectively used by the voluntary sector. It is argued that NGOs frequently are better change agents because they tend to be small, efficient, flexible, innovative, non-political and relatively unburdened by bureaucracy.

Power and culture are the principal reference points of this study. These concepts are important to the overall analysis of the actual struggle against poverty. Indigenous culture is a crucial, frequently missing link in the development equation. The value dimension, which is generally ignored or misunderstood by mainstream development agencies, more often than not, is part of the "tool kit" of voluntary agencies. On the other hand, these organizations are less conversant in the language and practice of power.

Power, as manifested in the politics of development in Thailand, is herein examined in the social and historical context of Thai society. The cultural variable is interpreted primarily within the traditional value system, informed first and foremost by Theravada Buddhism.

Alternative development is another conceptual focal point. Here, inferences, major lessons, and likely future directions of Thai society are the main concerns.

10

Overall, this study addresses questions regarding the concept of development and the meaning of the process in relation to the day-to-day reality confronted by people living in Third World societies.

ACKNOWLEDGMENTS

The success of any research undertaking is contingent on the assistance and kind support of many people. This study is no exception. NGO directors, country representatives, program officers, administrative staff, project administrators, academics, and many other development professionals gave freely of their time. By sharing their thoughts and insights, they facilitated my efforts and made the work more enjoyable.

I am very much in their debt. Because of the guidance and the information provided to me, complex issues were clarified and the overall picture of the development community in Thailand was shaped. I also value the friendships which resulted from many formal interviews and innumerable informal discussions. These experiences made my work especially rewarding.

My deep appreciation extends to all those who have contributed in some way to this study. While it is not possible to name everyone, I am especially grateful to the following individuals and organizations for their invaluable cooperation and support: Khun Amporn Wathanavongs, Director of the Christian Childrens' Fund in Thailand (CCF.), and Khun Asa Kanchanahoti, Sponsor Relations Coordinator, extended their hospitality, introducing me to field projects and to village life in Thailand's Northeast. Warren Scale, Director of the Adventist Development and Relief Agenc,; and Dennis Tidwell, ADRA Project Director, also helped to extend my knowledge of development work at the grass-roots level.

CARE-Thailand welcomed my inquiries and field research on its projects in the North. Marshall E. French, CARE Country Director Mike Carroll, Field Representative and Sarote Roskunpanit, Project Manager, made it all possible. I am also indebted to Terje Thodesen, Resident Representative of REDD BARNA, for his advice.

My research on the role of Thai NGOs in rural development was made possible through the professional guidance and friendship of Dr. Seri Phongphit, Executive Director of the Thai Institute for Rural Development (THIRD); Surachet Vetchapitak, Director of the Rural Development Documentation Center (RUDOC); and Apichart Tongyou, Founder and Board Member of the Center for Culture and Development (CCD). They taught me about the Thai NGO movement and the Thai way of life.

I also wish to acknowledge my debt to several authors. The landmark studies of Robert Chambers, Norman Jacobs, Judith Tendler, Somboon Suksamran, Sulak Sivaraksa and William Klausner provided important insights and major reference points that guided my inquiry.

A word of special thanks is reserved for my two research assistants, Solot Sirisai from Mahidol University and Sasithorn Wongsason, current Project Coordinator for PACT and the SVITA Foundation. I would have been lost without their communication skills and their diligence in arranging my schedules. Their work, in turn, was made possible with the financial assistance provided by a grant from the Faculty Research Fund of Eastern Washington University.

The entire project benefited from a United States Information Agency University Affiliations Grant, and Eastern Washington University generously provided me with a one year professional leave to complete the study. I am most grateful for the opportunities extended to me.

Last, but not least, my wife Heide and our daughter Tanja, deserve an award for their patience and tolerance. I am also grateful for their encouragement.

In the end, any remaining errors and oversights are, of course, solely my responsibility.

ERNST W. GOHLERT

Chapter 1

THE POLITICS OF DEVELOPMENT

What do they know about us?

They know that we're infested with worms and other diseases, that we're undernourished, corrupt, that there're conflicts among us, that our wealthy men are extremely rich and our poor are frightfully poor, that there're thieves in high places as well as low. Knowing this they send us experts, money, and materials to help us develop ourselves along their way to success and material wealth in the name of modernization, progress and industrialization.

What? When have they been doing this? I've never seen anything coming my way. If I ever get their money or their help, what will they take from me? My rice, my land, my buffaloes? My...

I don't know for sure, but the aid is believed to be free.

> ("Village Teacher and an Old Man." Pira Sudham, *Siamese Drama.*)

The images conveyed by this exchange are not confined to Thailand. They are typical of Third World societies, weighed down by poverty, hunger, disease, corruption and other social and political ills, as their own and foreign governments are attempting to deal with these problems.

Although similar in these respects, Thai society has certain advantages. A distinct culture, shared religious beliefs and deep devotion to the monarchy and the the King, combined with a common history (without an overt colonial legacy) afford the Thai people access to important and distinct development resources.

Whether and how these assets are applied has a direct bearing on Thailand's future development. These responses, furthermore, entail potential lessons for other developing countries and their partners in the industrialized world.

Key variables, such as culture, society, politics, resources, history, etc., which are inherently linked to development, are distinctly Thai. An examination of Thai ways in development politics provides a map on which current trends as well as potential future direction of the society can be traced and projected.

POWER AND CULTURE

The benchmarks of Thai society include a Buddhist *Weltanschauung*, a cohesive pastoral culture with deep roots in Thai history, dominated by the monarchy and a pervasive bureaucracy. With increasing exposure to external (mainly Western) influences, other forces, including the military and foreign political and economic factors, assumed greater importance. However, in all respects there are connections to core behavioral values, deeply embedded in Thailand's collective past.

Background

Thailand, the former Siam, is full of dualisms and contradictions. It is a country of more than 53 million people (as recent as 1960 Thailand's population was only slightly more than 26 million people) simultaneously traditional and modern, agricultural and industrial, rural and urban, rich and poor. More than 70% of the population is classified as rural and most of the villagers who live in the Northeast of the country, a high and arid plateau with strong geographical, historical and cultural ties to the Laotian people are poor (80% of Thai farmers earn less than $350 per year).

In 1985, Thailand ranked number 93 out of 142 countries in terms of per capita GNP, with an annual average income of $770.[1] There is also a wide gap in income and living standards between the urban and rural sectors and between the various regions of the country. Government statistics for 1984 indicate that per capita income, compares as follows: Northeast, $320; North, $511, South; $608, Central, $846; and the Bangkok Metropolitan Area, $2,241.[2]

The gap in income and living standards is widening every year.[3] The statistics are representative of other gaping differences between the city and the village, the elites and the masses, and their respective norms and modes of behavior.

Thailand, the capital city in particular, shares all the problems of a modern, industrialized society: urban sprawl, slums, chaotic traffic conditions, equally appalling pollution, and rapidly progressing deterioration of the natural environment, particularly the forests.

Accustomed by its history to authoritarian rule, the movement towards a democratic form of government is of relatively recent origin, dating from the abolition of the absolute monarchy in 1932. However, since that time democracy has been adhered to only intermittently.

Historically, Thai society is more familiar with military rule, frequent coup d'etats (although as a rule of the less violent variety) and personalized political leadership, sharing power with the pervasive bureaucracy. Even now, with nominal parliamentary democracy in place, the actual distribution and the exercise of power remain in the hands of the military and the privileged few.

While the small middle class—largely Western educated technocrats—is growing, its role in political decision-making is very limited, in part because of its own apolitical values, which, if anything, tend to favor authoritarian governments with their assurance of order and stability.

Pluralism, a major element in Western political democracy, remains a surface phenomenon in Thailand, although effective citizens, initiatives on environmental issues in 1987 and 1988 may signal a qualitative change. Groups are allowed to exist; diverse organizations function; interests do coalesce; many publications are available (Thailand's press, though not free is considered the freest in all of Asia); and people speak their minds—up to a point.

> The extra-bureaucratic elements in Thai society—political parties, professional associations, the media, academics, labor unions, etc.—not only lack power, as was drastically revealed in October 1976; they also lack authority. In accepting (however reluctantly) a subordinate role, they conform, like Thai citizens and institutions in general, to Thai traditional values.[4]
>
> Consciousness of power on the part of the bureaucratic elite accompanied by consciousness of lack of power by the rest were the twin norms of Thai politics.[5]

Existing constraints on the pluralistic tendencies and modes of behavior arise only in part from Thai politics; they are also the product of traditional values, which emphasize conformity and consensus in decision-making. On the other hand, individual expression and non-conformist tendencies are also tolerated in the context of the traditional Thai family.

The institutions which account most for continuity, stability and an overall but increasingly fragile consensus in Thai society are the monarchy and religion. Without doubt, the King is the most revered, the most loved person. The Royal Family as a whole, is beyond public criticism or blame.

The present monarch, King Bumipol Adulyadej (Thailand's longest reigning monarch), enjoys the deep admiration and devotion of his subjects in part because of his abiding concern for the farmer, the hilltribes, and the poor. He maintains regular contact with his subjects in all walks of life—particularly those in need— and supervises many Royal Development Projects.

Buddhism, the other pillar of Thai society, more than 2,500 years old, remains the *leitmotiv* of the people, particularly in the rural areas. Although popular Buddhism in Thailand, which is a mixture of animistic beliefs (particularly adherence to spirits) and the teachings of the Sangha (the community of Buddhist monks), has lost some of its principal functions to the state, for example, education. Tt retains considerable influence over Thai spiritual as well as every day life. Naturally, religious beliefs and practices have become most fragile and superficial in the metropolis, the cauldron of modernity.

As suggested by the slogan "Nation, Religion, and King," Buddhism is integral to the essence of being Thai. Except for the Muslim minority in the southern-most part of the country, over 90% of the population is registered as Buddhist.

POWER AND CULTURE

Given the importance of religion in Thai society, Buddhism has been harnessed by the state as a major force in nation-building. The Buddhist establishment was co-opted by the state to serve as an integrating and protective element in Thai society. The protective role grows out of the security concerns of the military in its struggle with communist and separatist elements, particularly in Thailand's border regions.

More recently, a growing number of Buddhist monks independently seized the initiative in re-shaping traditional roles, or in some instances, adopting altogether new roles for themselves. These development monks have taken it upon themselves to become catalysts and active participants in the development process. The nature and scope of this movement is the subject of the last two chapters.

This brief introduction hints at a traditional, culturally rich society, increasingly subject to the maelstrom of manipulative, external influences, which are largely beyond its control.

Except for the top 10% of Thai society, the majority of the Thai people pay a high price for "development" in the name of industrialization and modernization. The "cost" of development continues to rise, unavoidably, as some would argue.

Against the backdrop of poverty, malnutrition, farm debt, landlessness, slums, crimes and drug abuse, it is difficult to imagine that there was a time when the Siamese were relatively well off; when people did not go hungry and did not have to leave the village in search of work in the city or abroad. Yet, the pre-modern period in Thai history also had its problems, including serfdom, quasi-feudal structures and frequent wars.

Despite the ongoing transformation of Thai society, traditional beliefs, attitudes and behavior patterns persist, particularly among the rural population. The most pronounced and enduring features of traditional Thai society pertain to social structure and cultural patterns.

A constantly shifting network of patron/client relationships remains at the base of the authority structure today. Consequently, people think in hierarchical terms; subordinates seek to please their bosses, and people expect to do and to receive favors. Thai society is rife with this type of behavior, often stigmatized by corruption, as it clashes with the forces of modernity.

Other elements of continuity include the value attached to personal relations, the fear of losing face, the importance of appearances and an element of distrust. These cultural norms play a significant role at major junctions of the development process.

Underdevelopment and its Causes

The following interpretation of the origins of the development dilemma faced by people the world over is not shared by mainstream development thought. However, this framework is particularly appropriate, because of its empirical relevance. It also represents a significant undercurrent in both Western and Thai development circles.

The resulting explanation of massive poverty—generally regarded as the hallmark of underdevelopment—in Thailand today focuses on external and internal factors.

Briefly, although Thailand was not formally subjected to the abuses and the humiliation of outright Western colonialism; it did not escape this influence entirely. Growing out of the historical context, which includes the manipulations by European powers in the 19th century (e.g., the Bowring Treaty of 1855) and the stratagems of Thai kings, Thailand has and continues to labor under a form of hidden colonialism in its relations with major world powers, particularly the United States and Japan.

Through tacit alliances, the powers that be at home and abroad fashioned major economic, political and military policies, which do not serve the interest of the people as a whole. Thus, following the pattern of many, if not most, Third World countries, Thailand is a micro version of the international system.

In the words of the foreign minister, Siddhi Savetsila, the country's foreign policy has… "spearheaded our emergence onto the world economic stage. Thai foreign policy will therefore continue to promote active cooperation with others on matters of common interest."[6]

Consequently, the interests of outside powers, principally major governments and multinational corporations, are looked after by Westernized, self-serving elites. The supporting evidence is provided by the government itself, its actions (as distinct from policy pronouncements) and its cost-benefit analysis.

As implied, responsibility for the current plight of Thailand's millions of poor cannot simply be attributed to "evil, outside forces;" rather, this state of affairs is also caused by factors and circumstances inherent in Thai society, culture and history, a topic which offers fertile ground for speculation and hypothesis.[7]

Through the eyes of political economists…

> …rural poverty is seen as a consequence of processes which concentrate wealth and power…In general, they agree that the processes which concentrate wealth and power operate at three levels: internationally, the richer countries have made and keep the poorer countries relatively poor…; internally, within the poorer countries, urban and especially urban middle class interests gain at the cost of rural interests,….; and within the rural areas themselves, the local elites landowners, merchants, moneylenders, and bureaucrats consolidate their power and wealth. For their part, the rural poor stand to lose relatively and often absolutely through all these processes.[8]
>
> In this view, then, the rich and powerful get richer and more powerful; and the poor become relatively and often absolutely poorer and weaker.[8]

There are also numerous environmental factors which must be taken into account, including problems in population growth and resource depletion. From this perspective rural poverty is interpreted more in terms of what is physical, visible, technical, and statistical common sense. The two most commonly cited causes of poverty are population growth and pressures on resources and the environment.[10]

> The truth is that there are many causes of rural poverty; that it is difficult to judge to what extent one or more may be primary; that the balance of their significance varies over time, by season, and by country, region, community, village, household and individual; and that not only causes of poverty but opportunities for wealth are points of departure for rural development.[11]

According to another prominent thesis, Thailand has been able to achieve a level modernization but not development because, unlike Japan, Thai society is patrimonial in nature, i.e., it is qualitatively different due to inherent constraints.[12] This thesis maintains that the shortcomings of the development process are a function of culture and power, i.e., particular values and patterns of behavior which are inimical to conventional development norms.[13]

Thai Government Development Policies in Perspective

The Thai government's concern, expressed through public policy, on the subject of widespread poverty and underdevelopment, is of fairly recent origin, beginning with the first national development plan nearly 30 years ago. However, even if one were to ignore the time lag, the record is marked by governmental neglect, political expediency and mostly ineffectiveness.[14]

Following the adoption of Prime Minister Kukrit's *tambon* revolving fund scheme, which entitled rural areas to a larger share of national resources, the 1970s saw the enactment of two potentially significant pieces of legislation, the Land Rent Control Act of 1974 and the 1975 Land Reform Act. However, the record shows that rural poverty was not reduced, nor did meaningful land reform occur, and the only beneficiaries were local elites. The other major side effect of these policies was increased corruption.

From the late 1970s on Thai development policy was motivated mainly by explicit national security concerns, which in 1980 culminated in the adoption of Policy Order 66/2523. The measure called for a political strategy in fighting communist insurgents.

As a result, subsequent development programs—especially under the Fifth Social and Economic Development Plan (1982-86)—accelerated infrastructure improvements, particularly in the border regions. Ironically, this policy had the effect of rewarding rural communities which could demonstrate insurgent activity by providing electricity and new or improved roads. Villages without "communists" were not so lucky.

However, even prior to this shift, another priority of national development programs became apparent. Although the rhetoric highlighted the need to address the causes of poverty, especially rural poverty, the actual decisions of the government were guided by economic considerations which reflected the interests of the urban elites.

This position—favoring urban-led growth—has become a mainstay of the Thai government development policy in the 1980s. According to Thammasat University economist Prayong Netyarak:

> Government policy relating to rural development [has] failed to achieve its objectives because it [has] been determined in an urban context.
>
> The government [has] spent very little on rural development—some 6 per cent of the entire national expenditure budget—and [has] enforced policies which effectively brought down the income of farming families and further widened the gap between rural and urban populations.[15]

A review of current development policy in agriculture and commerce further underscores the government's priorities, which contrary to public pronouncements, do not favor rural interests.

A case in point is the government's Paddy Price Support Program, which is intended to allow farmers, with the aid of low-interest loans, not to sell their rice when prices are low. Some 5,000 million baht ($200 million), generated by commercial banks, has been set aside for this purpose.

While this policy appears to be a major boon to the farmer, in reality few farmers qualify for the low-interest loans. After periods of severe drought most of Thailand's small farmers, particularly those in the Northeast, do not have any paddy to pawn or mortgage. In other words, the loans are contingent on the availability of rice for sale. Consequently, only the well-to-do farmers and middlemen, including millers, stand to benefit from the government's program.

While giving the government the benefit of the doubt, the Paddy Price Support Program turns out to be another misconceived effort that fails to accomplish its stated objectives. It has been suggested that a temporary job creation program for drought-stricken farm communities should have been adopted instead.[16]

Commenting editorially on the Price Support Program, the conservative *Bangkok Post* observed:

> Despite all the efforts undertaken by the Government to alleviate their plight, today's farmers still live from hand to mouth with uncertain prospects. This may well be because some efforts were not targeted in the right direction.[17]

POWER AND CULTURE

Thai Government Development Policy in the Commercial Sector

The situation is rather different for the business community which is closely allied with the government, the military and the bureaucracy. After years of impressive growth based on government promotion of the manufacturing and service sectors of the economy to strengthen and expand export and tourism, Thai business leaders eyed the prospect of pushing Thailand into the ranks of the Newly Industrialized Countries (NICs).

There can be little doubt as to the direction chosen by the power brokers, particularly since the population employed in agriculture has been declining (from 83% in 1960, to 69.5% in 1984) and with the total share of agriculture in the country's GNP dropping from 39.8% in 1960 to 19.5% in 1984. Agriculture's 19.5% share compares to the modern sector (primary services) with 64.9% and the infrastructure sector with 15.6% in 1984.[18]

The critical observer may well be excused, thinking that the Thai economy is subservient to the international economic system. In order to survive and prosper in this system, national economies have to accept certain rules that may not be in the interest of the majority of the people.

Cheap labor, a docile work force, no strikes and generally favorable labor practices, along with readily available natural resources, are conditions very much sought after by international business and the major foreign powers. A quick perusal of some economic facts confirms that Thailand scores high in all of the areas mentioned.

For example, labor costs in Taiwan exceed those of Thailand by a factor of six. The minimum wage in Thailand, as of 1986, ranges from 73 baht ($2.92) for the Bangkok metropolitan area and in the industrial/commercial regions of the country (including Phuket and Chiangmai), to 61 baht ($2.44) per day in the rural provinces.[19]

Factories in Thailand are allowed to operate in three shifts around the clock whereas in Malaysia and Singapore, 16—hour days are enforced by law. Except for the brief period between 1973 and 1976 when strikes were a daily occurrence in Thailand, the work force is no longer militant, with only an estimated five percent represented by unions.

These are economic conditions which help to assure a favorable reputation in financial circles abroad and hardship at home. A noted foreign business consultant with excellent credentials in Thai academic, business and government circles, acknowledged that "...the country exploits its own labor cost," adding that "...Thailand is really in a growth mode—tremendous development and expansion."[20]

Thai society is also credited with the "right" cultural values and attitudes:

In particular, Theravada Buddhism puts a high value on the avoidance of personal conflict (Thais rarely express extreme emotions), and on the accumulation of merit in this life for the benefit of the next. This, together with an instinctive neatness and no post-colonial chips-on-the-shoulder about foreigners, goes a long way towards explaining the Thais' special talent for service.[21]

It is evident that Thailand's economic advantages in the international economy are purchased at the expense of the industrial work force and the farmers. In fact, government policies do not only compound the problems of underdevelopment, they are part of the problem.

To be sure, there is also a positive side to government performance. Selectively, benefits have accrued even to rural areas; for instance, in the form of improved access to hospitals, better communications, electricity, new roads and some curbs on the influence of middlemen.

Unfortunately, even "progress" has a dark side: improved access to the village has opened the floodgates to consumer goods on hire-purchase schemes, which, in no small way, contribute to the growing indebtedness of farm communities.

Aside from the introduction of consumerism, agriculture has been commercialized. Materialism, environmental problems, erosion of indigenous culture and technology, as well as the emergence of local elites, are by-products of modernization and "progress" offered by the government and other outside forces.

Thammasat economist Chirmsak Pinthong, assessing the current Sixth National Development Plan (1987-1992), adds to the critique of present public sector development policies with an outline of the Plan's principal features and its likely consequences. In his view the government's blueprint:

- Supports large agribusiness ventures,
- Allows for further forest encroachments,
- Continues with an overall basic needs strategy,
- Restricts NGOs to traditional welfare type roles in development (continuing in effect a long-term policy of subordinating or streamlining NGOs to government programs)
- Turns farmers into wage laborers, compounding the problem of rural/urban migration.[22]

Assessment

It is not surprising to find the government portraying its policies as "balanced," promoting "integrated development in the economic, social and political spheres," in order to "reduce social inequality through improvement of public participation in development as well as by giving people opportunities to advance in society." In addition, the government's policies are professed to "promote democracy at all levels."[23]

Aside from the obvious discrepancies between the rhetoric and the current level or lack of true development in Thailand, there are other, equally troubling concerns that derive from the Thai social context.

POWER AND CULTURE

Given the pervasiveness and deep roots of particular values and related behavior patterns; for example, the patron/client system,[24] the presumed inability to cooperate horizontally, distrust in personal relationships, belief in the law of Karma, and lack of discipline, what are the implications for future development? To what extent, if at all, do these beliefs and modes of behavior inherently circumscribe the nature and scope of Thai development?

Concerns of this sort tend to be voiced occasionally by people outside the government. It is an exceptional occurrence for Thai political leaders to address this subject. Bangkok Governor Chamlong Srimuang, speaking at a seminar on "Thai Youth and Quality of Life Development," made the argument that selfishness is the most intractable trait of the Thai people which hinders development, and went on to give the following advice:

> For Thai youth of today to develop their quality of life, besides the four basic necessities of life, they should also develop a sense of responsibility towards society as a whole.
>
> The present situation with a large number of selfish adults who are corrupting our society is already bad enough ...and if today's youth copy the same lifestyle, our future can be very dim and even worse than now.
>
> When we look at things around us, we may boast that our country is 'so developed'. Materially this is true because we have high-rise buildings, escalators, glass lifts everywhere but have we ever stopped to think why we are not yet really developed?

Concluding, he stressed that selfishness or selflessness among citizens is still the most important ingredient in any country's development, because selfishness can lead to disastrous action such as corruption. "I have one motto for today's youth: Eat a little, spend a little and work a lot, anything left should be for society as a whole."[25]

This study rests on the assumptions that all development is normative, relative and political in nature. In other words, the development of society entails qualitative as well as quantitative aspects within parameters determined by each society through political means. Consequently each society has to settle implicitly on its own definition of development and determine its direction accordingly, based on existing human and natural resources.

In Thailand, all crucial decisions regarding the development of the country have been the purview of the privileged few, thus preventing a more representative approach to the collective future of the country. Partially in defense against further erosion of indigenous culture, a counter-current to the government's Western concept and approaches to development—spawned and carried largely by the problems resulting from government policies—has emerged.

In view of the current constellation of power in Thai society—most of it concentrated at the top—whether this dissenting force will be sufficient to bring about a major redirection of conventional development policies, is an open, if not very promising, question.

However, all things considered, Thailand may well go its own way in pursuit of a more meaningful, humane development, taking into account both material and spiritual needs, along with a commitment to the natural environment.

The following reminder by Robert Chambers, on lessons learned, could be addressed to policy makers. It also leads to the next topic—the role of non-governmental organizations in development:

As is very well known, the development thinking of outsiders has shifted from the view that growth and modernization would be enough, with benefits trickling down to the poor, to the more realistic if depressing view that sometimes growth and modernization make the poor poorer; that the main gain from increased agricultural production often goes to urban populations and the rural rich; and that the better off and more powerful benefit more from rural services than do the poor and weak.[26]

CARE Mae Chaem, Chiang Mai Province, Agroforestry and Nutritional Project—development workers interviewing Villagers.

CCF community development project Don Pueng, Ubol Provinces—sponsored children and cement water tank in background

Chapter 2

THAILAND'S DEVELOPMENT COMMUNITY

The poorer rural people, it is said, must help themselves; but this, trapped as they are, they often cannot do. The initiative, in enabling them better to help themselves, lies with outsiders who have more power and resources and most of whom are neither rural nor poor.

(Robert Chambers, *Rural Development: Putting the Last First*)

Thailand's development community mirrors the humanitarian aspirations of the international system. It represents a kaleidoscope of potentially powerful agents of change and its raison d'etre is to affect improvements for the better—to enhance the quality of life for millions of poor, often hopeless people throughout the Third World.

Humanitarianism and idealism, joined ever so often to political will, provide the impetus to action which can make a difference in peoples' lives. After World War II, the human impulse to protect the less fortunate, those in need, was translated into practice by numerous national and international relief agencies. Although focused initially on war-torn Europe, attention was soon drawn to the plight of the former colonies.

On balance, pragmatism had as much or more to do with the institutionalization of international aid as did humanitarian and idealistic motives. Simply put, political self-interest on the part of the major Western powers—which reasoned that poverty and underdevelopment threaten democratic and capitalistic values, as well as international peace and security—prompted the establishment of aid and development programs. These in turn evolved into an expansive administrative apparatus.

At the country level throughout the Third World, scaled-down versions of the international system came into existence, implementing bi- and multi-lateral aid programs in collaboration with host government agencies.

In Thailand, the only country in Southeast Asia which escaped colonization, if not the influence of colonialism, domestic (particularly rural) development programs are of recent origin (dating from the early 1960s), largely in response to national and international security considerations. Of course, external assistance, in the form of foreign (mainly military) aid, has been a major aspect of Thai post-war foreign relations. Later massive amounts of money were invested in an effort to build and expand the country's physical infrastructure as part of the struggle against communism.

As an ally of the United States, the Thai government and particularly the military establishment sharing the American view of international communism allowed the country to become rapidly integrated into the global capitalistic system, in return for substantial economic benefits—foreign aid from the West, international (World Bank) financing of major capital projects, as well as access to markets abroad.

Thus, as far as its origins are concerned, the development community in Thailand is not atypical. Aid and development programs were initiated primarily for political and military reasons and only secondarily with altruistic and humanitarian considerations in mind. This explains why the plight of the villagers was ignored for so long by the government. Only after the threat of communist subversion fully materialized did the government move on the poverty issues. Relief aid and development activities became instruments for people in power to stay in power.

The practice of serving select, narrow interests at the expense of the community is but one of many problems which characterize the development process. Since all development activities are by nature interventions, confrontation between individual values, cultural, social, economic and political systems is axiomatic. The subjects of the intervention the people, their values, their culture and their lifestyle—therefore, are always at risk.

Examining the record of post-war international development, it is not unreasonable to ask who has benefited most, the development agencies (both public and private), the aid bureaucracies (at the national and international levels), universities, consulting enterprises, the business community and the privileged segments of society in general—or the poor? Since the legions of the world's poor are still here and their number is growing, the answer is not difficult to discern.

Imbalance is one of the obvious features of the development "business"—power is concentrated rather than shared. The international debt situation is a case in point. Today more money (in the form of interest payments) flows from the Third World to the industrialized societies than the other way around. Similarly, at the micro level, urban elites extract subsidies from the rural sector.

Biases in Development

Robert Chambers' analysis of these issues, highlighting the different types of biases that characterize the aid establishment generally, including Thailand, provides a useful introduction to the principal features of the development community, with special emphasis on the role of non-governmental organizations.

Conventional development inherently leads to the introduction of unfamiliar, even alien elements into the lives of people, the presumed beneficiaries. This applies also to local or indigenous change agents. In fact, there will always be a gap between the development community on the one hand and the beneficiaries on the other, particularly as long as conventional conceptions of development persist. To reduce this gap, the change agents need to become aware of their biases.

There are many types of biases as well as preconceived notions that affect the nature, quality and the ultimate outcome of development programs. For example, foreigners expectedly are particularly prone to a wide range of notions that do not facilitate the complex tasks of the development professional.

> Foreigners are also urban-based and urban-biased. Foreigners in third world countries who are concerned with rural development and rural poverty include staff in voluntary agencies and aid organizations, technical cooperation personnel of various sorts, and consultants.[1]

Most development practitioners also tend to think principally in terms of projects. This particular bias cuts across the entire development community because projects are convenient categories which help to organize an otherwise messy task.

> Rural development and rural research have a project bias.... Ministries, departments, district staff, and voluntary agencies all pay special attention to projects and channel visitors towards them. Contact and learning are then with tiny atypical islands of activity, which are repeated and mutually reinforcing attention.[2]

Unfortunately, ironic as it may seem, most development experts do not have a high opinion of the people whose interest they are supposed to have at heart. This patronizing attitude finds expression in what Chambers calls "development tourism" and outright disrespect for the poor.

> The persons with whom rural development tourists, local-level officials, and rural researchers have contact, and from whom they obtain impressions and information, are biased against poorer people.[3]

This version of elitism, furthermore, extends all the way to the grass roots level where progressive farmers, village leaders, headmen, traders, religious leaders, teachers, and para-professionals discriminate and look down upon their own people. As a result, "The poor are often inconspicuous, inarticulate and unor-ganized."[4]

There is also the dominant male perspective and the preference for what is visible and accessible. "Dead children are rarely seen. Much of the worst poverty is hidden by its removal."[5]

Many factors thus conspire to ensure that the poorest people are most seen at precisely those times when they are least deprived; and least seen when things are at their worst.[6]

Often politeness and shyness—"diplomatic biases" - as any visitor to the homes of the poor—be it in a village or in an urban slum - knows, tend to get in the way of effective communication and learning the facts. "Courtesy and cowardice combine to keep tourists and the poorest apart." [7]

Yet another set of prejudicial behavior, which is common among development specialists, derives from professional biases:

> ...agricultural extension staff trained to advise on cash crops or to prepare farm plans are drawn to the more 'progressive' farmers; ...[8]

Being the expert—having access to scientific knowledge, associated with major universities and other powerful institutions—often leads development specialists to ignore or look down on traditional sources of knowledge and wisdom. The benefit of the doubt tends to be given to the scientific, the tangible elements. Development workers often fail to realize that "Rural people's knowledge and modern scientific knowledge are complementary in their strengths and weaknesses." Combined they may achieve what neither would alone.[9] Thus, "The arrogance of ignorant educated outsiders is part of the problem."[10]

One way to address some of these issues is to encourage a systemic, interdisciplinary approach to development:

> Professionals should neither confine themselves to their own disciplinary territory nor fear trespass in that of others. If they are to see the gaps and help the rural poor to exploit them, outsider professionals have to be explorers and multi-disciplinarians.[11]

Discussion

Development biases are deeply entrenched. They are integral elements of the aid establishment. To overcome these barriers is one of the foremost challenges of the new development professionalism.

In the day-to-day world of development politics the preferred scenarios are overshadowed by quantitative development (materialism, commercialism, consumerism) and related outcomes such as non-equitable growth, social injustices, cultural pollution, spiritual confusion and environmental degradation. Of course no single factor accounts for this state of affairs. However, once we realize that the instrument, i.e., the development community with its extensive organizational apparatus, is a component part of the very system it is designed to change, a principal source of development pathology has been identified.

International development, at least when conventionally conceived and implemented, is not the solution to underdevelopment, rather it is part of the problem. In short, the development establishment needs to be transformed through a redistribution of power. Thailand's own development community is no exception.

The true features of the development establishment—its structure, functions and policies—are reflected in the conceptual triad of power, culture and development, which may be used to construct a hypothetical "power grid," consisting of concentric circles of "players," ranging from the core, the most powerful actors (government agencies, large bureaucracies), to the least influential participants, the poor, who provide rationale and legitimacy to the development apparatus.

In the periphery surrounding the core actors, a large number of other players with various degrees of influence cooperate and compete with each other. This group consists of foreign aid missions and international organizations, as well as the representatives of practically all sectors of society, including private enterprise (business and corporate entities) non-profit organizations (NGOs), foundations and religious bodies, universities and think tanks, democratic institutions including parliament, political parties and interest groups, the media, and finally the public and individual citizens.

The society and its culture, broadly conceived, establishes overall parameters, according to which the development "game" is played. In Thailand, an overwhelmingly Buddhist country, even though modernity is rapidly making inroads, the rules of the game derived originally from customary values and standards. To a considerable degree, the collective experience of the Thai people continues to shape their thinking. To understand Thai society and Thai politics, including the politics of development, requires familiarity with the social and cultural context including values and their history.

The development policies applied to society are the outcome of interaction between diverse players (the powerful and the weak) who generate and themselves are subjected to dynamic forces. Subordinated to the international development system (which is part of the international economic, political and other interrelated systems), the Thai development community seeks to maximize its own interests in the name of development for the entire society.

For example, the development strategy of the government firmly commits the country to policies of economic growth and expansion through greater reliance on the production and export of industrial goods, as well as cash crops produced preferably by corporate agro-business. Corollary policies limit financial credit to well-to-do farmers, keep wages down for industrial workers and generally favor the urban over the rural sector of society.

From a society-wide point of view, who, one may ask, is looking out for the interests of the majority of the people? More than 70% of the people still live in villages, and more than one third of the population lives in the Northeast, the most impoverished part of the country.

There are other players—principally in the private, non-profit sector—who are committed to quality development, but they do not make policy because they lack conventional power. Unable to enforce their will, they attempt to reason, to teach and to lead by example. They are the gadflies of the system.

This melange then is the backdrop for the following descriptive portrait—including critique and analysis—of the aid community in Thailand. While the discussion includes profiles of all the principal members of Thailand's development community, the emphasis throughout is on the role of the private, non-profit sector, based on the hypothesis that the non-governmental development agencies have the greatest potential for alternative development.

Development by Bureaucracy

The government "owns" national development in the sense that the political system reserves the right to control as much or as little as it chooses in the name of development. Generally, it decides to control more rather than less.

Depending on the nature of the political system—whether democratic or authoritarian—the development arena will be shared to various degrees with potential change agents from other sectors of society at home and abroad. The resulting relationships among members of the development community, therefore, are always relatively contingent on the general political climate and particularly the objectives and policies of the government.

Thailand, described as a "half-way democracy",[12] which followed years of political instability and military rule, did not fully enter the fray of development politics until the mid 1960s. Prior to this neither the government nor anyone else mounted large scale development efforts. A cynic might suggest, with some justification, that this was the case not only because of the dictatorial nature of the government, but also because major development problems did not exist until after the government became fully engaged in economic development.

Today, development politics—planning and administration—is big business for the Royal Thai Government. Four main ministries—Interior, Agriculture, Health and Education—numerous departments (e.g., the Community Development Department) and bureaucratic sub-divisions, plus a central planning agency—the National Economic and Social Development Board (NESDB)—along with review and control mechanisms such as the Department of Technical and Economic Cooperation (DETEC), represent the core of the government's development machinery.

However, this brief listing is only the tip of the proverbial iceberg. The national level agencies have their provincial and local counterparts through which programs have to pass before they reach the project level.

The Community Development Department (CDD), located in the Ministry of the Interior, is a case in point. CDD maintains nine Regional Community Development Centers charged with "rendering support and service to development projects in the region" and "to serve as Community Development Technical Assistance Center[s]."[13]

For example, Community Development Center, Region 3, located in Ubol Ratchathani in Northeastern Thailand, was the first CD Center, established in 1962 as the "Thai-SEATO Regional Community Development Assistance Center." Collecting data, running pilot projects, offering training courses, publicizing new ideas in rural development and serving as an office of inspection in Region 3 are among the specific functions performed by the agency. The latter responsibility includes supervision of all NGO activities and projects under its jurisdiction.

The following staff and organizational arrangements, provide an idea of the size and self-importance of the agency:

The administration of the Community Development Center, Region 3, Ubol is under the leadership of a senior official of the Community Development Department, Ministry of the Interior. This is a senior post of level 8 according to the position classification system. The occupant of this position is normally promoted to the rank of provincial governor or deputy director-general when his term [ends].

The director of CDC, Region 3 is assisted by 9 senior development officials who head 9 sections of the Center. They are the sections of the Secretariat, Supervision and Evaluation, Training, Community Education, Rural Engineering, Occupation Development and Marketing, Child Development, Youth Development and Women Development.[14]

Not until the adoption of the Fifth National Development Plan beginning in 1982, did community development emerge as a major focus of government policy, specifying "the role of village-level committees and village volunteers, especially in the field of primary health care."[15]

Again, this program, or more accurately the problems associated with it, are indicative of persistent shortcomings which continue to handicap government effectiveness in the development sector. One observer lists three major "limitations":

Firstly, many local government officials do not yet understand the concept of development. They are more used to governing the people than letting the people tell them what should be done. Secondly, the government civil service is still plagued by bureaucracy, incompetence and corruption. The most important limitation, however, is that government programmes stress material and environmental development rather than development of social consciousness at the community level, which is necessary for real social development.[16]

POWER AND CULTURE

In its relations with other members of the development community, for instance, the private profit and non-profit sectors,

> The Thai government,...expresses itself quite clearly that the role of private sectors in the development process would be very much appreciated. Yet what is meant concretely by the private sectors is rather private enterprises, such as banks, multinational corporations and others. Little is mentioned of ... NGOs for development...[17]

The private sector, for its part, is principally concerned about the government's excessive red tape, extensive clearances and controls for projects, the *mai pen rai* (a Thai expression, which usually means "it doesn't matter") attitude of many officials, the expectation of money under the table, and similar problems.

Government-to-government relations in the development sector are similarly afflicted. A recent study evaluating the USAID-Thailand Co-Financing Program addressed this concern, pointing out the need for streamlined, less time-consuming procedures in the development project cycle.[18]

Why are governments seemingly intent on complicating and hindering the very processes which they pronounce as central to their overall development policies? The answer, at least in part, comes from the realization that the Thai or any other government is not a homogeneous entity—it does not even begin to speak with one voice—and that the resulting policies, therefore, are often by definition, incompatible, even contradictory.

In general, most members of the Thai aid community view the government with reserve while at the same time maintaining good working relations. Of course, the working relationships between government agencies vary considerably over time, from case to case, and according to the issues involved.

By far the most skeptical "partners" of the government are the small, indigenous NGOs, which historically have been viewed by the government with a great deal of suspicion because of their close ties at the village level. Particularly after the 1976 coup, many NGO leaders were branded communists by the authorities, causing them to go into the jungle. Although the political climate has improved considerably for NGOs, uneasiness and lack of trust are still evident.

Under the government of Prime Minister Prem Tinsulanonda, attempts were made by both sides to improve relations and to set up a central coordinating mechanism.

In 1981, during the first major gathering of Thai NGOs, in Pathumthani Province, it was stressed (albeit not unanimously) "...that coordination with government agencies is necessary." Despite references to the "suspicious attitude of government officials towards NGOs" and "conflicts," the seminar participants recommended the establishment of a "joint working committee between government agencies and NGOs, ...to promote good relation[s] and cooperation with equal footing and each with full autonomy."[19]

It was also recommended at the conclusion of the seminar, which was opened by the Deputy Minister of Interior, that:

- Attempt should be made [by] the government to recognize NGOs more than it does now;
- NGOs should make an effort to approach the government and maintain good working relation;
- NGOs should present problems to the government regularly together with suggestions;
- When situation[s] of conflict arise, NGOs should play a supplementary role in trying to solve [them];
- NGOs should acquaint themselves with the political conditions of targeted communities.[20]

At the follow-up NGO meeting at Thammasat University in May, 1983, 70 representatives from 45 organizations, including representatives from 6 government agencies, a report was adopted recommending the establishment of a Joint Working Committee between NGOs and government agencies. One of the main functions of the Committee is: "To promote development work and coordination, including to further improve the relationship between NGOs and Government Agencies."[21]

On behalf of the Government, the National Economic and Social Development Board (NESDB) took the lead in supporting these NGO initiatives. Some NGO leaders have suggested with hindsight that the NESDB was principally interested in setting up a joint committee to harness the NGO community as a resource for the preparation of the National Development Plan. They point to the fact that the committee has been essentially inactive since the adoption of the plan.

A hypothetical "political" sociogram of the Thai development community would most likely display the following features:

- an interdependent set of players, with various degrees of influence, dominated by government agencies;
- a complex political relationship between domestic and foreign government development agencies, the host government deriving its power by controlling "access" and governmental aid missions basing their clout on economic muscle;
- power wielded by public sector agencies, being conventional in nature, i.e., it is derived from the traditional authority and legitimacy of the state, as opposed to influence that flows from the community.
- although relatively insignificant in terms of conventional power, the small, non-profit private sector, wielding considerable influence of its own, based on its grass-roots orientation.

POWER AND CULTURE

On balance, measured in terms of effectiveness and qualitative results in development, the "political" sociogram would reveal an inverted pyramid, contrasting the limited (principally due to lack of resources), but effective influence of a small local NGO sector with the extensive reach and power of the government's development bureaucracy.

Given the central position of the development bureaucracy in Third World societies, some observers warn against the "... danger of becoming 'development for bureaucracy' and not 'bureaucracy for development', arguing even that the state development apparatus "...has transformed itself into a 'monster' with a life of its own and with such tendency for continually getting bigger and bigger..."[22]

These developments are especially deplorable, because:

> Experience of this extensive overemphasis on the role of the state in national development with particular reference to developing countries has clearly shown that it has failed to deliver expected development results and has created additional problems. Of particular importance is the fact that the people themselves, who are the most important target for development, have not benefited from development commensurate with increased and increasing efforts on the part of the state....Thus relevant questions such as what development is for or even why development, have continued to be unanswered and, in fact, have less often been raised.[23]

As the discussion below will indicate, trends in Thailand do not support this pessimistic assessment, at least not at this time.

The Power Behind the Scenes

Thailand has a long history of military strongmen running the government, with coup d'etats a common occurrence in Thai politics. For several reasons, including the fact that Thai society has become more modern (Western) in outlook and increasingly more sophisticated in the conduct of public affairs, the military, during the 1980s, also opted for more subtle ways to wield power. Indications are that the application of brute force to influence or control internal politics is considered outdated in leading military circles.

Of course none of these developments have changed the overall distribution of political power. The military's association with the establishment continues to be the major source of political power in Thai society—power which, as necessitated by circumstance, is increasingly shared with business elites and supported by technocrats. Nonetheless, power remains concentrated in the hands of the few.[24]

An observant Thai citizen writes:

Everyone will agree that after the student uprising of October 14, 1973, the ruling class has learnt its lesson and become more responsible in their [sic] public duties and roles. However, they are still a long way from conscious responsibility. The authoritarian game is being played in a different manner, in which the ruling elite has gone underground and enjoys spending public money for their own personal interests.[25]

The fact that military influence has been given a more business-like face and that it is wielded in cooperation with other elites also reflects changes in the very nature of power. The military, by definition, is the wielder of conventional power, power derived mainly from physical control over human and material resources.

While the potential application of force—the element of threat—remains the major source of power, it is no longer the only source. Furthermore, as demonstrated by the complex challenges posed by development in all its dimensions (economic, political, social and cultural), military solutions are no solutions at all; they only compound existing problems.

As the guardian of Thailand's national security and thus of fundamental interests of Thai society, the military lays claim to a large share of the government's responsibilities for national development. Following largely the model pioneered in the 1950s in other developing countries, the army's role (the other military branches do not play a prominent role) is concentrated on infrastructure development and civic campaigns.

Most recently, prompted by the King, military resources were mobilized to battle the effects of a prolonged drought in the Northeast. Headlines in Bangkok proclaimed "Army ready to launch 'Green Revolution'." However, then Army Commander-in-Chief General Chavalit Yongchaiyudh cautioned:

The work will be a special task and the Army has no intention of expanding its role in the future to interfere in the work of other government agencies...[26]

The General also said that "The army was part of the government led by General Prem...and it knew its responsibilities were limited."[27]

Working through the military the government intends to "... spend 13,968 million baht ($558 million) on water projects and reforestation schemes in the region. Of that figure, 2,000 million baht ($80 million) will be invested in short- and medium-term development plans between 1987-88 and 1988-91."[28]

Assessing these developments, the editors of the *Bangkok Post* observed:

It is natural that the government agencies who have done their best with limited resources should now feel suspicious of military involvement in civilian development work. They need not. [in part because of the assurances given by the Army Commander-in-Chief].

Of course there will be skeptics, but the physical resources of the military, knowledge and experience of the civilian administrators and the blessing of the King add up to a strong formula for success.

This case does not only illustrate the current level of military involvement in development work, it displays also its competitive and potentially conflictive aspects, including bureaucratic politics.

But another ingredient is essential - cooperation. The military will need to reassure the civilian agencies throughout the scheme that the civilian officials are not being pushed on one side and the civilian agencies will need to appreciate that it is the urgency of the situation that has necessitated the unusual combination of a joint military-civilian effort.[29]

Prior to its new, highly visible and potentially risky development ventures, the army concentrated on development in the national security sector, working primarily through the Internal Security Organization Command (ISOC), an agency set up to eradicate the communist movement in Thailand.

In terms of the hypothetical sociogram of the development community in Thailand, referred to above, it is apparent that more often than not the government and the military are the same players. The distinction is essentially one of who wears which hat.

It is also true that the actual influence of the government cum military, results from the personality factor (witness the rising star of General Chavalit) and increased reliance on a more subtle, sophisticated type of politics. The people behind the army's push to make the Northeast green are also thinking of greener political pastures for themselves.

Development by Royal Command

Every society needs a focus, a common orientation and a sense of direction. In Thailand, the Monarchy serves as the major source of cohesion and stability. In the words of former Prime Minister Prem Tinsulanonda:

It is clear that, for Thailand, the role of the Monarchy has proven to be indispensable. The Monarchy is a moral force that binds all elements in the Thai nation. It is a force that works for the greatest good of the Thai people.[30]

Given the importance of concerted action for effective development, the potential influence of the monarchy in Thailand's national development can hardly be overestimated. However, the stature of the King is significant in this context not only for its own sake and its general political importance in Thai society, but its added significance derives from the potential contributions to an alternative development model.

The type of development represented by hundreds of Royal Projects is distinguished by a sense of urgency and priority, affinity with Thai culture, and the intent to minimize bureaucratic procedures and solutions.

However, in reality, Royal Development Projects must be sustained in the end by the Government. The King's own contributions and the resources continuously volunteered through extensive fund-raising activities do not suffice. After the Monarch initiates a particular development project - there are Royal projects in practically all development sectors, from agro-forestry and medical services to science and education - typically, a government agency will take over (in the name of the King), bringing its own resources - expertise, staff and material resources - to bear. In effect, therefore, Royal projects do not and cannot avoid bureaucratic influence in their implementation.

The King and the Monarchy as institutions occupy a unique place in Thailand's national development. Removed from ordinary day-to-day development politics, the Monarchy—both by law and custom considered to be beyond reproach— simultaneously serves as a model and guide for alternative development. This juxtaposition helps to explain why Royal projects are both a part of and at the same time separate from the government.

Organizationally, aside from the King's personal involvement traveling eight months out of the year to visit people and project sites, a special office attends to the principal coordination and supervision tasks, leaving government agencies and the people themselves in charge of project implementation.

Another important point is the growing financial scope of all the Royal Projects combined. In fact, the government recently institutionalized Royal development initiatives by making its own annual contributions a line item in the national budget. These funds, combined with public contributions, constitute an increasingly significant financial resource in Thailand's national development.

Foreign Aid Missions

Thailand has been highly successful in attracting bilateral development assistance over the past 30 years. Motivated largely by security and economic concerns, the governments of the United States (particularly during the Vietnam War), Japan, West Germany, Canada and Australia as well as those of several other countries, have contributed large amounts of money to many types of development programs, both large and small.

From 1961 to 1981, Thailand received grant aid of $189 million (4,726 million baht) from all foreign countries. Approximately 45% of this amount was agricultural aid provided by Japan, the Federal Republic of Germany and Denmark.[31]

POWER AND CULTURE

To administer these funds and to coordinate and supervise their development activities with the Thai government, numerous governmental aid and development agencies work out of Bangkok offices, employing a sizable proportion of Thailand's expatriate community. These organizations are significant players in Thailand's development politics, injecting both human and material resources, as well as an international dimension, thus linking Thai development efforts to the international system.

The foreign players work relatively independently from their Thai counterparts and from each other. They are separated by different cultural norms, varied development approaches and political strings controlled by home ministries. The foreign actors also tend to view their role vis-a-vis other members of the development community from their own more or less pluralistic and laissez faire national perspectives.

Their power derives from political leverage, national control over aid and development funds, diplomatic skill and the ability to relate to Thai culture. It is limited, at least in part, by the perceptions of other players. For example, in line with current development trends, USAID and other foreign aid missions are seeking contacts with Thailand's local NGO community in order to explore mutually agreeable avenues to enhance the development role of the private non-profit sector.

The NGO response to the foreign overtures thus far is shaped by individual, often culture-bound, perceptions. As a result the Europeans are often given preference as working partners over the Americans, who are viewed as too ideological and rigid and the Japanese who are considered too aggressive and profit-oriented.

In fact, given the choice, Thai NGOs prefer to work with selected foreign (principally European) NGOs, avoiding as much as possible bureaucratic entanglements and political strings associated with government assistance.

There is also the complicated issue of registration, required by the Royal Thai Government, before Thai NGOs are cleared for formal contacts with foreign governmental agencies. In addition, foreign governments often have their own registration requirements that bear directly on whether and what type of formal ties can be established.

Multilateral Aid

International organizations, United Nations agencies in particular, represent yet another "breed" of development specialists who are important members of Thailand's development community. Their presence is unmistakable. All UN development organizations are represented in Thailand, with Bangkok serving as the headquarter for the United Nations Economic and Social Commission for Asia and the Pacific (ESCAP). It is also the regional seat of several other UN agencies.

UNICEF, which recently celebrated 40 years of children's programs in Thailand, UNESCO, SEAMES, FAO, and WHO make their development contributions through multi-national programs with Thai participation.

The role of international organizations (IGOs) in development is defined by their multinational orientation and intergovernmental constraints. IGOs operate on a different plane from the other development agencies due to their international accountability and regional or global responsibilities. Their frame of reference transcends those of the other actors, with the result that often they do not "speak the same language." Thus differences in the scale of development activities and programs, the approaches used, and the amount of resources applied, sometimes create gaps between the UN and other development professionals, making communication and coordination challenging tasks.

Given the prominent positions of ESCAP and UNICEF in Thailand's development community, a brief look at these regional agencies highlights this discussion.

According to ESCAP's Executive Secretary, S.A.M.S. Kibria, the organization, which is composed of some 38 member countries and 9 associate members, should be considered a catalyst "...or triggering mechanism for international cooperation...ESCAP's role has shifted from originally being seen as a United Nations' agency for reconstructing wartime damages, to becoming the most important and unique inter-governmental forum in the Asia/Pacific region."[32]

ESCAP serves the international community as a forum, as a source of technical assistance, advice and training. The organization also conducts research, and sponsors seminars. Furthermore, the Commission implements projects.

ESCAP, according to Kibria, is a dynamic institution engaged in a constant learning process:

> We have learned that physical development involving infrastructures such as roads and dams may not necessarily lead to the proper development of human resources in terms of people's skills and health.
>
> I believe that to catch up and move forward we have to plan and act in the direction of developing the skills of the people...Thus there must be a plan to develop human resources and not leave them to chance.[33]

ESCAP's guiding themes are human resource development and transportation and communication. Specific activities of the organization include development planning for "industries, technology, population, trade, agriculture, transportation and social development."[34]

UNICEF also maintains its regional office for East Asia and Pakistan in Bangkok. Its programs in Thailand predate even the basic agreement, which was signed in December 1948 (Thailand joined the United Nations two years earlier), and have increased considerably in size and scope.

For example, "During the years 1983-1986, the UNICEF–supported Rural Kitchen educated the residents of hundreds of villages nationwide in the methods of kitchen sanitation."[35] Similarly, UNICEF works in cooperation with the Bangkok Municipal Authority on slum problems, providing assistance for the upgrading of crowded communities.[36]

The list of illustrative programs goes on. The important new development lies in the fact that while UN development professionals work in organizational contexts set apart from other development agencies, a convergence of development thought and strategies between the international and local levels appears to be taking place.

Briefly, major UN agencies such as the Food and Agriculture Organization (FAO) and the World Health Organization (WHO) as well as UN-related agencies such as the World Bank (IBRD), while they still think "globally," are also beginning to "act locally," thus moving closer to a fundamental premise of NGO action, namely recognition of grass roots movements as being a key factor in rural development.

"In Asia, as perhaps nowhere else, the small farmer has for centuries been the backbone of civilization, of family trust, of traditional morals, of wisdom..." In recognition of his plight—earning perhaps as little as $75 a year and mostly landless—FAO has now made the small farmer the focal point of its programs. According to FAO Director-General Edouard Saouma: "To assist the small farmer is to respect the past and, even more important, to respect the future."[37]

Following in the footsteps, so to speak, of rural development NGOs in Thailand and elsewhere, FAO and the World Bank now agree that "...the way to help the small farmers is to meet them in the villages," to listen to them and to allow "peoples' participation" to take its course.[38]

Listen to the People, written by Lawrence Salmen and published for the World Bank, is indicative of the inroads made on traditional thinking at the Bank:

The only way to learn what people in borrowing countries want from development projects is by listening to what they have to say...[through the participation-observer method]

...development has got to touch people's lives...and then be carried on so they believe in themselves and strive to increase their own opportunities. And that isn't pure economics. Clearly it goes beyond that. And that's where communication and understanding are essential.[39]

To match words with action, World Bank President Walter Conable announced in October 1987 that the Bank is drafting lending programs for Asia and elsewhere which are designed "to reach the grass roots level," because:

One cannot assume automatically that the poverty that has been so endemic in Asia will be alleviated everywhere by the spectacular economic growth now registered by that continent as a whole.[40]

Given the characteristic features of IGOs and their activities in Thailand, how much influence do they wield within Thailand's development community? Gauged by the assessments of other members, UN agencies are less influential than foreign aid missions. Perhaps in the opinion of some, this same judgment would also apply in a comparison between international and non-governmental organizations.

In part, this evaluation derives from perceptions which portray UN development agencies as large, highly bureaucratized, and aloof from the plight of the people their programs supposedly assist. Such criticisms, in conjunction with the global or at least regional responsibilities of IGOs, help to explain their status of separateness, if not of isolation, from most other members in Thailand's development community.

Development Incorporated

Business and development are separate realms: one is preoccupied with economic gain and the other is concerned mainly with the welfare of the whole community. Yet, as in the case of economics and politics, the business world is intimately connected with national development.

Given the preference for the growth model of development, one would expect a central role for business, industry and the multinational corporate sector in government development plans. This has in fact been the case from the beginning of national development planning.

As for the Sixth National Economic and Social Development Plan, the business community lauds the government for pursuing the following economic goals:

- An economic growth rate of over 5%
- Conservative fiscal and monetary policies
- Promotion of export-oriented industries
- Encouragement of foreign investment
- Privatization of government enterprises.[41]

The government, for its part, but rarely passes up an opportunity to underscore its commitment to a development policy based on economic expansion and growth, thus prioritizing commercial, financial, industrial and urban interest over rural interests. While the agricultural sector cannot be—and is not—ignored, it is being transformed by government policies. The long-standing government support for cash crops for export has fundamentally changed farm economics in Thailand, giving rise to a new way of life and, equally important, a new set of problems, particularly farm debt.[42]

POWER AND CULTURE

According to a spokesman of the Association of Thai Industries,

> Thailand is not using Asian industrialized countries like Japan, South Korea and Taiwan as a model to achieve its economic development objective, despite the country's heavy promotion of export-oriented industries.
>
> Rather, the way we are proceeding is that agriculture will remain the vital factor of our economic development…
>
> [The] Thai government has a comprehensive programme to promote agro-based and related industries, including tax incentives, credit and production assistance, material supplies, marketing and general management.[43]

Government and business in Thailand is a profitable partnership; the government is responsible for maintaining a favorable business climate (which translates principally into political stability) and the business community sustains high profit margins for the elite.

Expressing confidence in the current state of affairs, the chairman and managing director of Esso Standard Thailand said: "Despite all the political activities, smoke and heat, the fact is that Thailand has a very stable government and politics."[44]

As a result of this widely shared perception in international business circles, "Thailand is now [according to a senior Thai political observer] one of the most attractive countries for foreign investment in Asia."[45]

Similarly, an economic advisor for UNICEF gave Thailand high marks for a "much expanded export sector, …diversification in the agro-based, textile and semiconductor businesses, import reduction, migrant remittances, promotion of the service sector, particularly tourism, and direct investment."[46]

Without making any connection to the above success, the same analyst pointed to three persistent problems: a fiscal deficit, deforestation, and income inequality.[47] As critics of this business-oriented development model are quick to point out, these problems are the direct result of the very policies for which the government is given credit and praise.

A major role is reserved for the international corporate sector, which, according to Professor Prapas Ouaychai, the president of the Thammasat University Council, has "…operated in Thailand in various fields including commerce, industry and finance for more than 100 years. [Presently there are] …some 60 multinationals from 12 countries operating in Thailand, many of them producing pharmaceutical products."[48]

The multinational corporations are expected to assist the country with human resource development and technology transfer. Thus far, however, human resources development does not go much beyond the extensive use of Thailand's cheap labor and as far as technology transfer is concerned, observers freely admit that this has yet to happen.

Thus far "…no multinational companies [have come] to Thailand to transfer their technology, except to those local firms which purchase the knowledge or when it is part of [*sic*] the joint venture deal." Before meaningful technology transfers can happen, the government would have to provide more incentives, including tax incentives and better telecommunications.[49]

Confident in the economic future in Thailand, business leaders project that Thailand "…will in the long run be able to effectively compete with other countries…" in the 21st century.[50]

By the same token, the government is mindful of the implications. Foreign Minister Siddhi Savetsila noted in addressing a workshop on peace and security in Southeast Asia: "Thailand's efforts to expand its exports have resulted in greater exposure to the impact of protectionism and the world economic situation."[51]

Business in Development: A Case Study

Against this general background, a brief synopsis *cum* analysis of a concrete situation where business and development interact will help clarify the role of the private sector in the development community.

This example involves the partnership of some 50 farm families in the central region of Thailand (Chachoengsao Province) joined with the Charoen Phokapan (CP) agro-corporation to raise chickens for local and foreign markets.

The arrangement calls for the company to provide feed and broiler stock and to facilitate bank financing of the farm operations. The farmer, for his part, "…has only to concentrate on maintaining a high quality crop." Participation in this scheme is limited to farmers with land. Farmers are classified into to three categories: big, medium and landless.[52]

Seemingly, this approach has been highly successful to the extent that it has been copied by other companies, both in Thailand and abroad. According to the managers of the project, the farmers are also pleased.

The company pooled initially a group of 50 farming families in Chachoengsao province to try out a 10-year contract. It worked so well that when the contract expired, the collective had owned their individual plots—made possible by a monthly payment scheme.

The Chachoengsao farmers now hold title deeds to their plots. They have also formed their own company.[53]

Looked at from a developmental, non-business perspective, a different assessment results. This agricultural strategy is not unique; it has been tried before with less than satisfactory results:

In 1977, an agro-industrial group of companies in cooperation with a commercial bank introduced a 'new integrated package project' for raising swine. The local authorities joined this project by providing utility services and recruited farmers to participate in the project. The bank provided a credit fund of over baht 25 million. And the private company was in charge of land consolidation, establishment and improvement of the infrastructure including roads, reservoirs, and irrigation systems, construction of houses, pig pens, and offices, training of farmers, production management, and marketing of farmers' products. Farmers were supposed to provide the manpower.[54]

Again strictly from an economic standpoint—as far as the company, the bank and the government were concerned—the project was successful, even though each family ended up with a debt amounting to approximately 500,000 baht ($20,000). In fact, NESDB has adopted this scheme "…as a solution to rural development in Thailand."[55]

From the farmers' standpoint and in terms of the long term interests of the agricultural sector, Heim reached the following conclusions:

The 'integrated package' scheme is a purely commercial undertaking in which farmers supply labour, acquire specialized knowledge and skills….They are not persons who operate and manage a farm but contract labourers hired by the company. The company therefore profits from the farmers who produce piglets for its large-scale pig fattening enterprise.

These kinds of schemes…are detrimental to such a country as Thailand. [They] …limit the choices of small farmers as they can never compete with large agro-industrial companies and their subsidiaries, … What remains are more and more unemployed migrating to Bangkok and populating the slums there.

These schemes have nothing to do with development as they only aim at profit maximization and economic growth.[56]

In addition, the charge is made that these schemes are also detrimental to the national interest, because the country cannot afford to subsidize multinational corporations in the form of infrastructure provisions and tax privileges.

Finally, giving the private sector an increasingly larger hand in running Thailand's agricultural system with an emphasis on processed food has profound implications, because it:

…is an ultimate expression of selfishness on the part of the elite of a country. They want to work the hands harder for the benefit of their mouths and stomachs, and yet how little they think of the chains of economic, cultural and social trappings that keep farmers down. When farmers realize that to work harder gives them no real benefits, and refuse to do so, they are blamed for that by saying that they are lazy. This gives the elite further justification for not really helping them, and for oppressing them the more. Little is it realized that the farmer's refusal shows their wisdom and pragmatism which can be a great asset in development work if only it is known how to treat them well.[57]

Academia and Development

Intellectuals contribute concepts and theories to national and world development. This indirect, yet pivotal influence, contrasts with the material resources brought to bear by government and the private sector. The academic establishment by and large accepts and supports the mainstream model of development with its emphasis on economic growth and material progress.[58]

Ideally, academics should shape the direction of world development in a creative, catalytic, energizing manner. However, in reality, the failure of "developmentalism," the development ideology of the West with its blind commitment to materialism, resulted in part from an intellectual paralysis, a seeming default of intellectual leadership to transcend existing frontiers.

Since the late 1970s the situation has begun to change. New ideas, concepts and theories are gaining ground, although still hardly acknowledged in official development circles. Under the heading of "alternative development" the ideology of conventional developmentalism is scrutinized and challenged, subtly changing the power status of the various players. As the 1980s drew to a close, a promising trend—witness the phenomenon of the "Barefoot Revolution"—became apparent.[59]

In Thailand, reviewing the history of the indigenous NGO movement from its roots in the political events of the early to mid-1970s, one finds that most if not all of the leadership emerged from the universities—activist students and progressive lecturers.

Following the period of underground activities—from the 1976 coup and gradual liberalization initiated by General Kriangsak, until the assumption of political power by the Prem Government—many Thai PVOs continued to receive their intellectual stimulus and pragmatic guidance from academic leaders in Thai universities.

However, this movement constitutes only a small minority in the academic establishment because the Thai university system is afflicted by the same pathologies which hamper the entire state apparatus, "where bureaucracy and inertia reigns supreme."[60] One should, therefore, not expect too much in the way of innovative leadership on development issues from the academic institutions as a whole.

Chulalongkorn University and Thammasat University, the nation's most prestigious universities, have each established programs which reflect the new trends in development thought, pointing out alternative approaches, capitalizing on the development situation and development needs specific to Thailand.

Included among these programs is Chulalongkorn University's "Alternative Development Study Project" and Thammasat University's "Graduate Volunteer Program," which over a period of ten years evolved into the Thai Khadi Research Institute. This program, for example, began as an opportunity for graduate students to work with villagers for an extended period of time—getting to know the rural way of life and the problems faced there—before writing their dissertations.

In a more traditional and conventional mold, with financial assistance and tutelage from abroad, two major institutions—the National Institute for Development Administration (NIDA) and the Asian Institute of Technology (AIT)—were established to specialize in development and related subjects.

NIDA was initially supported by the Ford Foundation, whereas AIT receives funds from a consortium of foreign, public and private institutions. These programs fall within the mainstream of traditional development practice and thought, thus conforming closely to the thinking in government circles.

In addition, following the pattern in Western countries, Thailand also has its own think tanks concentrating on development issues, foremost of which is the Thai Development and Research Institute (TDRI), which was also set up principally with external funds and continues to be supported by donor agencies such as The Asia Foundation.

TDRI represents Thailand's most comprehensive institutional effort to focus the country's intellectual resources on all the major issues confronting Thailand in a stage of transition. However, given TDRI's origin, its small size and very close ties with the government, TDRI-sponsored research is not likely to break conventional molds. Innovative thinking will more likely continue to be more characteristic of individuals and small groups in academic and NGO contexts, as the following illustration demonstrates.

In 1987 Thammasat University's Department of Dramatic Arts, led by Professor Mattani Rattnin, inaugurated a new "social theater" program supported financially by the Australian government. The intent of the program is to involve Thai rural youth in the development process, and its philosophy is based on the premise that:

> The country's economy has developed, science and technology have progressed strikingly, but the lag in religious, cultural and ethical values has grown drastically as our society has turned more materialistic.
>
> Human values have changed, and today's youth lack knowledge and understanding of traditional culture, a heritage handed down through many generations.
>
> To reach the young generation of today in an attempt to reinstate the age-old traditional values, beliefs and culture, there is no better medium than the performing arts, which can be entertaining as well as educational.[61]

"Suwannaphum Village"—'Thai Village'—one of the plays performed by Thammasat University students, takes a leaf from Orwell's *Animal Farm*. Five characters—a dog, a hen, a buffalo, a cow and a cat—are portrayed getting along fairly well sharing the hard work in the rice fields until some of them begin to think there must be an easier way to make a living. Just then along comes Pig, a prosperous rice miller with all the right ideas—but there is a catch:

...the rice milling service offered by Pig costs farmers one out of every four grain baskets they bring.

Soon, there are other tempting opportunities that the animals find impossible to resist. They discover that they cannot get along without modern conveniences—electricity, radio, television, and luxury goods—and when the money runs out, they find it easy to borrow more, promising to repay after the next harvest.

The handwriting is on the wall. When the harvest fails due to drought there is no money to repay debts, and the animals get more and more desperate. "A poor mother hen has to sell her beloved daughters, represented by three little chicks, to agents who promise a good life in the city."

Finally, the dog, representing the village leader, fetches the chicks and returns them to their mother as the play ends.[62]

Dramatizing not only the debt problem and the whole question of what kind of development the people want, but also such topics as drug addiction and child prostitution, the group has been enthusiastically received by village audiences.

The intellectual community is clearly engaged in the development process. The work of these individuals and organizations is critically important to Thailand's development, and their influence is likely to be more extensive then their numbers suggest. They are in the forefront of a countervailing movement, the "Barefoot Revolution."

The intellectual leadership in Thai development circles also provides a major link between the old and the new schools of development thought, between the city and the village, between the government and the non-governmental agencies, as well as between foreign and indigenous development organizations. This pivotal position is the context of a significant and potentially powerful change agent.

Democratic Institutions

Thailand has adopted most of the trappings of a democratic society—parliament, political parties, interest groups and the media—but has yet to develop the ethos of a pluralistic society. The people are not well versed in the democratic process. There is a general sense of uncertainty and insecurity regarding the democratic nature of Thailand's political system. (In a 1988 by-election in Bangkok only 16% of the eligible voters went to the polls.) Editorial writers in the major papers (particularly the English language press), politicians and opinion leaders in general, regularly voice their concern over the nature and direction of Thai democracy.

The issues raised, for example, include whether or not to adopt the 'one man—one vote' principle, whether the prime minister should be elected, the role of the military and the bureaucracy in the decision making process, rampant corruption (including vote buying), lack of discipline on the part of parliamentarians, and the caliber of Parliament as a whole. While there is no lack of criteria by which to examine and judge Thai democracy, the fact that these issues are aired is in itself a healthy sign.

Unfortunately, authoritarianism rests heavily on Thai society. In fact, according to a recent study, "… the legacy of Thailand's traditional patterns of authority have worked against an effective institutionalization of the formally adopted democratic system … ."[63] Deeply imbedded negative attitudes towards "politics" as messy, chaotic and dirty, contrast with "administration," which is regarded as the proper practice of government. Not surprisingly, therefore, Thais do not perceive democracy to be popular sovereignty and power exercised by the people through their elected representatives.[64]

However, these traditional doubts have not escaped untouched by the major events in modern Thai history, most notably the revolutionary period of open politics in Thailand from 1973 to 1976. Consequently, people in all walks of life have become politically more conscious and various segments of the population, including farmers, are mobilizing.

These changes reflect the growing tension between society and politics—the forces of modernization and change confronting stagnant oligarchic institutions, giving rise to " … a search for a new definition of legitimacy as the basis for the contemporary political system."[65]

Except for the Monarchy, there is no institution which has the undivided support of the people. There is an evident lack of trust. People are not sure whether the military will accept democratic rules. They wonder whether the bureaucracy can be reformed and corruption be stemmed. Above all, they wonder if there is hope for a more equitable, more just distribution of resources.

The condition of Thailand's contemporary political system determines the environment in which the development community labors. Major political problems inevitably affect all aspects of national development—the players as well as the process and the outcome. Thus political insecurity, lack of trust, corruption and other major issues delineate the parameters of development—what can and cannot be done, under what circumstances and in which time frame.

Chapter 3

POVERTY AND THE NGO RESPONSE

The past quarter century has been a period of unprecedented change and progress in the developing world. And yet despite this impressive record, some 800 million individuals continue to be trapped in what I have termed absolute poverty: a condition of life so characterized by malnutrition, illiteracy, disease, squalid surroundings, high infant mortality, and low life expectancy as to be beneath any reasonable definition of human decency.

(Robert S. McNamara, Quoted by Robert Chambers)

Fortunately, there are also entries on the other side of the ledger. Since the 1950s life expectancy in developing countries has increased on an average of nearly 30%, from 42 to 54 years, and literacy among adults has jumped from 30 to 50% of the population. Overall, improvements in the quality of life are uneven. Some sectors of society—especially women and minority groups—as well as entire world regions, are left behind.[1]

Clearly, the battle against poverty and underdevelopment is not being won. Asia, according to ESCAP data, with an overall estimated population of 2.7 billion, has "…hundreds of millions of people … engulfed in widespread poverty, hunger, and malnutrition." An estimated 300 million people suffer from malnutrition. While food production has increased from 549 million tons in 1976 to 764 million tons in 1986 (an average annual growth rate of 3.7%), the population growth rate stands at 1.7% per year. Furthermore, as a measure of environmental dependence, 70% of the region's farmland remains dependent on rainfall.[2]

Primary Health Care: A Case Study

The following report shows what can be accomplished under government auspices in primary health care, but it also indicates the major problems experienced by government programs and why NGOs may be more effective. Sumitr Hemasathol, a reporter for the *Bangkok Post* writes:

POWER AND CULTURE

I have often wondered why we are not able to do more for the unfortunate and the deprived. You have probably heard a great deal about the many efforts to help the poor, the slum dwellers, the undernourished, and other, less fortunate people. But we have been doing so much for so long, why haven't we been able to solve some of these problems for once and for all? We have spent what must be billions of baht, and employed thousands of gifted people over decades to try to relieve the suffering from poverty, ignorance, and disease. We should have some concrete results by now.[3]

The story begins with the UNICEF/WHO conference, at Alma Ata, USSR, in the late 1970s. This meeting is credited with the establishment of a new development approach and a new movement in primary health care, which rests on the following premises: first, all development problems—poverty, ill-health, low education, etc.—are interrelated; second, governments are not in a position to provide all the services people require; and third, people have a right to be involved in seeking solutions to their own problems.

Accepting this framework, Thailand decided to start a new program entitled the "Quality of Life Campaign," under the auspices of the four principal ministries concerned with development: Interior, Education, Public Health, and Agriculture and Cooperatives.

A list of basic minimum needs and minimal goals was drawn up and the government agreed to provide some assistance, including consulting, technology, and limited financial support. The bulk of the resources, both human and material, had to be provided by the villagers themselves. Mahidol University's ASEAN Training Center for Primary Health Care Development, the Ministry of Public Health and the WHO were asked to collaborate in making this approach work. The principal challenge was how to induce government officials, particularly at the provincial level, to adopt new attitudes and to acquire new skills.

Professor Tavisak Svetsreni of Mahidol University devised a research and development strategy designed to allow the villagers and civil servants to identify the community's problems and to seek relevant solutions. Successful pilot projects, for example, set up cooperatives to raise funds for development projects (including 'banks' for chicken, cattle, and fish) and initiated campaigns to eliminate health hazards (e.g., mosquitos and other disease carriers) and to improve road safety.

In analyzing this program, the reporter recounts:

The important thing to stress is that these are all activities which are contributing to an improved quality of life among the rural population with minimal input from central ministries. The people themselves, have been able to mobilize their own resources with their own initiative and a little guidance from officials.

The project has also made a difference among the government workers in the project area. They have learned to adopt new roles as consultants for the villagers. Once they have understood the meaning and implications of the new approach to development, they have realized how much more successful they can be—in terms of benefits for the people—when they use the research and development approach along with the people.[4]

Unfortunately, these new approaches were not universally successful amongst all participants:

> But the barriers to the success of this approach can now be identified as the attitudes and skills of government officers; the ones in central offices that insist on controlling local-level activities with which they are not familiar, and the ones at the periphery who cannot or will not adopt new ideas. We can do much. But first, we must give the power back to the people.[5]

The principal lesson regarding government development programs concerns the inevitable and pervasive influence of the bureaucracy. Its unwillingness or inability to go along, in this case, is symptomatic of bureaucratic behavior in general. At issue is the bureaucratic mindset, which resists change even if it might ultimately enhance the effectiveness and thus the power of government officials themselves.

Furthermore, by inference, the tendency of officials to be unyielding and superior in attitude underscores the obvious advantage enjoyed by non-governmental organizations, which tend to be more flexible and willing to learn with and from the villagers.

Unsurprisingly, the "Quality of Life" campaign under government auspices has not been as successful as anticipated—or hoped for.

What Kind of Power?

Viewed in the broader trinity of power, culture and development, there is another totally possible interpretation of this case study. The conventional referents of power are influence, control, even force—perceived as means towards ends. In this sense, bureaucratic agencies, representing the state, embody power. Individual actors are conditioned to think and act accordingly, i.e., to wield power.

As suggested in the previous case study, the poor—be they indebted and/or landless farmers or urban slum dwellers—are powerless, or at least this is what they are told and what they have come to believe. Consequently, the poor are conditioned to think in terms of outside assistance. Improvements in their condition are thus contingent on the good will of individuals and organizations with power.

To change these traditional dependencies would require a redistribution, a sharing of power. Conventional Thai wisdom does not favor a redistribution of power, believing that sharing power is a zero-sum game: your gain is my loss. Few organizations in positions of power—least of all governmental agencies, charged with upholding the authority of the state—are inclined to engage in meaningful power sharing, jealously guarding their prerogatives instead.

Unlike recalcitrant government agencies seemingly unable or unwilling to change their attitudes allowing bottom-to-top development to work, thus bringing about an empowerment of the people, the success of this approach under the auspices of non-governmental agencies is a function of a different concept of power.

The bottom-to-top approach does not accept the assumption that power sharing inevitably produces winners and losers. Instead, and this is borne out by experience, shared power, e.g., through devolution and decentralization of decision-making, may result in retaining the same level of power, or even lead to increased influence.

Government officials who are prepared to give local communities a say in their own affairs gain respect, enhance stature and better cooperation, which translates into more power for the officials concerned. In the end, the tradeoff amounts to exchanging the presumption of control with the reality of improved conduct of official responsibilities.

This is the lesson learned by a growing number of private development agencies— the rationale for empowerment of the poor, i.e., for effective development programs and for development approaches which put people first.

Empowerment, as a concept, also links culture to development, because once communities are allowed to practice self-help, to assume responsibility for their own destinies, they inevitably capitalize on all of their inherent resources, especially their accustomed ideas, norms and traditional modes of behavior.

Accordingly, freed from the preconceptions of outsiders, development needs are redefined, "…starting with the priorities and strategies of the rural poor themselves" and "…by concentrating on what outsiders and the rural poor agree in saying no to." As a result empowerment, has come to mean "… enabling poor [rural] women and men to demand and control more of the benefits of development."[6]

Without implying one-or-the other choice, this alternative concept of power helps to clarify the differences between public and non-governmental development agencies. Many Development NGOs have yet to realize their *comparative advantage* vis-a-vis public development agencies:

> Plans, projects and programs are often nowadays intended to benefit 'the rural poor', 'the vulnerable groups', 'the backward classes'. Projects which are targeted to such groups, and especially those run by voluntary agencies, have had some successes. Programs run by large-scale government field bureaucracies have a less good record.[7]

Comparative Advantage

Proponents of the non-profit development sector frequently claim that non-governmental organizations have certain advantages over their public counterparts in administering development programs. In particular, they point out that as a rule

NGOs or PVOs are more efficient and more effective because these organizations tend to be less bureaucratic, more flexible in their management approaches, less expensive, relatively free from political considerations and constraints, as well as culturally sensitive and better informed about local conditions in the host countries.

In general, these characteristics fit the preferred NGO strategy of concentrating on the grass-roots level and the promotion of community self-help programs.

The question of comparative advantage is not only of academic interest. Indeed, the extent to which the stated claims are born out has attracted growing interest from government and international aid agencies, prompting a series of studies. For example, a USAID-sponsored analysis by Judith Tendler[8] critically examines the major presumed advantages attributed to private development agencies. Her general findings and conclusions provide a good point of departure for an assessment of the NGO response to poverty.

The PVO literature, as summarized by Tendler, reflects a series of assumptions about organizations in the voluntary aid sector that only too often are taken for granted as facts. These assumptions regarding the nature and functions of NGOs result from organizational self-descriptions and efforts to draw distinctions between themselves and other members of the development community. Because, according to Tendler, the characteristics attributed to NGOs are plausible, they have been given the benefit of the doubt in and outside of the NGO community and thus tend to escape critical scrutiny and empirical examination.

A brief review of the major themes—what Tendler refers to as the PVO community's "articles of faith"—supplemented by illustrative data from the Thai NGO experience, provides a concise introduction to the nature and potential of the Thai NGO community.

Reaching the Poor

The primary "mission" of most development agencies—public or private—is to improve the lives of the poor. This seemingly clear and widely accepted goal belies an immense complexity, beginning with the identification of the "poor" and the means by which their lot is to be improved most quickly and most effectively. Thus, reaching the poor—how best to provide services and to affect changes in their condition—is a major and contentious issue for development agencies.

Considering the origin, philosophical orientation (mostly religious and humanitarian) and the development strategies of volunteer agencies, it comes as no surprise that NGOs lay special claim to the subject of Third World poverty. In fact, they consider themselves as particularly well qualified and generally more or at least as effective in alleviating poverty as their governmental counterparts:

> PVOs contrast their 'comparative advantage' in reaching the poor to the inadequacies of large donor organizations, particularly AID, and third-world bureaucracies. These

organizations, they say, have less experience with the poor and only a spotty record of commitment to them.[9]

Many NGOs in Thailand readily subscribe to the charge directed at public development agencies, criticizing the government for its seeming inability to reduce the gap between rhetoric and action. On the one hand, as indicated above, the government hardly misses an opportunity to stress its commitment to assisting the country's poor. Yet, the actual record in urban, rural and general community development is marred by too much bureaucracy, inefficiency, incompetence, corruption and, most importantly, lack of political will to seriously affect the existing distribution of resources and thus power.

The Thai government, to its credit, is beginning to recognize (at least implicitly) the nonprofit sector's claim regarding greater competence and efficiency in reaching the poor. This is illustrated by the preceding example of the government-sponsored primary health care program, which is actually a replication of approaches pioneered in the private sector.

It should also be noted that major foreign-based NGOs working in Thailand do not only cooperate closely with various government agencies in addressing poverty issues, but actually rely on the government for program implementation. The NGO community in Thailand, as in most Third World countries, does not have a uniform orientation on most major development issues, including attitudes and relationships concerning the government.

Participation

Participation of the poor in decision making, some PVOs say, is a distinct characteristic of their projects. The only way that the benefits of development programs can reach the poor, in turn, is said to be through a participatory process in which the poor make decisions about what they want and how they will go about getting it.[10]

The desire to share responsibility for all facets of the development process, which informs much of the NGO literature and is particularly dear to the hearts of indigenous development organizations, is based on the sound assumption that people have to be the subject, not the object, of development, thus giving communities the power to determine the nature and direction of their collective future for themselves.

In practice, however, the call for community participation frequently fails to be matched by appropriate action. More often than not, major NGOs are guilty of the same top-down approaches for which public donor agencies are generally criticized. Upon closer examination, the reasons for failing to implement community participation in both private and public development projects become readily apparent. Such causes for failure include preferred management styles, the nature and particular requirements of a project, specialized expertise, cultural differences, limited time frames, donor requirements, etc. There are also unstated reasons which frequently turn on the question of who is in charge. In short, community participation in development projects often fails to materialize because NGOs want or need to be in charge.

Field studies show that community participation generally translates into various degrees of cooperation with local elites who facilitate the work of development agencies. Natural or formal leaders, village committees, and community organizations already in place, tend to be the contacts and channels for program implementation.

Seen from the vantage point of the development professional, given the absence of a Western-style pluralistic society, the leadership-oriented approach to participation is the only realistic one. This leaves visions of community-wide participation principally for purposes of public relations and fund raising.

There are exceptions, particularly, if expatriates are not involved. However, even in the case of indigenous development organizations, gaps still exist between the agency and the target community.

The fundamental problem inherent in community participation derives from the fact that all development agencies, to various degrees are outsiders. Mindful of this, some NGOs (for example Redd Barna Thailand), adjust their hiring, training and development policies by employing local field workers, following appropriate training and allowing field workers time to live in the communities before a project is actually started.

If a major aim, perhaps at times the ultimate purpose of community-wide participation, is to assure equitable distribution of outside and community resources (reaching the poor), there may in fact be more than one way to accomplish community participation. Experience shows that effectiveness in reaching this goal will vary in accordance with the nature of the project and the interests of the elites. Tendler identifies three types of projects involving local elites:

(1) Activities or services in which a conflict between the interests of the elites and the poor is inherent; (2) the opposite case where elites will help the poor simply by helping themselves; and, finally, (3) the intermediate case where there is little conflict between elites and poor interests if the project is designed in a certain way.[11]

In the first instance, the concern for participation by the poor is real and justified. Empowerment of the poor should be a goal. In the second case, participation by the poor is less urgent on the assumption that benefits will be shared more equally. In the third situation, particularly dealing with projects in education and health, a top-down approach may be appropriate and defensible.

POWER AND CULTURE

In sum, it is suggested that reality calls for a more sophisticated approach to the participation issue. In Tendler's view the top-down vs. bottom-up decision making dichotomy is spurious.

Process vs. Outcome

PVOs feel that the emphasis on process is distinctly different from the 'dominant ideology' about economic development—adhered to by governments, large donors and development economists—which looks for results in the form of growth in output and other physical measures. The poor usually do not benefit, the PVOs say, from the growth achievements so valued by the 'developmentalists'. This PVO emphasis on process, and the contrasting of it to the way large donors think, contributes to the PVO fear of having their projects evaluated by 'outsiders'.[12]

Placing project implementation ahead of particular outcomes or results is a function of qualitative as opposed to quantitative development. This is a basic philosophical or ideological fork on the development road as seen from an NGO perspective.[13] While infrastructure, for example, is obviously important to a community's economic development, capital projects of this type, being highly visible and therefore quantifiable, represent only a part, according to the argument, of the overall development process.

On the other hand, the ability of the people to identify the source of their problems, to formulate, implement and assess responses to these challenges entails a complex, subtle and usually slow learning process that is reflected in a gradually growing awareness and consciousness of critical factors in their economic, social and political environments. This is a process of empowerment, a feeling of achieving greater control over one's destiny, at least in the short run.[14]

These aspects of the development process are non-quantifiable; they are normative. They are not the result of outsiders taking charge, of experts presuming to have the answers; in short they are the product principally of grass-roots initiative.

There are valid reasons why development programs are generally assessed in terms of their quantifiable outcomes. For one thing, material development is essential. Another very important reason is accountability: donors wish to see results. Proof of so many schools and hospitals built, children vaccinated, fed and educated, is gratifying. Statistics speak of progress; they represent what development is all about to most outsiders and development professionals alike.

In fact, most NGOs, of necessity highly sensitive to the wishes of donors and funding agencies, are very much output oriented. For example, CARE and ADRA (the Adventist Relief and Development Agency), following their initial refugee work in Thailand, now concentrate their development projects in agriculture, agro-forestry, small enterprise development and environmental education (CARE), as well as providing medical services to rural people in remote areas (ADRA).

These are traditional development activities, based on budget allocations, which in turn support concrete and by and large quantifiable programs.

In the end, the process vs. outcome controversy is not an either/or proposition, i.e., development assessed either in normative or quantitative terms. A scale combining both elements clearly is more useful and more realistic.

Focus on People

PVOs work 'people-to-people', they say, whereas large donors establish government-to-government working relationships. Like large donors, in turn, third-world governments are said to work through large bureaucratic organizations, which in many cases are too corrupt, uncommitted, or inefficient to reach the poor. Because PVOs are committed to people rather than governments, organizations, or physical outputs, they can achieve things for poor people that no amount of money channeled through the public sector can. That money cannot do the job is a corollary theme of PVOs, and a basis for their criticism of large donors..[15]

Practically all members of the Thai NGO community—with few exceptions—maintain relations with government agencies. These contacts range from formal clearances (generally in the form of signed agreements), periodic reporting on their activities and the exchange of information to very close working relationships, involving program implementation and shared funding. These relationships exist with the Thai government and foreign governments.

The NGO claim to the people-to-people approach, therefore, is tempered, in fact, by the requirements of program implementation. This is not to deny that significant differences exist between the respective development models. Deeply rooted first of all in philosophical differences—private agencies are predisposed to work on a person to person, non-bureaucratic level and secondly, reinforced by the presence of organizational constraints—public sector agencies need to abide by different sets of rules. Differences, both theoretically and operationally, do exist. But these differences should be viewed more in terms of degree rather than kind.

For example, Redd Barna, the Norwegian Save the Children Organization, and the Christian Childrens' Fund are committed to people-to-people-oriented development. Redd Barna sees itself as "a humanitarian organization" promoting better understanding and friendship between peoples by concentrating on community development, which, according to its own definition "...includes all aspects of life: food, housing, income generation, education, health, etc. and also more importantly culture, religion, social values, and foremost involvement of the community members in the decision making process.[16]

Similarly, the Christian Childrens' Fund Foundation (CCF) in Thailand, describes its organization as "An international nonprofit and non-sectarian humanitarian organization…dedicated to serving the needs of children worldwide through person-to-person assistance programs."[17] Its principal aims are to help "…bring together all available resources to benefit the child, his family and his total community," and to "…increase international understanding."[18]

Both NGOs maintain close links with the Royal Thai Government through various liaison activities and (in the case of CCF) the actual implementation of programs through government agencies. Redd Barna selects project areas according to the incident of poverty and malnutrition. Local willingness to cooperate and the availability of governmental support for the project are other factors to be considered.

Government ties are even more pronounced in the case of CCF. In fact, partnership with the government is very important to the agency. About 50% of CCF-sponsored children in Thailand are supported by government co-sponsored programs. CCF works mainly with the Ministry of the Interior (which includes the Community Development Department and the Public Welfare Department) and the Ministry of Agriculture (particularly the Cooperatives within the Ministry.) According to an internal fact-finding report, the Christian Childrens' Fund "…is working very effectively with the government programs."[19]

At the project level the people-to-people philosophy is actually put to the test. Redd Barna, relying on an all-Thai field staff, allows for a period of several months during which field workers have an opportunity to become as much as possible members of the local community before any effort is made to define problems, assess possible approaches and initiate projects. The entire process is centered on community input and participation. In sum, the people-to-people approach is maximized through decentralization and bottom-up decision making.

CCF on the other hand, is only indirectly and intermittently represented at the project level. Visiting "CCF Villages," for example, in Thailand's Northeast, one meets officials from the Community Development Department (CDD) who work directly with the headmen and the various village development committees. Funds provided by CCF for designated projects in the areas of child care, education, agriculture, income generation, and community infrastructure are administered by local committees, working under the auspices of provincial government agencies. The CCF child sponsorship program, the heart of its people-to-people strategy, thus depends on national, regional and local agencies for its implementation.

Furthermore, the link between individual sponsors abroad and the recipient CCF-sponsored families in Thailand is important primarily on account of its fund raising potential. The actual person-to-person connection is subordinated because most sponsors find it easier to write checks than letters. Mothers of CCF-sponsored children generally express regret that more or less regular correspondence from sponsors tends to be the exception rather than the rule.

However, this assessment does not deny the fact that sponsor-child correspondence is a top priority for the agency, both in terms of its philosophical orientation and its resource allocation. With thousands of letters requiring translation and transmission by the field office every month, considerable resources in terms of personnel and time have to be mobilized.

According to Tendler:

> Though the PVO-government contrast is understandable as a form of self-definition, it also obscures the rich and complex relations with government that some PVO projects have, and the contribution that PVOs are making in this supplementary way.[20]

Thus, given the relations between the public and the private non-profit sector, a more relevant conceptualization of this issue would be to think in terms of a division of labor, of a continuum between the public and private development agencies.

In sum, closer examination of NGO programs supports the conclusion that NGOs prefer and to the extent possible, do work within a people-to-people framework. However, the extent to which they succeed in this endeavor varies considerably from case to case and often from one project to another.

Flexibility and Experimentation

The smaller the organization, the greater is the potential for flexibility and experimentation in programs. The trade-off consists of the need for adequate resources before flexibility and experimentation can come into play. Ideally, development agencies should not be too large, falling victim to their own organizational or bureaucratic weight, but should be large enough in order to have an adequate resource base.

The CARE Mae Chaem Agro-Forestry Project in Chiang Mai Province, Thailand, illustrates the parameters of flexibility and experimentation in a large non-governmental development organization. In fact, CARE International is "…the world's largest private, nonsectarian dispenser of foreign aid with a budget approaching $250 million."[21]

CARE Thailand's Mae Chaem Project is a small-to-medium size program involving approximately 1,400 participants or beneficiaries. The main purpose is to assist dryland farmers, Karen Hilltribe people, through improved agricultural practices in order to stem the rapid worsening of environmental conditions, including deforestation and soil erosion. Crop production had been declining at an alarming rate, exacerbating already high poverty levels with all its associated problems, prior to CARE Thailand's Mae Chaem intervention which began in 1983 with a small pilot project, in the wake of the large-scale, inter-governmentally (RTG/USAID/UN) funded Mae Chaem Watershed Project.

A small, all Thai CARE team led by an experienced Project Director, initiated a learning process in the context of the pilot program, starting from the experience of the various Thai government, AID and UN agencies which were still working in the area. The Royal Thai Government was quite cooperative because it had invited CARE to develop a project of its own.

The project's long-term goal was to measurably improve the quality of life for some of Thailand's poorest people. CARE's strategy contained the following key components:

First, gaining first-hand experience and knowledge of the root causes of the numerous problems encountered by the Karen people in the Mae Chaem area, by hiring and training local people and/or experienced staff from the government/ international agencies, working already in the area.

Second, linking research with project activities at the field level was done by establishing personal contacts with villagers throughout the project area, obtaining information through informal discussions on agricultural practices, soil, water and related environmental conditions, as well as by gaining a better understanding of the general economic and social problems (opium addiction is a serious problem in the area) faced by the people.

Third, gradually introducing soil conservation techniques and other appropriate technologies in a phased approach, relying extensively on human resource development within the target communities. Principal project activities consisted of community/farmer motivation, field demonstrations, training and follow up.

A review of the CARE Mae Chaem development activities, beginning with the pilot project, includes numerous setbacks and disappointments in an overall record of gradual improvements. It also highlights considerable flexibility and responsiveness on the part of the CARE Mae Chaem staff. Field data show, how particular approaches were changed, how plans were altered, crop substitutions made, etc., frequently in response to suggestions from the farmers.

On visits to numerous Karen villages, the receptivity to the wishes of the community, sometimes expressed jokingly in an informal meeting with some members of the CARE staff, who regularly spend several days at a time in a given village, became readily apparent.

The Mae Chaem Project evolved and matured as both sides came to know and trust each other. The fact that nearly 40% of the staff shares the ethnic background of the villagers, obviously is a major contributing factor.

By the same token, there are also major resource limitations, both human and material, which affect the project's overall flexibility and ability to engage in experimentation. Despite extensive decision making authority, being part of a large organization means that budgets have to be adhered to and time lines have to be met. Worries about future funding and time consumed by internal and external reporting requirements, are two major concerns that plague most projects, Mae Chaem being no exception.

However, on balance, while the project activities were not particularly innovative— for example, terracing as a soil conservation technique, although new to the Karen villagers, has become standard practice in many dry farming areas throughout the Third World—human and material resources were used flexibly and to some extent experimentally. The pilot year by definition was an experiment, given the high degree of uncertainty encountered by the staff.

Local Institutions

As private organizations, both Thai and foreign NGOs say they have a special ability to work with and strengthen local private institutions, thus helping to create American-style pluralism in the countries they are working.[22]

Unlike the NGOs discussed so far, The Asia Foundation functions as a donor agency, working through indigenous NGOs and numerous other institutions, including civic, academic and religious bodies. In Thailand, The Asia Foundation's primary goal is to strengthen local institutions in the interest of a more pluralistic society, a theme supported by many NGOs.

Present in Thailand since 1954, The Asia Foundation established itself as a major U.S. private organization providing grants in accordance with the country's needs and the Foundation's priorities. "In fiscal year 1985 the Foundation made 195 individual grants in Thailand, expending a total of $1,183,331."[23]

Briefly, its major support activities include the Books for Asia Program (with more than 200,000 books distributed in 1985), parliamentary and legislative reporting internships for journalists, training programs for government officials, promotion of the recently created Thailand Development Research Institute (TDRI is a private think tank with close ties to the Royal Thai Government), as well as support for various academic professional associations.[24]

In addition, the Foundation has been instrumental in advancing major academic programs at national and regional universities. Its support for local community organizations is particularly significant. As early as 1955, the Foundation supported various Buddhist programs, including the Sangha Social Service in Northern Thailand and vocational training programs conducted by Buddhist monks.[25] The budget for this program alone was approximately 400,000–500,000 baht per year, from 1975 to 1985.[26]

Concentrating initially on educational programs at the two Buddhist universities—Mahachulalongkorn and Mahamakutra—which were not fully accredited until fifteen years ago, Foundation grants led to the establishment of new faculties, leading up to major curriculum revisions (including moral teaching, environmental and vocational education, and population planning), English language instruction, books, and scholarships for monks. A small number of scholarship recipients went to study abroad. Upon completion of their studies, monks were expected to engage in community service activities.

Without government or private support, these programs were coordinated by the Buddhist Universities and in close consultation with The Asia Foundation. The monks' activities in the outlying provinces, however, were viewed by the government as supplemental to its national security activities.

To facilitate administration of these programs, two Regional Centers—one in Ubol and the other in Chiang Mai—were established to administer Asia Foundation grants.

According to the Foundation's own assessment, the Buddhist program was effective because it provided the monks with the necessary material support and in turn, the monks were able to exercise considerable influence in rural communities throughout the north and the northeast of Thailand. It is also pointed out that direct employment opportunities were created for graduates from the various vocational programs. As a result the pressure for leaving the village was reduced.

It is interesting to contrast the Sangha's vocational training (made possible by Asia Foundation funds) with parallel government programs run by the Community Development Department. While CDD provides certificates, which the Buddhist programs were not allowed to do, its graduates are almost unemployable because of the programs' poor reputation. On the other hand, students with Buddhist vocational training were sought after, but they lacked official recognition of their training.[27]

This raises several important issues regarding relations between the government and the NGO community in general and ties between the government and the Buddhist establishment in particular.[28]

The Asia Foundation is almost the only major foreign NGO which extends its local organization support programs to the South of Thailand. Working largely with regional universities and Islamic educational institutions, the Foundation has become well established in a region which has traditionally been neglected, if not ignored, by the NGO community.

In view of the political difficulties faced by the government stemming from a disaffected Muslim minority (94 % of Thailand's population is Buddhist) and the presence of various separatist movements (the Communist Party of Malaysia was until recently active in the southern border region), the work of the Asia Foundation has had an integrative effect.

It is apparent from this brief synopsis, that the Asia Foundation supports pluralism in Thai society by strengthening public and private institutions at the national, regional and local level. Serving as a donor agency the Foundation does not implement development programs itself, but functions instead as a catalyst.

A review of the Thai NGO community reveals a general consensus on the critical importance of pluralism in the development process and the struggle against poverty in particular. In a sense, the NGO community itself stands for diversity and individual organizational identity. This commitment to pluralism is, *ipso facto*, also a weakness because it limits organizational willingness and the ability to cooperate.

Lack of coordination, for example, is a major shortcoming of development NGOs in Thailand, which will be discussed at a later point.

By far the most important factor in the work of NGOs, particularly of those NGOs which are specifically concerned with the promotion of local and regional organizations, is the overall political climate. Obviously a fearful society and a government paranoid about national security make for a highly insecure environment which is not conducive to the broadening and strengthening of pluralistic tendencies.

Development and politics are two sides of the same coin; one cannot advance without the other. This is a major inference of the NGO role in promoting institution building and pluralism.

Costs

A final theme is that PVOs can benefit the poor at lesser cost than large public-sector organizations. This is because of their commitment, their ability to draw on voluntary or 'unpaid' help, and their freedom from the inefficiencies and lethargies of large organizations.[29]

…PVOs typically operate with a streamlined, modestly paid, and in many cases volunteer staff, thus reducing their administrative costs to a rather low level by comparison to the rather bulky and expensive U.N. and governmental bureaucracies. PVOs can typically make an aid dollar stretch much further than bilateral and multilateral agencies can, while focusing those dollars directly upon the needs of the poor.[30]

Although comparative data on NGO/government cost effectiveness are not extensive, the available evidence speaks in favor of the non-profit development agencies for two principal reasons: lower staff salaries and lower overhead.

According to a 1982 analysis of this subject, based in part on USAID assessments, "…the first year annual cost of one AID field staff member is $150,000, with all support costs added in. By contrast, a PVO field worker, with all support costs included, will require just under one half of that amount."[31]

Furthermore, NGOs are in a much better position—their limited size, development philosophy, styles of operation and management, among other considerations—to keep administrative expenses down.

[In 1976] A study of ten large PVOs showed that the percentage of expenses earmarked for administrative costs and promotion was an astonishingly low 3 percent of total cost as compared with 20-30 percent spent on overhead by most businesses and the estimated 20-30 percent spent on overhead by government-to-government AID programs.[32]

If anything, administrative expenses of public agencies are even higher when the development records of host governments are scrutinized. In 1979 when Thailand's population stood at 44.3 million, some 800,000 officials absorbed 30 per cent of the national budget through salaries and wages.[33] The Ministry of the Interior's Community Development Department, which shares extensive responsibilities in rural development, alone has 4,000 employees.[34]

Similarly, the NGO record on in-country cost effectiveness looks better when secondary costs—e.g., inefficiencies, incompetence, negligence, and corruption—are taken into account. Government projects, although to varying degrees, depending on their size, scope and the responsible officialdom, are afflicted by these problems, thus reducing program effectiveness and impact. Unfortunately, only estimates rather than accurate data are available.

For example, the Royal Thai Government's Rural Job Creation Program (RJCP), initiated by Prime Minister M.R. Kukrit Pramoj in 1975 and continued intermittently, until the government of Prime Minister Prem Tinsulanonda decided to resume the program, involved massive expenditures, but without being "…able to improve the overall economic status of the country."[35] The Kukrit government allotted 2,500 million and 3,500 million baht ($100 and 140 million) to this program in 1975 and 1976 respectively. Under Prime Minister Prem, the Thai Government spent 15,000 million baht ($600 million) over a period of six years or more than 2,000 million baht ($80 million) annually from 1980 through 1985.[36]

The Job Creation Program, designed "…to help provide income throughout the year for the rural people," has been widely criticized, particularly during its early years, for its high degree of politicization, gross inefficiencies and wide-spread corruption.[37]

Addressing the failures of government development programs in general, the following excerpt is quoted in *How to Develop the Small Farming Sector*:

> …for the Thai public, hardly a day goes by without their hearing or reading about the Government's conceiving, planning, or implementing yet another agricultural development project aiming to improve the quality of life for the country's farming population. In the eyes of the people, however, despite these often expensive projects, rural life in Thailand hardly seems to have changed at all. Low incomes and resultant low living standards in the rural areas continue to be the biggest and most difficult problems facing any government, and the favorite panacea seems to be to channel more and more funds into the rural area through what are often poorly conceived agricultural development projects…
>
> …nearly all of the agricultural development projects which have been completed in Thailand have been very expensive. In economic terms the rate of returns on investment has been very poor…When questioned, Cabinet ministers or senior government officials often claim that the slow progress, or lack of progress, in Thailand's agricultural development, is due to an insufficiency of funds…however, lack of funds is not the reason. Instead, a poor understanding of problems basic to the

development of agriculture in Thailand has resulted in the Government's incorrect spending of funds and consequent paucity of achievements.[38]

Of course, the average NGO development project does not even begin to match government programs in terms of budget allocations and program size. Yet, mindful of economies of scale, micro-level NGO programs compensate for their limited resources through greater cost effectiveness. The tradeoff is frequently quality over quantity in their impact assessment.

The Moei River Health Project

Following a successful 1985 pilot project, the Adventist Relief and Development Agency (ADRA) in Thailand proposed to implement a five-year primary health care training program for Karen villagers living on the Thai-Burmese border.

The Moei River Health Project's primary goal is to improve the health of the Karen people, who are among the poorest and most neglected minority groups in the region, by addressing the major health problems, including malaria (one third of all patients visiting the current health center suffer from this disease), the lack of immunization for children, the absence of oral re-hydration therapy and the absence of family planning.

Focusing on the existing health center—a compound of traditional thatched-roof huts, located in a jungle clearing on the Burmese side of the Border—the project proposal called for the expansion of the present health worker trainee program for young Burmese women. The program consists of a year-long course for six women during the first year, followed by the establishment of no less than two primary care clinics (PCC) in selected villages.

> Each PCC will provide basic health services to the surrounding community. It will be the local center for malaria control, immunizations, primary health care, mother-child well clinics, family planning, health education, etc. The health worker will promote health teaching in the community through regular health presentations in the clinic, teaching mothers in their homes and teaching health in the village school.[39]

The final goal is "90% of households in 8 target villages have received health service(s) from a project primary care clinic" (PCC) by March 1991. Thus, "by far the greatest benefit will be that the Karen people enjoy a better state of health."[40]

The relevant point is that the cost of the entire program for a five-year period totals 4,826,000 baht ($178,741), which amounts to less than $36,000 per year for expenses including capital ($5,370) and operating expenditures ($173,371).[41]

Small programs like the Moei River Health Project, multiplied many times over, while still insignificant in budgetary terms when compared to public sector undertakings, tend to produce results which often elude government-sponsored development programs. These data suggest that NGO claims regarding their comparative advantage appear to be more justified on the grounds of cost effectiveness, than on any of the other alleged advantages discussed above.

Free of Politics

"One of the major strengths of PVOs has been their ability to maintain a largely apolitical focus on the human needs of prospective aid recipients."[42] The presumption is that choosing not to take a political stand, avoiding strong ideological positions, and not becoming too closely identified with government agencies makes NGOs more effective development organizations. In theory, this is a plausible argument because it suggests the concentration of human and material resources on the problems at hand.

Even governments accept this position almost at face value. One of the reasons why USAID, for instance, is mandated to channel more government aid funds through private non-profit agencies, is based on the assumption that:

> PVOs can take on a much lower profile than the U.S. government in development assistance efforts in the Third World. In regions that are sensitive to or hostile to U.S. intervention, PVOs are more capable of winning acceptance by the local governments and the people. In some cases the PVOs work under contract with the host governments and thus 'blend into the local landscape'.[43]

As indicated, some Third World governments go along with the alleged apolitical character of NGOs. However, there are also instances where this position has backfired, in the sense that NGOs are viewed as Trojan horses precisely because of their alleged apolitical nature.

The important distinction to be made, in order to clarify the issue, is between the appearance and the actual situation. In terms of power and culture, it is not difficult to see that all development agencies—public or private, profit or non-profit, bilateral or multilateral—function in a political environment. Development does not take place within a vacuum. Nearly every facet of the development equation, regardless of time or place, is imbued with political considerations.

It follows that NGOs, whether they believe themselves to be in fact apolitical or non-political, derive considerable tactical advantage from this assumption. Appearing to be free from politics turns out to be a source of power that enhances the position of NGOs vis-a-vis other players in the development game. Trading in this currency allows private development agencies greater leeway in pursuing their particular objectives, e.g., through government cooperation, access to the poor, and greater acceptance by local communities.

Clearly, the proximity between NGOs and governments varies considerably with each actor and corresponding situation. Although unable to escape politics, at one end of the spectrum are organizations such as OXFAM, which refuse almost all government funding and on the other (far more popular) end—are organizations such as CARE, Catholic Relief Services and similar-minded foreign NGOs, which receive up to 80% of their funds from government sources.

The independence-from-government theme, is particularly characteristic of Catholic social action and other church-related groups, who teach the poor to learn what their own resources are, and how to mobilize them, instead of counting on help from outside the community to materialize.[44]

Viewed from a systemic perspective, private and public development organizations are part of a division of labor that entails choices as to who will perform which preferred sets of roles. For example, NGOs sometimes function as brokers—mediating for local communities, treating them almost as their clients—at other times, the emphasis will shift to advocacy, defending the poor against hostile outside forces including government agencies.

For example, the Human Development Center (HDC), working with people in Bangkok's Klong Toey Slum, made famous by Prateep Ungsongtham Hata (the "Slum Angel"), does not only maintain educational, medical and income producing programs, but also provides assistance in the constant struggle against eviction. Legal advice and sometimes bail money are made available.

Funded by a Dutch NGO, the legal assistance program of the Human Development Center relies on a high-powered lawyer and a prominent Thai woman with excellent social and political connections to open doors and smooth the way in eviction cases which involve Klong Toey residents.[45] HDC, according to Tendler, belongs to the category of NGOs described as as "enlightened patrons."[46]

Other relationships may involve cooperation, competition or direct conflict between private and public development agencies. If there is competition, duplication of programs is likely and NGOs may be getting in the way of the government, which usually reduces their effectiveness and results in the termination of their activities.

On the other hand governments also replicate programs pioneered by NGOs.[47] When this happens the division of labor between the private and public sectors is working. Under the best of circumstances, this may not only strengthen NGOs but government agencies as well. On the other hand, outright conflict may also result as government programs and objectives change:

Previous to major public sector moves into an area, a government may have been perfectly content to allow an outside organization to 'occupy' that area.....Thus it is that in some countries with extreme problems of poverty and little political will or institutional capability to deal with the problems, PVOs are like para-governments, "dividing up territory between them," [the reference is to Haiti]…When governments suddenly move into the areas previously occupied peacefully by PVOs, they sometimes find it difficult to tolerate the power or prestige that the PVO has come to hold in that area. Bad relations may ensue…[48]

Comparative Advantage: Additional Considerations

This chapter began with a case study summarizing key features and major problems of a Thai government program in primary health care before exploring the alleged comparative advantage enjoyed by private sector development agencies. Throughout these discussions, the focus has been on the poor, specifically on how NGOs seek to reach and empower the poor.

Summing up, Tendler points to three additional considerations that affect the ability of NGOs to reach the poor. They are related to the recent shift from relief to development activities—from first to second generation NGOs.[49]

First, there is the shift to projects focused on income-earning activities, particularly in agriculture.

> The most recent thinking in development assistance, … has focused on ways to incorporate these poor into the economy through development or income-generating projects—rather than on the poor as objects of welfare.[50]

Unfortunately, NGOs do not always have the expertise to manage these projects, plus they tend to run into opposition from local elites. In other situations they may actually end up working with the not-so-poor (communities which are receptive and qualified), thus reinforcing their sense that the poor are difficult to reach.

> The new development focus on income-earning activities, … is a commendable transition away from the perception of the poor as fit only for charity. At the same time, this attempt to treat the poor as producers has sometimes resulted in the inadvertent exclusion of the poorest from the new production-oriented projects—leading full circle back to a perception of the poorest as unreachable. The dilemma can be partly resolved by a greater awareness of the 'trickle-up' dangers inherent in projects involving income-earning and agriculture. With some extra thought and sensitivity to these dangers, as suggested above, PVOs (and large donors) will find that the poorest are not so unreachable.[51]

Secondly, many NGOs find it difficult to change their welfare thinking in line with the new focus on development:

> Many PVOs started as relief and charity operations, and some still continue to do considerable work in this area. The welfare way of thinking about the poor may be more

difficult to shake off, as the PVOs become more 'developmental', than the welfare techniques themselves.[52]

Thirdly, there is the shift from specialist to generalist:

The transformation of PVOs from relief and welfare to development agencies has meant, for some PVOs, the taking on of more community needs than might have been done in the past….In certain ways, this multi-component or 'integrated' vision of development and development projects looks similar to the emphasis of the large donors on integrated rural development projects, a result of the shift of development assistance toward the poor during the 1970s. The broadness of the developmental approach of some PVOs may be diminishing their ability to do effective projects and reach the poorest.[53]

These three considerations—the emphasis on income generating activities, the persistence of welfare thinking and the shift from specialist to generalist—are symptoms of the evolution from first to second and third generation NGOs. First generation NGOs concentrate primarily on relief efforts. The second stage is represented by those organizations which see development as a long-term strategy in the struggle against poverty and injustice.

Finally, the most recent change concerns the evolution of so-called "strategic organizations," which see their mission principally in managerial, intermediary and supportive (sustainable systems development) as opposed to operational terms.[54] It follows, with reference to cost analysis, that the overhead of strategic or third generation NGOs is higher. The cost/benefit ratio, therefore, will also be different.

The evolutionary stages are not mutually exclusive. In fact most large NGOs combine relief with development programs, although the shift is clearly towards the latter. Thus far, relatively few NGOs, except for private foundations and other similar donors, see themselves primarily as strategic organizations. However, the presumption is that comparative advantage applies to all three types of non-governmental organizations.

CCF community development project Don Pueng, Ubol Province—cottage industry promotion.

CCF community development project in Don Pueng, Ubol Province—fish production as part of diversified agriculture.

Villagers gathering water at the community well in Chik Du, Ubol Province.

"Grassroots power"—villagers gathering in Chik Du, Ubol Province.

CARE Mae Chaem, Chiang Mai Province, Agroforestry and Nutritional Project—Karen women and children waiting for health workers.

CARE Mae Chaem, Chiang Mai Province, Agroforestry and Nutrition Project—development worker dispensing medicine and advice.

Chapter 4

THAI SOCIETY: PARAMETERS OF DEVELOPMENT

The East is being changed. The West is the Model. However, as in the case of Thailand, the roots are still there. This makes the difference between Thailand and the West which has to go back to its remote past in order to find its roots. The wisdom of the East is still alive and in evidence in the daily lives of many individuals and communities.

Seri Phongphit, Religion in a Changing Society

The survey of Thailand's development community begun in Chapter II stopped short of the interface between Thai society—its structure and characteristic features—and the development process. Embedded in this relationship are also implications regarding the position and the potential of the various development agencies, including NGOs.

The assessment of the approximate status and relative degree of influence exercised by these actors—ranging from governmental agencies, the monarchy and the military to the business community, international organizations and democratic institutions—implicitly assumed that conventional power, measured in relation to force and/or material resources, does not hold the key to meaningful, qualitative development. This assumption is based on the premise that development is a voluntary process that depends on a community's internal dynamics. In other words, true development cannot be imposed from the outside. The process may start, as in fact it often does, with an external stimulus or catalyst, but it can be sustained only by the individuals and the community concerned.

There are members of the development community who are not powerful in the conventional sense, because they are not part of the state apparatus, nor do they command extensive material or financial resources. Yet they do have influence that manifests itself in successful development programs, which, even if they were not conceived by the local community, benefited from its early participation in the planning stage and from acceptance of full responsibility for their implementation and continuation.

POWER AND CULTURE

While NGOs do not have a monopoly on "non-conventional" power, they are more advantageously placed, as demonstrated in the preceding discussion.

Again, this is not to infer that all NGOs fit into this mold. Many of the large private sector agencies are allied too closely with the conventional centers of power to pursue true grassroots development strategies. Consequently, they are afflicted by the same pathologies that come with the accumulation of traditional power, based on formal authority and access to material resources. 'Developmentalism', the Western ideology of development, is characteristic of this type of imposed development. Chambers, linking grass-roots development strategies with the idea of a learning process, observes:

> The learning process approach is easier to achieve for small voluntary agencies than for the great field bureaucracies of government. A major challenge over coming decades is bureaucratic reorientation, including a change from authoritarian to participatory styles and a shift in responsiveness from orders from above to demands from below.[1]

By the same token, those NGOs that successfully practice alternative development strategies, by relying on influence which derives from partnership, mutual respect, and self reliance, will be most successful. This is also true for organizations that are able to reduce the number of barriers between themselves and the community to a bare minimum.

Therefore, foreign-based NGOs, compared to their indigenous counterparts, have to work harder to overcome social and cultural barriers. However, no matter how favorable the conditions may be concerning the role of outside NGOs, there will always be an inherent division. But this does not mean that local development organizations are entirely free of these constraints. For example, the background of rural development workers generally differs from the village environment. The villagers and the rural development workers are separated by identity, status and outlook.

Thus, to understand the position and the role of NGOs working in Thailand, a brief descriptive analysis of Thai society its structure and principal cultural norms— is necessary.

The Patrimonial Society

Thai society is fundamentally autocratic in nature; it is benevolent, not absolute or despotic, but it is autocratic nonetheless. Strong leadership is accepted because it is considered essential to the smooth and proper functioning of the ideal, i.e., a moral society. The ruler, the supreme decisionmaker, may act arbitrarily, but he also has a clear obligation to be compassionate and not overly demanding of his subjects.[2]

These are key aspects of Thai patrimonialism—a model of Thai society, which conceptualizes its fundamental structure and behavioral norms, explaining the functioning of this society over time—advanced by Norman Jacobs in *Modernization without Development: Thailand as an Asian Case Study*.

Jacobs makes a clear distinction between patrimonial and feudal societies. Feudalism, as was found in Europe and Japan, according to Jacobs, produced a qualitatively different society with correspondingly different goals. Thai society, in his view, should be analyzed within the context of a patrimonial society. The development paths of patrimonial and feudal societies does not follow the same course.

Power Structure

Historically, land was the basis of wealth in Thai society. It was transmitted, not through lineage and kinship, but bestowed by grace through the benevolence of the superior. In this society "power is generated and maintained not by individual, military, or political sagacity over limited terrain in constant competition but by membership in a bureaucratic structure owing allegiance to a sovereign of a national state." In effect, in this system office equals power.[3]

Traditional Thai society was ruled by autocratic and bureaucratic politics, which were superimposed on a stratified, hierarchical social system and an economy characterized by "prebends." Combined, these structures engendered rules and behavior patterns that continue to dominate most aspects of life for the Thai people today.

Political Authority and Power

First, political behavior is oriented towards deference, inequality, submission to bureaucratic rules, highly personalized and centralized decisionmaking. Pertaining to the relationship between the rulers and the ruled, these patterns have remained remarkably unchanged over time, despite the fact that the center of political authority has experienced systemic change:

In spite of these formal changes, the basic patrimonial posture of an arbitrary policy maker, often indifferent to the rights of the public, did not change, although formally Thailand has evolved (or modernized) from the feudalism of the Sukhotai to its present constitutional democracy. The people are not the staff-constituents (or clients) of the patrimonial decisionmakers, as those constituents remain the administrative staff. Officials, decisionmakers, and staff alike, continue to consider themselves above and apart from the public and in no way accountable to it, free to pursue their own interests as they see fit. The decisionmakers in particular not only are indifferent to popular political participation but often even are indifferent to communicating government policy to the general populace. Officials are notoriously difficult to see and are indifferent to requests and complaints from below. Conversely, officials too often are impatient with public compliance of their requests, and the police frequently are accused of bullying citizens. Appeals by certain officials to the administrative staff to go out and serve the public and listen to complaints are taken for what they are intended to be—model, ceremonial rhetoric.

In sum, the nonofficial Thai, although hardly subject to a despotic authority, is certainly subject to an often arbitrary and capricious one, without, at the same time, having at his disposal either the moral right or any legitimate formal channel to challenge that authority. At best, a private individual who believes he has a political grievance or interest to pursue can only hope to establish some personal, individual (i.e., patrimonial) patron-client relationship with an official to insure that authority will not operate to his disadvantage, especially at a time when he is least prepared to deal with it.[4]

Morality is basic to the patrimonial political order. It is assumed that the state exists to uphold the moral laws that govern the universe. Consequently, power and morality are intimately connected, "…the more powerful one is assumed to be, the more moral one is expected to be, or to appear to be. At the apex of the political pyramid stands the very moral symbol and moral protector of the society, traditionally the king, with the wheel of mortality (*Cakkrii*) as his symbol—a moral symbol that doubles as a weapon of power against evil."[5]

Furthermore, patrimonial politics thrives on the distinction between the center and the periphery, with the latter distinctly subordinate and at the disposal of the former, thus reinforcing the behavioral norms. In Thailand peripheral authority (provincial and local government) are characterized by urban bias and control, as well as by the absence of decentralized decisionmaking.[6]

Consequently, the village matters little when compared to the town; power always emanates out from the city and flows down to the rural communities; and provincial cities are principally administrative centers and only secondarily the focal point of commercial activities.

The village is formally governed by two officials, one headman or *phuu yai baan* and one commune head or *kamnan* who is in charge of a district with an average of twenty hamlets). Each of Thailand's more than 52,000 villages are, according to a 1914 law, elected but in fact are chosen by superior authority.

Both the headman and the commune head are instruments of the government, which gives their positions power and prestige. At the same time, however, it is important to note that local officials are not part of the governing elite because they are not civil servants. The commune head, for example, is only an "unofficial official" or "a glorified hamlet representative."[7]

Concurrent with this structure of formal authority at the village level, are the natural leaders who frequently also hold the position of headman or commune head. Informal or natural leaders—sometimes made assistants to the headman—exercise potentially greater influence than the formal office holders, by virtue of the support and confidence of the community. As Jacobs points out:

> The ability of the informal leaders to act on village problems is important to the villagers because, in spite of the well-laid, patrimonial official plans, the villagers' faith in the ability and motivation of the formal leadership (and indirectly of local authority), is less than the central government would desire.[8]

These two kinds of leadership are distinguished by external manipulation, lack of motivation, insufficient interest, and more often then not by sheer incompetence, in the case of the government's village-level representatives; while the informal leaders enjoy the confidence and support of the community itself, facilitating their work.

In general, the relationship between the urban and the rural spheres, from the perspective of the villagers, continues to be characterized by the principle of patrimonial obligation, i.e., as long as the village meets its formal obligations to the urban authorities, they should be able to pursue their own affairs relatively undisturbed. Such feelings are still part of the behavioral norms of the rural areas, despite the intrusion of government, rural and community development programs, particularly under the auspices of the Interior Ministry's Community Development Department.

> …the political relationship between the urban and rural peripheries, in spite of many modernization programs and many alleged attempts to make it otherwise, has remained patrimonial. All lines of political communication and power are still directed down from the urban center, and there are still no institutionalized means by which the average villager can have his interests (as he conceives those interests) represented in the councils of political decisionmaking.[9]

As a result of the division between the two spheres, all aspects of Thai society—political, social, cultural, etc.—are affected by discontinuities that find expression in wide-spread distrust and prejudice.

Social and Cultural Norms

Closely tied to the political values, social and cultural norms evolve around the principle of patron-client relations, i.e., an asymmetrical exchange of benefits. Given the established features of authority (autocratic, erratic, arbitrary, personal and centralized), in order to achieve personal goals, to get ahead in all spheres of daily life, Thais look for patrons willing to further and protect their interests in return for allegiance and service.[10]

POWER AND CULTURE

Ideally, the patron is akin to the benevolent head of the family. In reality, however, the principle engenders exploitation and increases distrust. Another set of significant consequences derive from long-standing practice of patron-client relations: the belief that one's own efforts and contributions (e.g., hard work) do not matter, only an effective, powerful patron can assure success; the common phenomenon of factionalism, which characterizes all sectors and levels of Thai society, and the resulting inability to cooperate over an extended period of time; and the widening gap between rich and poor—as the concentration of power in the hands of the few, the patrons, increasingly polarizes Thai society.

Furthermore, social behavior, especially in a rural context, is typified by distinct traits that help define the development parameters of Thai society. A pronounced individualism, for example, is frequently noted by observers, suggesting that the seeming inability or unwillingness to cooperate on a long-term basis, is at least partially the result of this tendency in Thai society. This characteristic in turn generates little social pressure to take collective action in response to major problems. Instead, people tend to shift responsibility to public agencies.

From another perspective, individualism generates egocentric behavior, which is evident in the widespread selfishness of people and entire sectors of Thai society.[11] The attitudes of the urban-based middle class towards national development problem, are prime examples. In the past, when Thailand did not experience material deprivation; this type of individualistic behavior was unproblematic. However, in the wake of a population explosion, this traditional norm has become a liability. "The smile on the face of Thai farmers and their unwillingness to co-operate with each other for a long-term benefit is a sign of culture lag."[12]

Thai farmers as a class are known for their fortitude, magnanimity, hospitality, generosity, fun loving and pragmatic outlook, and innovativeness, among other positive traits. However, they are also said to be envious, suspicious, and fatalistic in their attitudes.

There are apparent connections between these behavioral traits and development issues in contemporary Thai society. A case in point is the shortage of leadership at the village level. Farmers are hesitant to volunteer for leadership positions for fear of being considered too ambitious. This, for example, makes agricultural extension work difficult. To cite another example, when leaders are chosen, Thai farmers tend to select those who are better off, implying the search for a patron.

Behavioral Norms and the Economy

Patrimonial economics is characterized by the right and obligation of political authority to manipulate the society's production and exchange facilities at its own initiative and according to its own design in the name of public welfare (service) and to appropriate and dispose of the society's economic benefits (prebends) as it wishes in recompense for its service.[13]

The political and the economic spheres in the patrimonial society are joined by their mutual dependence on morality. As already indicated, morality is at the center of an integrated and stable social order. It is maintained, therefore, that:

> Without moral compulsion, ... neither the patrimonial apparatus nor the practical, economically oriented masses will be materially productive because without a sense of morality, political leadership will not reward the moral and punish the evil. Rather, they will raise up to positions of political responsibility and support in the general society those who will only support their own service needs rather than the needs of others.[14]

Although laudable for its idealism, in practice this economic model proves itself rather problematic because, particularly in conjunction with the patrimonial principles of authority (autocratic and arbitrary rule) and social organization (patron-client relationship), patrimonial economics seemingly sanctions behavioral norms, e.g., corruption, which seriously compromise and undermine national development.

According to a report by the Anti-Corruption Committee, in the five-year period from 1982 some 10,559 cases of corruption were reported, with most of the incidents occurring in the Interior Ministry, followed by the Ministries of Education and Defense.[15]

The pursuit of personal aggrandizement at the expense of society has become the norm in Thailand. So-called "influential people," usually in high government office, abuse their positions by instructing subordinates or persons in their entourage to violate the law in order to obtain material benefits solely for themselves. Examples of this type of behavior are manifest in the rapid deterioration of forest and other environmental resources, as well as in a thriving drug business.

The fact that the patrimonial society sanctions much if not all of this type of behavior underscores the depth of its roots in Thai society and helps to explain why public efforts to address these issues seldom go beyond the rhetorical stage. Again, the implications of this economic model for development are readily apparent, which leads to the broader relationship between the patrimonial society and development.

Parameters of Development in Thai Society

Jacobs' thesis is that Thai patrimonialism is responsible for modernization without development. "Modernization" denotes "the maximization of the potential of the society within the limits set by the goals and the fundamental structure (or forms) of the society." While "development" refers to "the maximization of the *potential* [emphasis added] of the society, regardless of any limits currently set by the goals or fundamental structure of the society."[16]

POWER AND CULTURE

Modernization may be part of development, but the reverse is not necessarily true. Jacobs sees development as a "special case of modernization," which is associated with feudal but not with patrimonial societies.[17]

In essence, Jacobs' thesis, whether one wishes to accept it or not after examining the evidence, raises a critical issue: namely the impact of a society's inherent limitations on its development.

While uneven development of societies certainly cannot be attributed to internal factors alone, the empirical record of international development leaves little doubt that a society's collective experience, traditional structures and widely shared modes of behavior, based on common beliefs and cultural norms, will affect the quality of change.

Mindful also that development, a process of unfolding and change, is a relative phenomenon that each society has to define and determine for itself, it is impractical to prescribe formulas for development and to judge societies accordingly.

The important consideration is to be aware of the society's assets and liabilities with reference to the collective development goals, i.e., the type of change which is desired. This stock-taking process allows for the option of minimum change in a cultural heritage that continues to promote the general welfare of the society.

Thailand, as is the case with most other developing countries, still lacks a national development concept of its own making. Instead, the society has been subjected to change induced by external factors with little regard to its long-term consequences and inherent merit. Employing Jacobs' thesis, it is apparent that only quantitative, in a sense superficial change, could result. Modernization introduced material change (progress) into Thai society, grafting as it were the symbols of Western development on to a traditional society.

As a result, contemporary Thai society is afflicted by discontinuities. There are divisions and gaps that will become more pronounced as modernization takes its course. Pending a re-assessment of the society's collective goals, which does not appear likely in the foreseeable future due to the prevailing power structure, true development will remain only a hope.

It is this belief in a more humane, more just society that motivates a growing number of foreign and Thai private development organizations.

Non-Governmental Organizations in Thai Society

Private, non-profit development agencies represent a growing, albeit subordinated part of Thailand's development community. Their importance, i.e., their influence or power, does not flow from their material contributions (although these contributions are increasingly significant), but derives from the attributes shared by many private agencies, i.e., their comparative advantage, including their small size (no large bureaucracies), their flexibility, grassroots orientation, cultural sensitivity, local expertise, and relative political independence.

Although, as pointed out before, comparative advantage is not triggered as a matter of course, collectively NGOs do offer a significant alternative to the development strategies pursued by other members of the development community.

To what extent then, if at all, are these NGO attributes and their overall roles circumscribed by the assumed patrimonial aspects of Thai society? More specifically, what are the actual limitations imposed on NGOs by social and cultural constraints? And finally, how much influence does the NGO community wield, with reference to a reassessment of Thai development goals?

The 1987 *NGO Directory*, published by the Thai Volunteer Service (TVS), listed a total of 136 active non-governmental development organizations, 22 of which are foreign based.[18] The actual number is probably closer to the original TVS estimate of 240, 170 of which are indigenous NGOs.[19] The discrepancy between these figures is the result of revised criteria for classifying local NGOs.

The profile of foreign NGOs working in Thailand—between 50 and 70 agencies— is characterized by differences in size, orientation and program scope. Financially and in terms of staff, major NGOs (e.g., CCF, CRS and CARE) maintain annual budgets ranging from 60 to 120 million baht ($24 to 48 million), with staff support of 24 to 120 people. It should be noted, however, that staff size does not necessarily correlate with the agency's financial resources. The corresponding budget figures for smaller foreign-based NGOs range from approximately 10 to 40 million baht ($4–16 million) (e.g., Save the Children Fund/U.K. and The Asia Foundation, respectively).[20]

Most NGOs came to Thailand during the mid-1970s and early '80s, in many cases starting out as refugee and relief agencies. The recent shift from relief to development work is continuing. CARE and Redd Barna, for example, are consolidating their initial development experience in Thailand, while completing the transition from relief to development work.

This evolution is a reflection of dominant trends in the international NGO community. As indicated above, in the post-war era, NGOs moved from first generation (relief and welfare) to second generation (longer term development projects), and most recently to the third stage, which casts NGOs as catalytic or "strategic" organizations. Most foreign-based NGOs in Thailand fall into the second generation category.

Their program activities cover all development sectors, including health, nutrition, education, agriculture, environment, small enterprise development and income generation, among others. Most NGO projects are concentrated in the Northeast and the North of Thailand, where the incident of poverty is highest, leaving the Central Region and especially the South less attended.

POWER AND CULTURE

Programs generally target the rural sector since more than 70% of the Thai population still lives in villages or small towns. Rural and community development programs, therefore, claim most of the NGO budgets. However, due to the causal connection between the plight of the farming communities in the North and the Northeast and the abysmal conditions in Bangkok's slums, a growing number of programs address urban development problems as well.

For example, The Christian Childrens' Fund (CCF) provides partial support for the Human Development Center (HDC), which devotes its widely recognized educational and income generating programs to the improvement of living conditions in Klong Toey and other Bangkok slums. Redd Barna also has become increasingly active, initiating community development and special projects for members of Bangkok's crowded communities, for example, fire rehabilitation and a program for street children.

In order to work in Thailand, all foreign NGOs require clearance from the Royal Thai Government, which usually takes the form of a signed agreement between the agency and the Department for Technical and Economic Cooperation (DETEC). Other government agencies (e.g., the Community Development Department) may also be part of the original arrangements or NGOs may collaborate with them at a later stage.

On the whole, the relationship between NGOs and the government, with few exceptions, has been smooth. Unlike the local NGOs, their foreign counterparts have not experienced the same level of official suspicion and mistrust. The government feels better informed and exercises more control over the activities of external agencies, many of which are working in close cooperation with the public sector.

Still, from time to time, the government has made efforts to extend its control over the private non-profit sector by expanding reporting and related requirements for NGOs. Generally, the impetus for seeking expanded government controls stems from national security considerations. Many NGOs maintain programs in or close to sensitive border regions, which present serious military and political problems.

Coordination among NGOs and their programs is limited. Unlike refugee affairs, which have benefited from the work of the Committee for Coordination of Services to Displaced Persons in Thailand (CCSDPT), few comparable mechanisms exist for development NGOs. A recent exception is an NGO Coordinating Committee on Slums, composed of a total of nine foreign and indigenous NGOs, which agreed to coordinate their activities and to support each other.

Other coordinating efforts involve principally local NGOs. In general, private development organizations in Thailand tend to work relatively independently, thus lending more importance to informal channels of communication.

Similarly, NGOs are not known for joint ventures. They prefer to concentrate on their own projects, for reasons which have more to do with fundraising and expeditious program implementation, than with objections to the principle of coordination.

NGO Influence on Thai Development

Private development agencies derive their strength from several sources, including a sense of purpose (moral obligation or religious mission), the nature of their organizations and their characteristic development approaches and strategies (comparative advantage), as discussed above.

In an attempt to assess the effectiveness of these resources within the context of Thai society—referring to its principal institutions, shared values and dominant modes of behavior—the following discussion will attempt to review the issue of comparative advantage in the context of Jacobs' "modernization without development" thesis.

To summarize briefly, Jacobs observed that the Thai people are individualistic and pragmatic; that they are not accustomed to plan ahead because in the past the people did not experience major economic deprivations; and that by tradition, they are fun-loving, reflected in "Sanuk", an expression which implies care-free, good times.

Furthermore, the availability of ample resources in the past, including food, helps to explain another frequently observed characteristic, namely the inability or unwillingness to cooperate on a longer-term basis. This does not contradict the "culture of mutual help," which finds expression in the practice of assisting each other during planting *long khaek* and harvesting.[21]

As any visitor to a Thai village will confirm, the people are most generous and hospitable. These characteristics are reinforced by tolerance and understanding of foreign ways. However, in-depth study of village life also find evidence of the following traits: egocentrism, narrow horizons and limited timeframes, suspicion and envy.[22]

These stereotypical attributes must be seen in context, i.e., within the dominant institutional framework of Thai society, which is autocratic, hierarchical, and bureaucratic in nature. The moral leader, an integrated and balanced order, two classes (small elites and the people as a whole) and the patron-client system are the hallmarks of this society. And to a large extent they are still part of contemporary Thai society.

The dominant attitudes and resulting behavior patterns produced by a patrimonial society encourage individuals, for example, not to be overly ambitious, not to depend on their own abilities, but to rely instead on the influence and benevolence of a patron. Furthermore, in this system people learn to be deferential, highlighting the importance of power and status symbolized by public office.

POWER AND CULTURE

Deference in an autocratic context also leads the individual to expect capricious, erratic and often unfair behavior on the part of superiors, in particular holders of public office. This implies also the subordination of the many to the few and of the village to the city.

The system is reinforced by the law of Karma, the belief that people receive in this lifetime what they earned through either good or bad deeds in an earlier one. Injustices therefore are not to be blamed on others or on society at large, but are the result of personal conduct. Consequently, except under the most extraordinary circumstances, a relatively public which is relatively submissive tends to be the norm in Thai society.

In this context, what happens to NGOs with their preoccupation to reach the poor, the intent to foster community participation in all aspects of the development process, to work at the grass-roots level, to be flexible and experimental in outlook, to strengthen local institutions, to promote efficiency and to avoid political involvement as much as possible?

Reaching the Poor

Allowing for the persistent gap between rhetoric and practice, the goal of reaching the poor, as discussed earlier, is inherently difficult to achieve and is compounded further by some of the attitudinal patterns germane to Thai society. The belief in Karma, tempered by the practice of merit making, and combined with the hierarchical, status conscious social system, tends to moderate compassion. Also, within the context of the patron-client relationship, prospects for the poor to improve their situation are definitely circumscribed. In addition, selfish behavior and envy are traits that are not likely to advance the interests of the poor.

Are these circumstances, at least in part, responsible for the fact that NGOs frequently end up working with the more well-to-do, the leading groups in their target communities, at the expense of the poor? Furthermore, are the described attitudes, in effect, representative of additional barriers to the goal of reaching the poor? Given the existing social stratification, are villagers not likely to perceive this objective as symbolic output and not as a concrete policy objective?

These questions do not yield clear-cut answers. Field data permit various interpretations. For example, compiling community baseline information, the village leadership may experience difficulties in deciding who, and how many, are poor. From their perspective, often only a handful of people are seen as poor.[23]

The goal of reaching the poor is at the heart of the NGO development process. While this commitment generates support from practically all other members of the development community, it may not carry as much weight at the project level.

Both, the issue of participation and the NGOs' preoccupation with process over outcome (i.e., seeking qualitative as opposed to mainly quantitative development)

86

represent major challenges for non-governmental and public development agencies alike. However, the declared desire to engage the people in their own development rings more true in theory than in practice.

Community or peoples' participation is difficult to obtain in Thailand at the village level for a number of reasons, which include the authority structure, the patron-client system, socio-economic divisions, the erosion of traditional practices and cultural norms, negative attitudes, and time constraints.

The patrimonial society with its emphasis on autocratic and highly centralized authority does not favor widespread participation in decisionmaking. Bureaucracies monopolize power and exercise their authority in a top-down manner. There are no inherent expectations of participation by the people—either on the part of the authorities and even less so on the part of the individual citizen. With the official shift in emphasis towards establishing a more democratic political system in Thailand, changes are introduced, but thus far principally at the margin.

The pervasive patron-client system is synchronized with the top-down authority structures. People are conditioned to look to their superiors (their boss, formal leader or patron) for instruction, advice, support, favors, etc. Personal initiative is not encouraged; it may simply backfire by incurring the patron's displeasure. At the group level independent initiative also is a risky business because such activities could be misconstrued by the authorities as instances of insubordination and worse, as political subversion, particularly in security-conscious Thailand.

Yet by far the most significant constraint on popular participation imposed by the system derives from considerations of power. Sharing power, according to conventional wisdom, translates into loss of influence, something that is entirely unacceptable.

Both participation and qualitative change in essence concern empowerment—giving people control over their own lives with minimum outside interference. Thus the concern for maintaining the existing center of power and corresponding relationships goes a long way to explain why these NGO objectives are fraught with difficulties.

There are other constraints caused by the class structure and the abandoning of cultural norms. Studies of poverty in Thailand often assume that poverty-stricken communities are homogeneous, when in fact real socio-economic distinctions exist.[24] These differences lend themselves to factionalism and conflict at the community level, which tends to discourage entire community segments from participation.

Another critically important force are the the changes in cultural norms, which are the result of a clash between tradition and modernity, the struggle between "authentic culture" and the "culture of alienation," a capitalistic, commercial pseudo-culture.[25] Traditional culture includes self-help practices, for example *long khaek* and important festivities such as Songkran. These practices evolve around the

POWER AND CULTURE

Wat and tend to incorporate folk wisdom as a major resource. These traditional elements are inherently participatory in nature and thus provide a counterpoint to the superimposed systems of domination and control.

Finally, long-established negative attitudes on the part of individuals and groups (often a sense of ineffectiveness, inferiority and powerlessness, giving way to fatalism) in conjunction with little time to spare for meetings and or training activities conspire further against widespread participation at the local level.

Despite these formidable odds, NGOs, perhaps more than any other development agent, do have a chance to make a difference in the overall quality of life of village communities because of the by now familiar reasons derived from their comparative advantage. NGOs are potential agents of empowerment.

Under the best of circumstances, governmental (i.e., bureaucratic) opposition to community-wide participation in the development process will be neutralized by co-opting, as it were, government agencies; elitist socio-economic structures at the community level can be harnessed by demonstrating that all or nearly all elements of the community potentially stand to gain from inroads against poverty by shared participation; the culture of cooperation ("mutual help") can be revived and or adapted by cultivating informal leadership, including abbots, former monks, wat committees and the heads of credit and savings groups; and attitudes and negative values can be changed through active learning processes, given sufficient time.[26]

Case Studies

The following data are based on two NGO project evaluations Anan Ganjanapan's assessment of the Integrated Rural Development Project (IRDP), funded by the Friedrich Naumann Stiftung (FNS), and the Akin-Yupin evaluation report of Redd Barna projects in the Northeast. These projects cover a ten-year period starting in the mid 1970s.

In 1975, the Friedrich Naumann Stiftung (FNS), a German NGO (funded through public channels), set up its first development project in Northern Thailand (Samoeng District), in response to pervasive conditions of poverty, caused by fundamentally unequal relationships and widening gaps between the villages, cities and markets. Following some initial successes in relieving rural communities from their "structural paralysis," FNS extended its programs to include additional villages in Lamphun Province, under its Integrated Rural Development Project(IRDP).[27]

The IRDP has the fundamental objective of promoting rural development through an integrated approach. The idea is to be able to see all aspects of rural life as interrelated, increasing production, health care, pre-school activities, etc.. Efforts will be made to involve peoples' participation as much as possible in carrying out most activities, especially through the principle of self-help organization.[28]

Redd Barna has conducted similar development projects in the Northeast (Khon Kaen Province) since 1981. "The purpose of this development program is to improve the well-being of children, particularly the well-being of their families in the context of the community in which they live."[29]

The underlying factors that both organizations had to consider very carefully include: one, a long-standing record of government neglect (at least until the adoption of the Fifth National Economic and Social Development Plan, with its Rural Poverty Eradication Program and the subsequent establishment of Tambon Councils); two, growing commercialization, facilitated by improvements in the physical infrastructure; three, a marginal agricultural area; and four, rapid deterioration of the environment through commercial and illegal logging and other kinds of damage caused by human beings.

FNS' development philosophy finds expression in a holistic view of the entire development process, beginning with the assumption that the problem of underdevelopment and poverty in rural communities is a result of the following conditions:

- Insufficient knowledge among the people on how to respond adequately to economic, social and psychological situations;
- The lack of organizational capabilities to represent interests effectively and to institutionalize self-help;
- The shortage of measures which reach the people directly–especially the most disadvantaged, socially and economically.

An emphasis on integration and participation informs the overall approach aiming at these conditions. FNS' development methodology relies principally on education and training, demonstration (largely through motivators and contact farmers), credit and marketing assistance, direct assistance and infrastructure improvement.[30]

Redd Barna's philosophy and approach are comparable:

The Redd Barna Thailand concept of community development …is that improvement in the health and well-being of people in a community rests primarily in the will and understanding of the people themselves, both in identifying community needs and in [program] implementation … Development is therefore the development of the people…another aspect …is one of linkages, or the linking of available resources such as services of various government ministries, technical expertise from universities or industry, or access to new markets to community needs.[31]

POWER AND CULTURE

This approach rests on the following premises:

- Government cooperation is essential, serving the poorest people is the highest priority;
- All programs must be participatory and self-help in nature;
- Direct aid should be made available through revolving funds;
- Programs need to be integrated with a focus on basic needs;
- Self-reliance and independence from outside assistance should be final outcomes;
- And assistance should be provided only where requested and approved by the authorities.[32]

Power and Leadership

Especially during the preparatory stage of the Integrated Rural Development Project (IRDP), FNS sought to obtain government support and to build trust in the communities. Eventually, specific project activities—particularly in the fields of education and training—were jointly organized with the Agricultural Extension Department, the Community Development Department and the District Health Office.[33]

Redd Barna was also successful in its governmental relations. According to the evaluation report:

> It can be stated clearly that co-operation of government agencies have been obtained particularly as regards training, equipment and assistance in solving health problems of villagers, controlling plant disease, and construction of water resources. Reasonably smooth relationship between Redd Barna and the Government have been obtained at all levels including the Provincial level and the village level. Such co-operation was obtained in the period when non-government village workers in general were looked at by the government officials unfavorably.[34]

The history of IRDP (1979-1984) reflects many of the problems and issues discussed earlier, including autocratic authority, bureaucracy, class divisions, lack of cooperation and conflict. Formal leadership—village headmen and Kamna—generally from the rich peasant class, often proved to be unreliable and not interested in the project, or they might be interested only for reasons of personal enrichment. However, due to their pivotal position as gatekeepers, the formal leaders were of neccessity informed, consulted, and included in the affairs of the project.

The degree of cooperation by these leaders had a direct bearing on the community's overall level of participation:

> For those villages whose headmen still remain, as in the past, serving the community, there will be a high degree of people-participation in the development activities, based on

cooperative efforts. In contrast, low degree of people-participation will be found in those villages whose headmen, as is often the case, become more exclusively like government functionaries or work only for their own personal benefit. The reason is that in these villages there are big gaps or conflicts between villagers and their leadership.[35]

IRDP learned that two other factors—informal leadership and the support of the middle class—are critical to its influence in the community. Working through its team of eight motivators, IRDP gained experience in identifying and training (interestingly enough, with training assistance provided by the government) natural leaders, some of whom might become contact farmers, "to take the leadership role in the development of their own community."[36]

The IRDP was rather successful in most cases of group formation where it supported informal leaders running the cooperative stores, because generally there was less [of a] gap between those leaders and their members than in the case of the formal leaders.[37]

However, with hindsight a number of problems became more evident: the training courses payed too little attention to the root problems of rural development, too many contract farmers came from the better-off sections of the communities, and women were almost entirely excluded. These shortcomings reflect both preconceptions of the organization and skewed community power structures.

Another, rather ironic problem stemmed from the very success in mobilizing informal leadership for income producing activities, including the running of cooperative stores. The short-term economic benefits created demands for more consumer goods, which in the long run resulted in new dependencies for the communities. This situation raises a troubling issue for many NGOs wishing to promote self-reliance and independence.

Redd Barna's experience casts additional light on this issue from a different angle. The project villages closest to the city of Khon Kaen, which had experienced considerable commercialization, proved to be the most difficult to work with, and in the end, this is where Redd Barna's efforts were least successful. In fact social differences and hostilities between the rich and the poor increased. These results led the project evaluators to speculate whether "...it may be too late and impossible to reverse the trend..."[38]

The role of the motivators, which was critical to the success of IRDP, also illustrates comparative advantage at work. Motivators are development workers who stay and work with the villagers. They see themselves not so much as advisors, but as coordinators who encourage people in taking charge of their own affairs. Motivators are confidence builders and catalysts.

Their tasks are complex, requiring human relation skills and intimate knowledge of the community. A considerable amount of time may pass before they become accepted and trusted by the community. For example, IRDP's first team of motivators was suspected by some villagers of being communists:

> The problem was quickly overcome when the motivators proved themselves by working very closely with their official counterparts. In fact they later were even more trusted by the villagers than government development workers, as the motivators were able to live longer and work more closely with the villagers.[39]

For Redd Barna leadership selection was also a major issue. Particularly in two out of six project villages in Khon Kaen Province, field workers were confronted by major socio-economic differences. Also, during the early development stage, leaders were selected too hastily.[40]

Well-trained development workers who rely on face-to-face contact with villagers are the key to the NGO grassroots approach. Although intrinsically difficult, there is no substitute for close, regular contact with the target community. Trusted development workers are the NGO's most effective and most valuable resource.

IRDP's goals are improving all aspects of village life, encouraging community participation, and promoting better cooperation between the government, IRDP and the villagers according to the IRDP evaluation report:

> The motivators have generally been able to implement a fair number of these goals. However, they are most successful through their work in the development of themselves. This can be seen from the fact that some motivators have been able to recognize the limitation of a strict formula approach to community development work and have turned to look for a more open approach.[41]

Through an ongoing learning process and a willingness to be flexible, NGOs potentially increase their influence and overall effectiveness. These are lessons from which large bureaucratic development agencies appear to be unable to profit.

IRDP also demonstrates how NGOs may establish what amounts to a parallel power structure, composed largely of informal leaders and self-help groups, functioning with quasi-official support. This amounts to tacit recognition by the authorities of an empowerment of community, limited as it may be.

> Judged from the standpoint of the IRDP's two main objectives—promoting self-help organizations and improving the quality of community leadership—the project has achieved a great deal. Only in terms of quantity, the achievement might be considered moderate, because less than half of the communities within the project area were able to set up self-help groups of some kind and some of these groups managed to carry out their work themselves, after the withdrawal of IRDP. The great achievements, however, are found to be mostly qualitative and rather unexpected. Most villagers who are active in

some kind of self-help group think that they have gained more confidence in dealing with officials or outsiders....these villagers pay more attention not only to their community's own problems but also to the problems in society at large. Many of these villagers realize how much they have learned ...about management...as well as the power of bargaining.[42]

Culture and Participation

Since learning on the job, as it were, as a relative newcomer to development work in Thailand, the Friedrich Naumann Stiftung failed to capitalize on a major source of influence for NGOs—indigenous culture, local technology and knowledge—and concentrated instead on the material aspects of development. Only in the later stages of the project did field workers come to realize the value in studying and incorporating these factors into IRDP.[43]

In the Redd Barna projects considerable emphasis was placed on religion and traditional practices. For example, rice banks were established on the basis of *tam bun* (merit making), as opposed to the share-holding principle. Also the traditional practice of mutual help (*long khaek*) was adapted to counteract individualism, selfishness and the negative impact of commercialism. The cultural approach was most effective in the villages farthest removed from the urban center.[44]

There is a direct connection between culture, participation and power. Once a community is encouraged to activate old cultural practices and institutions, people will have an incentive to become involved. The activity in turn will support a sense of self-control and independence that promotes greater confidence and influence with external forces.

As it turned out, IRDP villages were the purveyors of a rich heritage of cultural beliefs and institutions—spirit cults, Buddhism and the spiritual essence of life (*khwan*) or vitality. The entire village organizational infrastructure is connected to these basic beliefs, collectively referred to as a "subsistence ethic."

These groupings and small, informal organizations include communal irrigation organizations, wat committees, inter-village wat networks, and exchange networks.

The most important lesson to be learned from this experience is this: given the right leadership, these functional groupings can be modified to accommodate various other tasks. It is more effective to activate these traditional organizations than to establish new ones.

Similar considerations apply to the use of indigenous technology and knowledge, also called "folk ecology."[45] Traditional farm practices, for example, in conjunction with appropriate technology, will facilitate NGO program implementation and enhance the project's cost effectiveness. In this situation the NGO role is essentially that of a facilitator and catalyst.

The difficulty faced by NGOs (and by all other development agencies) is one of cultural gaps—gaps between efficiency-oriented and formula-ready Western conceptions of what needs to be done and the traditional, generally unhurried and indirect approaches of the target community.

This is the difference between the "culture of practitioners" and the culture of rural people. More specifically, it has been noted that:

> Outsiders polarize into two cultures: a negative academic culture, mainly social scientists, engaged in unhurried analysis and criticism; and a more positive culture of practitioners, engaged in time-bounded action. Each culture takes a poor view of the other and the gap between them is often wide.
>
> A balanced view may best be sought in a pluralism which straddles both academic and practitioner cultures, which accepts both social and physical explanations, and which is open to the third culture, of rural people in a particular place.
>
> Practitioners have a sense, too, that their actions or non-actions make a difference. So while academics seek problems and criticize, practitioners seek opportunities and act.
>
> The third culture, of the rural people in a particular place, is the true center of attention and of learning.[46]

Another lesson derived from the experience of both NGOs suggests that these cultural gaps can in part be bridged through appropriate research methods cum development approaches. Thus, participant observation, participatory research, and participant organization "…describe methods in which rural people and outsiders are partners."[47] Explicit emphasis on the "third culture" effectively encourages approaches to development which work from the bottom up, from the remote to the central.

Balance Sheet

Negative values and attitudes in the communities account for some of the failures experienced by FNS and RB. For example, in the case of the IRDP, many cooperative group efforts came to naught for reasons of individual selfishness when leaders pursued their tasks principally for personal gain. Self-centered values, exacerbated by growing commercialism and materialism are at the root of most of the problems encountered on the projects in the effort to promote participation and self-reliance.

IRDP was unable to avoid getting enmeshed in the existing socio-economic power structures that always succeed in manipulating development programs aimed at the poor to promote their own ends. For example, the IRDP evaluation report states:

> In most cases, the well-to-do and the village leaders seem to benefit more from training than other villagers, especially in leadership training. This condition may widen the gap

between village leaders and other villagers at large who are increasingly unable to follow or keep control of their leaders.[48]

On the positive side:

It was found that there were an increasing number of village leaders who have joined various self-help groups (as ordinary members) enthusiastically without any aim of taking office in the administrative committee. In the past, these leaders were rather suspicious of the groups and only joined the group in order to enhance their personal reputation and benefit. This change is helping to solve the tensions between the well-to-do and the poor groups in the communities which used to be high because of the personal benefits the rich got from development projects.[49]

As indicated, successful self-help organizations, such as cooperatives, proved to be a mixed blessing—producing both more income and higher consumption of goods. This, plus greater dependence on the market economy, resulted in more debt for the villagers. Farm debt has become the number one problem of most rural areas in Thailand.

Redd Barna also experienced the negative influence of commercialism when young girls declined to participate in weaving groups set up by the project. The girls wanted to work in the city. They did not like having to wait for their wages.[50]

The overall record of both NGOs—the Friedrich Naumann Stiftung and Redd Barna—underscores the findings of the earlier discussion on NGOs' comparative advantage, which indicate that the presumed strength of non-profit development organizations are not automatically triggered with each new project. On the contrary, any advantages claimed by or on behalf of NGOs are a function of the agency's effort, experience, and professionalism.

The case studies suggest also that the various constraints inherent in Thai society and culture (Jacob's patrimonial society) need not be insurmountable. But it is imperative for NGOs to concentrate on the local culture and to work within that system. This approach requires a competent field staff residing as much as possible with the villagers.

Furthermore, there is no guarantee that the overall impact of successful NGO programs will lead to qualitative improvements in peoples' lives if short-term material improvements coincide with new, long-term dependencies. This is a key issue and a major point of contention between the growing number of indigenous development organizations and foreign NGOs. The adoption of the socio-cultural approach by Thai rural development NGOs will be closely examined in the following chapters.

Finally, the experience of the Friedrich Naumann Stiftung in Northern Thailand demonstrates that community participation in self-help organizations can generate greater self-confidence plus inter-personal and organizational skills. In short, despite the inroads of modernization and Western developmentalism, community self-reliance is a realistic development goal for Thai society. This, in essence, is the meaning of empowerment.

> Without reservation, villagers' participation in self-help organizations can be considered the strongest impact of IRDP development work in the communities. Although such impact is the most difficult to quantify, it can be seen in the development process itself, in terms of knowledge and abilities gained by participants, in carrying out group activities and in solving their problems.[51]

The headman of a Redd Barna project village, noting that the arrival of the NGO had made his job a lot easier, summarized the changes brought about as follows:

> Prior to Redd Barna's work in the village, no one could leave woven clothes and things around. They could be stolen. Things often got lost and stolen. Nowadays, there is no theft in the village at all…there used to be drug addiction …now there is none…[Also] it is far easier [now] to ask villagers for cooperation in communal work…it was not like this before.[52]

Chapter 5

THE ROLE OF LOCAL NON-GOVERNMENTAL ORGANIZATIONS

In the midst of generally passive voluntary associations …there has now emerged a new trend of private non-profit organizations with the specific aim of active social development. This is to a large extent a reaction to the adverse effects of planned development during the past two decades. The exclusive focus on economic growth gives rise to major social problems: income inequality, urban-rural imbalances, poverty, and unemployment ….there has been increasing awareness of the plights of underprivileged masses. Out of this common sense of social obligation, there arise increasing numbers of a new type of privately organized activities which could be grouped as development non-government organizations.

(Saneh Chamarik)

By far the most interesting and increasingly important participants in Thailand's development are the indigenous NGOs. They represent a concrete response to the status quo in Thai society, culture and its political system.

Compared to other members of the development community (government agencies, bi- and multi-lateral aid missions, and foreign NGOs) local development organizations do not carry much weight. Although they are rapidly increasing in number—the Thai Volunteer Service (TVS) Directory lists more than 100 active local NGOs—material and human resources are still insufficient. Their development approaches are generally considered outside the mainstream.

The apparent irony of this situation underscores the realities of national and international politics where domestic private agencies are often politically suspect or they become pawns in power plays. However, an underdog position contains also potential advantages, particularly when fresh ideas and alternative approaches are called for. Furthermore, the benefits of comparative advantage attributed to non-profit development agencies apply to foreign and indigenous NGOs alike.

The history of Thai development organizations reflects the actual record of national development policy, particularly the inability of the government and the foreign development community as a whole, to improve substantially the quality of life for all the people. Today the struggle against poverty in Thailand remains as much in the forefront of Thai politics as ever before.

The movement of local NGOs experienced its greatest expansion in the late 1970s and early 1980s due to a general liberalization of Thai society and in response to the need for alternatives to centrally planned, top-down, government-controlled national development programs. Their evolution, therefore, is both a measure of the gradual democratization of a traditional, authoritarian society, as well as an indication of potential future directions in Thailand's national development.

The history and current status of Thai NGOs is indicative of the shortcomings of predominantly public sector development because these local organizations were spawned principally by the government's inability to deal effectively with society's fundamental problems. This situation corresponds to the experience of the private development sector elsewhere. "NGOs exist because Governments have not responded sufficiently to the problems of the poor and the powerless."[1]

Once again, the primary reference points for the following discussion are the three concepts of *power, culture* and *development*, plus democracy as an indicator of favorable conditions for NGO development. In the Thai context, power is the name of the game. Government agencies, as a rule, respond to NGO grass-roots initiatives and programs with suspicion, seeing them as potential threats to their status and authority. For example, the NGO call for local self-determination and self-sufficiency, free from government controls, poses a continuing challenge for most government officials and agencies. Officials as well as NGO development workers often misunderstand the true nature of community empowerment.

Many Thai development organizations accept the premise that indigenous culture holds the key to alternative development. Based on traditional values, folk wisdom and Buddhist principles, culture has emerged as the major ideological current in Thai NGO circles.

While power is generally recognized as an inevitable factor, the essence of development and the ultimate direction for society the future of its social, cultural, economic, and political systems—remains the subject of heated, frequently divisive debates. Insisting on "qualitative" or "social development"—societal change which minimizes external intrusion, while balancing material with spiritual needs—local NGOs offer alternatives to traditional, growth-oriented, public-sector development programs.

Furthermore, the theory and practice of democracy is also very much part of the philosophical roots and general orientation of the Thai NGO community. Without, albeit limited steps in the direction of a more pluralistic, more liberal society—particularly following the 1973-1976 period and throughout the 1980s—local development organizations could not have come into existence.

THE ROLE OF LOCAL NON-GOVERNMENTAL ORGANIZATIONS

In the past, Thai society has not been hospitable to pluralistic movements and relatively free from government control. Recent NGO history, therefore, is illustrative of the "half-way democracy" practiced in Thailand today.

As beneficiaries of political liberalization, Thai development organizations contributed in turn significantly to the advancement of democratic institutions, by promoting popular participation, local autonomy and self-reliance at the grass-roots level. For example, guidelines regarding the responsibilities of NGO development workers stress democracy as a goal:

> [A] Development worker must foster the spirit of unity, mutual help and perseverance in seeking the solution to …village problems. He must be open and plan the long-term strategy and participate in planting the basis for democracy.[2]

The Early Period

The following brief historical overview provides the background for an analysis and evaluation of the role and likely future impact of Thailand's own development community—particularly in relation to the work of government development agencies and foreign NGOs.

The synopsis touches not only on the broader social context from which Thai NGOs emerged, but it includes also a brief survey of NGO/Government relations, NGO ideology, followed by an assessment of the strengths and weaknesses of local development organizations.

Speaking of the period from 1932 to 1957—the start of the constitutional monarchy in Thailand to the dark years of despotic rule, under Field Marshal Sarit Thanarat—Professor Likhit Dhiravegin observes:

> The social milieu was characterized by the absence of organized groups as countervailing forces necessary for power balancing and for bargaining in the democratic process. The Thai organizational setup was clearly seen in two areas: governmental and religious. The bureaucracy (military and civilian) and the Buddhist order were two institutions which were organized. Among the masses, an institutionalized organized group was absent. Unlike the Sinic culture where the family system served as a social organization below the state, such a system was nonexistent in Thailand…. The Thai were by necessity atomized individuals.

Given the social milieu in which social organization below the governmental and religious setups was absent, the formation of organized entities such as political parties and interest groups was hard to implement successfully. It had to center around the personality, and it had to be organized in a vertical manner.[3]

Commenting on the implications of the social context for contemporary voluntary associations, another prominent student of development affairs in Thailand states:

POWER AND CULTURE

> The fact is that in a centralized state like Thailand, there existed no tradition of voluntary associations like in the west or in the feudalistic Japan of the old days. And this, in spite of the oft-quoted traditional practice of mutual help in Thai agrarian setting [sic]. One even suspects that organized groups on a permanent basis were, and still are, to be discouraged. And whenever they are allowed to emerge, they are to be kept under control one way or the other by the authorities.[4]

Given the absence of a pluralistic tradition in the Western sense and in view of the fact that contemporary Thai NGOs are as much a response to the negative consequences of government development programs beginning with the national development plan in 1961 as they are the product of political liberalization, there were no Thai NGOs prior to the mid- and late 1960s, with the exception of the Thai Red Cross.

> …"Sapaunalomdaeng" was the first NGO established in Thailand, in the reign of King Rama V. …[it] became later the Thai Red Cross.[5]

All previous private efforts were initiated by missionaries. During the 1950s any development work outside of the public sector was branded as communist. "Even the Red Cross which is supposed to be an NGO was started by the government."[6]

The main catalyst in the evolution of Thai development NGOs were activist university students and leading academicians. Their influence is not only reflected in the early stages of Thailand's NGO movement, but continues to shape the character and the direction of the NGO community. Former student activists and university lecturers still provide intellectual guidance, practical leadership and training for development workers.

Credit union activities were among the first private efforts to help alleviate the plight of the poor. They gave rise to an entire movement that continues to inspire self-help development programs throughout Thailand. After many difficult years under precarious political circumstances, the dream of a handful of caring individuals was realized when the first Thai credit union, the Soon Klang-Thewa Credit Union, was established in July 1965.[7]

The credit union movement evolved from a voluntary action center for the poor (located in Bangkok's Dindaeng slum), which was established in 1959 on the initiative of Father Alfred Bonningue, a French Jesuit priest; Dr. Chavalit Chitranukroh, a medical doctor; and Mrs. Prakhin Xumsai, a Chulalongkorn University professor.

Their idea to establish a credit union for poor people gained momentum after Amporn Wathanavongs, a Buddhist monk, joined the center in 1960. His vision of a self-help organization based on brotherly love provided constant inspiration to the credit union's co-founders and later for Thai NGO leaders.[8]

THE ROLE OF LOCAL NON-GOVERNMENTAL ORGANIZATIONS

Also, "The western idea of Work Camps, encouraged by the Americans, enabled the young elites in Bangkok to go out and see how the people in the country lived. And through these Work Camps, they could show that they had some care for the country without being regarded as communists."[9]

Cited as the first rural Thai development NGO, the Thailand Rural Reconstruction Movement (TRRM) was set up in 1969. Founded by Dr. Puey Ungphakorn, "who thought that NGOs were possible..",[10] TRRM, led by prominent businessmen and civil servants, was a pioneer in integrated rural development.[11] The Foundation's lasting influence is felt especially through the training provided to its field workers, many of whom are still active today.

Another critically important organization among the early NGOs was the Catholic Council of Thailand for Development (CCTD), which was formally established on February 16, 1973. CCTD evolved into a large, nation-wide organization with 10 regional activity centers and 25 other member organizations. Its Secretariat has 16 staff members, and funds are obtained from foreign and domestic sources. CCTD's legacy is twofold: represents the prototype of a comprehensive, traditionally-oriented NGO with a wide spectrum of responsibilities and functions, ranging from education to culture and religion.

Secondly, CCTD contributed indirectly to the establishment of several local NGOs, especially the Village Institution Promotion (VIP) Project and the Rural Development Documentation Center. The entire leadership of these NGOs, as well as other staff members, emerged from the ranks of CCTD in 1985.

The Komol Keemthong Foundation (KKF)—named after a murdered former student activist and teacher, and suspect to both the government and the communists— is another major Thai NGO, which is part of Dr. Puey Ungphakorn's legacy. Registered in 1971, with Dr. Sulak Sivaraksa as the Managing Director, the Foundation's far-reaching goals include higher levels of idealism within Thai society, the promotion of Buddhist values, community education, social welfare, and support for the arts and culture.[12]

Despite government criticism, particularly in the context of the 1973–1976 student revolts, the Foundation is still active. Its annual budget exceeds 1.5 million baht ($60,000), of which 70% comes from domestic sources.

A few months prior to the violent attacks on the Komol Foundation and its supporters in October 1976, another NGO with similar aims, the Coordinating Group for Religion in Society (CGRS), was established in March of that year by prominent activists, including Professor Sulak. Its purpose remains "To promote basic religious principles toward the development of love, humanity, solidarity, justice and peace in society." The organization concentrates on human rights, rural life development, religion and nonviolence.[13]

The brief democratic period from 1973 to 1976 proved to be a watershed for NGOs. Political liberalization made the initial growth of NGOs possible while subsequent years of severe repression strengthened the resolve of the NGO leadership to continue their struggle for a free and just society. After 1976 the Thai NGO community was forced under ground, with its leadership going into the jungle and ideologically moving more to the left.

As the 1970s ended, the political climate allowed new NGOs to emerge and to work in public, giving rise to the need for coordination, which is a constant issue.

> From 1978 and 1979 onwards, those who were involved in various activities started to work in small organizations. However, a number of pioneering founders of NGOs thought that more co-ordination among these small groups should be initiated to strengthen their efficient activities.[14]

One of the early coordinating bodies was the Thai Inter-Religious Commission for Development (TICD), which began in December 1979 with the support of six Thai organizations, including Mahachulalongkorn (Buddhist) University, the Catholic Council of Thailand for Development (CCTD), and the Credit Union League of Thailand, Ltd.[15]

The Commission was to function as an independent body and its objectives were (1) "to co-ordinate individuals and organizations involved in religion and development," (2) "to exchange experiences and knowledge about religion and development among interested parties," and (3) "to provide training programmes and other facilities for organizations in need of support."[16]

Similarly, another coordinating body, The Thai Development Support Committee (TDSC), was established in August 1982, "…in order to bring the small NGOs together to tackle their common problems and support one another in their work."[17] Its primary objectives are threefold: to make NGOs more effective, to serve as an information clearinghouse, and to promote NGO cooperation.[18]

TDSCs many activities include publicity and public information campaigns (seeking wider public support), providing contact with foreign sources of NGO support, regular publications (e.g., the *Thai Development Newsletter*), hosting conferences, seminars and workshops. TDSC's budget is in excess of 1 million baht ($400,000), 80% of which is derived from foreign NGO sources. Some of the European contributors are: MISEREOR and Danchurch Aid.[19]

Both the Inter-Religious Commission for Development and the Thai Development Support Committee encouraged the current trend to establish more development-oriented NGOs and for others to switch to development work.

The lessons of the turbulent 70s continue to affect the direction of the local organizations, particularly in the eyes of the Thai public, which tends to associate NGOs with leftist or radical causes. Furthermore, the bitter experience of Thai intellectuals in the NGO movement, during the years of repression, reinforced their long-standing antipathy towards government development programs. Although there is today a greater willingness to seek accommodation between NGOs and government development agencies, as Professor Sulak points out, strong reservations remain:

> More and more people were convinced that to follow the government was not really the thing. And many people with a deep commitment wanted to work outside of the government. From 1978 to 1979 onwards, those who were involved in various activities started to work in small organizations.[20]

In view of the close ties between academics and development NGOs, it is not surprising that the movement has been characterized by persistent gaps—socio-economic differences—which derive from the middle class origin of its leadership and the working class background of the target population in the rural and urban areas.

These discrepancies between Thai NGOs and other members of the development community, including the villagers, the public at large and the government, are still, according to some observers, a "major burden" for local NGOs.[21] However, greater visibility, growing legitimacy and successful development programs, are improving the public image of Thai NGOs. Progress is particularly evident in formerly strained relations between government and NGOs, as officials have become increasingly aware of the positive contributions made by the NGO community.[22]

Taking Stock

Non-profit development organizations are inherently predisposed towards critical views of the government. Their attitudes are "...conditioned by the [sic] sense of alienation from the bureaucratic, centralized, and depersonalizing features of contemporary government and business. In this sense, we can say that the new NGOs are reactive, however, they are not revolutionary."[23]

The following discussion illustrates the important and complex roles that Thai NGOs perform. In February 1984 a major seminar on "Rural Development in Thailand," sponsored by the Royal Thai Government's Department of Technical and Economic Cooperation (DETEC) and the Canadian International Development Agency (CIDA), was held in the resort city of Pataya, south of Bangkok.

Although this was certainly not the first conference of its kind in Thailand, this meeting was remarkable for two reasons. First, it provided an opportunity for key development specialists, representing government as well as private development agencies, to engage in a thorough and frank exchange of ideas.

Secondly, it produced a surprisingly critical assessment of the government's own development record over the past two and one half decades. In particular, the various formal and informal presentations confirmed the dual thesis that government programs are largely responsible for the widening gap between the rich and the poor, which in turn, led to the rise of Thai non-governmental development organizations.

POWER AND CULTURE

According to the Seminar Report:

> Thailand has implemented its Development Plans for more than two decades. Throughout the first four Plans covering the period 1961-1981, economic development was based primarily on a growth oriented strategy aiming at the increase in national income and production.[24]

Because of the strong emphasis on economic growth, the Western-oriented model produced the following conditions, now fixed features of Thai development:

- increased dependence on world markets
- relatively high economic growth
- expanding government development programs
- comprehensive foreign aid programs
- a substantially improved and expanded infrastructure

Consequently the government's ability to penetrate society down to the village level increased significantly; rural communities became more dependent on external market forces; and the gap between the rural population living at subsistence level and the small, but expanding and increasingly wealthy middle class widened.

From the peoples' perspective their part of the bargain included:

- malnutrition affecting 51% of the children
- farm debt (with the average debt slightly above the average annual cash income)
- rapid deforestation
- prostitution (affecting at least 3% of young women)

The following, related problems, listed by the Thai Volunteer Service (whose representatives participated in the seminar), are also part of the overall situation:

- lack of community participation in decision making
- uncertainty regarding land tenure
- an unstable market system
- government bureaucracy
- lack of social consciousness [25]

Cognizant of these serious problems, the DETEC/CIDA Seminar Report admitted:

> ..it turns out that a large segment of the Thai population has not benefited from the overall national development....The 1981 data...revealed that about 63% of the rural people suffer from parasite disease and 90% of the Northeast farmers are suffering from anemia.

The illiteracy rate is also as high as 14.5% of the total population, the majority of which lives in the rural areas.[26]

Elaborating on the problems and obstacles, the Report also states:

...These [problems and obstacles] include the inconsistency of the projects with local conditions, the lack of adequate participation of the people in implementing projects, the lack of proper understanding on the part of field officers, the delays in budget disbursements and projects implementation, etc.[27]

Interestingly, even the charge that government development programs are not only ineffective but harmful and counterproductive, a key proposition in the local NGO literature, managed to find its way into the printed Seminar Report:

In some cases, the introduction of government policies and measures to raise rural income may also backfire. It is claimed, for example, that the rural job creation program in some areas has threatened the existence of the tradition of assisting one another in planting and harvesting seasons. The case is often used as an example in which the lack of knowledge of local culture and conditions on the part of the government may lead to failure of development objectives as well as the failure to translate appropriate micro policy into meaningful measures and actions at the micro level.[28]

Giving public credence to NGO positions that are highly critical of the government did not stop with a frontal attack on the public sector's long-standing development policy. It went on to question the government's true motives and its commitment:

Finally, questions are raised by certain groups of people concerning the government's commitment and sincerity toward rural development. The government's intervention in the agricultural market via taxes and export quota, its refusal to intervene in the market where monopolistic practices exist, its considerable subsidy to industries in the Bangkok-centered region, its reluctance to relinquish power to local people, etc., all point to the conclusion that in fact the government may have played a major role in creating rural-urban disparity.[29]

While the government's development strategy has changed relatively little—its intention from the start has been to advance the material well-being of the people—Thailand's development NGOs, on the other hand, have experimented with several approaches, although some of these are indistinguishable from the public sector's development orientation.

Dr. Seri Phongphit, a scholar and leading member of the Thai development community, points out that during the 1960s Thai NGOs concentrated on economic assistance for villagers through income producing activities, vocational training and related projects.

As the number of indigenous NGOs began to grow during the 1970s, development approaches also proliferated, including socio-cultural and purely political approaches. The socio-cultural approach concentrates on community organization and bargaining, while the political approach advocates "power and structural change," with less attention given to economic concerns that might only "delay the revolution."[30]

According to Dr. Seri, it is only recently that Thai NGOs adopted the "socio-cultural" approach, which incorporates all community resources—material, human, cultural and religious. This eclectic development concept does not entail a preconceived model. The thrust of "socio-cultural" thinking is captured in the slogan "Back to the Roots" (which is also the title of a book edited by Dr. Seri's).[31]

If one accepts the premise that Thai NGOs received their primary impetus from failed government development programs, a certain learning process becomes apparent. NGOs experiment with appropriate development alternatives, free from the restraints and vested interest which afflict the public sector.

However, it should be pointed out in this connection that the ability to learn on the basis of past experience is not a monopoly of private, non-profit agencies, although, as argued below, NGOs appear to be more adept at it.

For example, the DETEC/CIDA Seminar produced evidence of progressive ideas very similar to the "socio-cultural" approach advanced by government development officials. Defining rural development, Khun Pracha Laphanan, a District Chief Officer, spoke of "...rural development...involving improvement in the standard of living, attaining security of life and property, freedom, and maintaining moral standards and culture."

Furthermore, as a guide to rural development, he recommended the following measures: ascertain "the true conditions and problems of villagers, improve the villagers' education (including ethics), encourage villagers' participation, promote managerial skills of villagers, promote appropriate technology, promote reforestation, allow foreign agencies to play a supportive role."[32]

The historical record shows that the political era beginning with the inauguration of the first administration headed by Prime Minister Prem Tinsulanonda marks a new period of growth, reconciliation and dynamism for the Thai NGO movement.

In its own assessment of the past decade and a half, the Thai Volunteer Service (TVS), a major development NGO promoting training and coordination, reports:

> Most of them [Thai NGOs] have grown up in the last decade. Yet they are beginning to make some impact on public awareness and public opinion concerning social and development issues, and are emerging as a small progressive force for social justice and social change in Thailand.

THE ROLE OF LOCAL NON-GOVERNMENTAL ORGANIZATIONS

The NGDO movement, in any case, is still weak and lacking in support from the general public. It is still building experience and working out methods and directions. In the last four years, nevertheless, there has been considerable progress. NGDOs have benefited from more exchanges of views and experiences and have modified their approaches to bring them more into tune with target groups' needs. In addition, they have developed their ability to publicize the problems of the underprivileged and have improved coordination and staff development. Professionals, students, and recent university graduates are all showing new interest in NGDOs.[33]

In sum, in Thailand the record of government—NGO relations has been characterized from the outset by mistrust, antagonism and major differences in attitudes, motives, ideas and development approaches. As recently as 1981, Chamniern Voraratchaiyaphan, a Thai NGO leader, observed in an interview:

But if we are all going to discuss the essence of developmental work or the true objectives of development, we have to talk about liberation. Strictly speaking, our society [is] ever changing. In the process of changing or in the process of developing, there must be a transformation in the state of what we consider advantage taking and economics, social and political oppressions.

There are only two cliques, whether you are developing to liberate or you are developing to dominate [sic].[34]

More recently a softening of positions and a search for accommodation has taken place.

Eclectic Ideology

The attitudinal and behavioral changes that Thai NGOs have experienced are the result of diverse and shifting ideological currents. As already suggested, one of the characteristics of the indigenous agencies is heterogeneity of development concepts and approaches, ranging from relief or welfare to future-oriented systemic models.

Nor is there a consensus among analysts regarding appropriate categories to distinguish between NGOs. Some observers apply political criteria, emphasizing various ideological persuasions. Others use development activities and/or the target communities as distinguishing features of NGO orientations.

For example, Philip Hirsch points to traditionalists, like Apichart Thongyou, who use the small village—its inherited values, traditions, and Buddhist principles—as the ideal type.[35]

On the other hand there are those who maintain that it is too late to turn the clock back. They subscribe to development programs which seek "…to raise the poor farmers within the wider system, by increasing their bargaining power through group purchases, marketing, and even group production enterprises."[36]

POWER AND CULTURE

Yet another system-wide approach supports overall efforts to develop local leadership and to involve groups in agrarian reform and rural development. This includes the establishment of networks through exchange visits between villages.

Often a particular approach to development is a function of professional training and background. Doctors and health professionals, along with religious leaders, especially Buddhist monks, are increasingly associated with NGO work.

"With such a mixed bag of results of official rural development policy [sic] and with the scattering of NGDOs, it is not surprising that there is currently considerable confusion."[37]

Jon Ungphakorn, Director of the Thai Volunteer Service, makes a distinction similar to David Korten's first and second generation NGOs, referring to development agencies that maintain a welfare or social service orientation and others that concentrate on community development. He relates the difference to a change in the concept of social development over the past ten years. Given the nature and magnitude of the social problems confronting society, he argues, the handout approach was bound to fail. Instead, people need to take stock of their own human and material resources; they need to organize themselves and deal with their own problems.[38]

Some NGOs, logically drawing the inference from community developmentwith its emphasis on self-reliance and self-sufficiency, went one step further by calling for "community organization," which implies empowerment. According to Dr. Seri:

> The basic assumptions of community organization are (a) the elites will take control over the resources after the development process has taken place for some time, (b) the powerless or the ordinary farmers have no means to take control of the benefits and resources, (c) the power must be returned to the poor and the oppressed or else the situation will get worse.[39]

Consequently, the role of the outside agency is changed from implementor to catalyst. Community organization, at least to some observers, even implies the replacement of NGOs with "people organizations", i.e., local communities relying exclusively on their own independent power. "However, the basic conclusion to any discussion on community organization is that the poor must share the power and partake in social development."[40]

> Peoples Organizations have arisen (both spontaneously and with the stimulus of NGOs) as organizations of people who all share the same problem and do not see Government as answering their calls to deal with these problems.[41]

Regardless of the particular development orientation and the nuances of a given approach, they all constitute to one degree or another an alternative to the conventional public sector development approach. They share the idea that basic needs are important but not exclusive goals of development:

> There is also the quality of living and experience the value people set on the familiar, on being needed, on a purpose and role in life, on love, on religious observations, on dancing and song, festivals and ceremonies, on things in their seasons, and bringing in the harvest. Perhaps the most one can say is that for the full enjoyment of these, secure and decent livelihoods may be necessary but not sufficient on their own.[42]

Shared Assumptions

Although eclectic in outlook and program orientation, Thai NGOs share basic assumptions regarding their purpose and role in society. This is largely the result of the circumstances that gave rise to the Thai NGO movement in the first place. As alternative development agents, Thai NGOs began with essentially similar values and assumptions about fundamental problems in contemporary society, as summed up in the following statement:

> Thai NGDOs reject the use of power conflicts or violence as a way of solving problems. They associate such methods with dictatorship and feel that their use can only lead to further misery, conflict, and violence. NGDOs feel that developing peoples' consciousness and carrying out small-scale, peaceful, practical activities is a more appropriate and secure path to social change in Thai contexts. Thus NGDOs view social development not as an overt struggle but as a long, painful process of change in consciousness. A great deal of theoretical orientation is rooted in prevailing cultural values and an appreciation of current political realities, particularly local government officials' distrust of NGDOs. The unhappy experiences of many Thai intellectuals with constitutional and rapid popular mobilization efforts, right-wing violence, and an ideologically-backward Communist Party during the 1970s have also played a part in producing a reaction against much radical social theory and the confrontational political activism practiced in other Asian countries.[43]

More specifically, many PVO leaders and their organizations subscribe to four assumptions: One, the raison d'etre of development is poverty in all of its dehumanizing dimensions. Two, poverty is caused first and foremost by "oppressive structures" (principally the state, economic, social, cultural, educational and religious systems). Three, these internal forces are linked with their international counterparts. Four, people have to regain the ability to control their own affairs.[44]

> The people themselves, after prolonged oppression, have lost self-determination and awareness for their own potentials. It is not as easy as putting the switch on and then people can suddenly start movement for their own development.[45]

POWER AND CULTURE

Quoting Dr. Soedjatmoko in *"Development is Learning,"* Dr. Prawase continues:

> Learning itself is the keyword for development. Without learning there is no development. Participation without learning does not lead to development. Learning by all sectors concerned is development.[46]

NGO thinking regarding rural development strategy, according to Jon Ungphakorn, rests on similar assumptions: for villagers to obtain true economic and political power in the long run (instead of merely focusing on increasing productivity and income or promoting national security), they need to be placed first of all in a position where they may obtain basic minimum needs (food, health, education, and decent employment); and secondly, their political and social consciousness needs to be promoted, along with local organizations and activities, involving the people in the development process.[47]

To summarize, ideologically Thai NGOs typically see themselves as legitimate critics of government development programs, offering viable, albeit small-scale, alternatives, based on the concept of community development, with its emphasis on self-reliance, self-sufficiency and political empowerment.

These values do not correlate with the conventional conception of power (defined as influence, derived from political, military and related sources); instead, they imply a redirection (power emanating from below) and a redistribution of power (allowing more people to share in community decision-making).

Because of these conceptual differences, the interface between non-governmental development organizations and their public counterparts is fraught with complications. For instance, while local NGOs stand ideologically in opposition to public sector development programs, they need to accept a modicum of cooperation with government agencies in order to remain viable.

By the same token, although government personnel basks in the authority of the state, at times they reluctantly concede greater efficiency and effectiveness to the private, non-profit sector. While some enlightened government agencies have come to regard NGOs as useful laboratories and even as partners in development, the opposite view—NGOs perceived as troublesome and unprofessional rivals in community development—tends to predominate.

Realistically, compromise is both necessary and possible. Furthermore, efforts to change long-standing prejudices and to seek accommodation are no longer isolated occurrences as the willingness to recognize each other's strengths and weaknesses grows.

NGOs, by their very nature, tend to promote pluralistic and democratic tendencies within society, while at times being severely limited by countervailing forces, including factionalism, lack of expertise, insufficient material resources, etc. Government agencies, on the other hand, control extensive resources which frequently

110

remain either unproductive or can have a regressive impact. These are the results of pathologies that afflict all large organizations.

Primary Health Care: A Case Study

The following synopsis focuses on Primary Health Care (PHC), a major development sector. This subject is also illustrative of the ideological differences as well as the areas of compromise and cooperation between non-governmental and public development agencies.

Dr. Prawase Wasi writes:

> ...PHC is a very large platform for social development. It equates democracy which equates social structural change that will enable the people to liberate themselves from perpetual powerlessness and dependency. This must come from social learning. Innovative learning process [*sic*] through information, reasoning and meditation is needed to develop true intelligence to emancipate humanity from their failure to live and work together to achieve health and happiness for all.[48]

The presence or absence of health care serves as a prime indicator of development, in both its quantitative and qualitative dimensions. In Thailand, equitable health care is still a goal. While the wealthy urban elites and to a lesser degree the middle class have access to the most up-to-date medical services and facilities, the vast majority of the people—particularly those living in the remoter areas of the country—have to manage with little or no health care at all.[49]

Providing quality health care to the total populace has thus far been mainly a matter of public policy pronouncements rather than policy implementation. The government's health budget amounts to 5.1% of the total budget. This compares to 2.2% and 6.8% respectively for Indonesia and the Philippines. Thailand has a total of 12,966 physicians, 5,700 pharmacists and 2,600 dentists. However, only approximately 3,000 doctors work in rural areas.[50] From an NGO perspective the "inequitable health care allocation is caused [by] the government's prejudice to benefit urban dwellers rather than those in the countryside, as is the case ... in every other [development] aspect."[51]

Major responsibility for this inequity is placed on the government bureaucracy, which is viewed as a conservative force monopolizing authority and resources. The mentality of government officials is seen as that of rulers who are firmly in charge. Furthermore, presumably no serious efforts have been made to reform the system.

The government's and the NGOs' concepts and approaches to PHC are different: The government concentrates on ten aspects of primary health care, including health education, nutrition, and common disease treatment, relying heavily on the training of village health communicators (1 per 10 households) and village health volunteers (1 per village).

The NGOs perceive the problem in a different way. They feel that the Government's targeting of problems such as malnutrition, poor sanitation—while ignoring the factors leading to these problems, such as poverty, infertile land, inability to earn a living—is again only looking at 'diseases and germs' instead of 'the whole patient'.

PHC according to health NGOs implies a development strategy which aims at developing society through people's movements and people's participation, bringing about public health justice…. They target the reformation of health, economic, social and political systems.[52]

The NGO strategy for Primary Health Care in Thailand calls for equity and social justice through decentralization of decision-making and services instead of the current preoccupation of state agencies with centralization and maintaining the status quo and national security.[53] The NGO agenda is summed up as follows:

Undoubtedly in the future, a major restructuring will have to take place, with more networking, less bureaucracy; more initiative from the people, less control by the government; with a re-allocation of resources and power. Only by supporting the people's efforts towards self-reliance and community participation, can we hope to strive towards "Health for all by the year 2000."[54]

Government/NGO Cooperation: A Case Study

Cooperation between a government agency (e.g., a District Government Hospital) and health care NGOs is possible, as was demonstrated in the Korat area in Thailand's Northeast. A close working relationship between the organizations came about as a result of one individual "wearing two hats."[55]

Dr. Sanguern Nittayaramphong, Director of the District Hospital (which has a staff of approximately 70 people), is also chairman of the Primary Health Care Group of Buayai, as well as former chairman of the Rural Doctor's Association. At his initiative, a new working arrangement—a division of labor—was implemented, which has yet to be replicated elsewhere.

It rests on the premise that medical care entails three stages: the curative, preventive and promotive stage. While the hospital is in a good position to perform the curative function, support from other sources is required to properly attend to the preventive and promotive stages of medical care. This is where NGOs fit in.

For example, in this case study, malnutrition is a responsibility of the Primary Health Care Group. The program is staffed and financed by an NGO, but the hospital provides the facilities. Similarly, the Health Care Group assists the hospital with the training of Village Health Volunteers at the Tambon (subdistrict) level.

Dr. Sanguern is convinced that although successful collaboration between public and private agencies is possible, whether it actually comes about depends on the people concerned and their concept of development. He has demonstrated what a successful formula may look like.

> ...Doctors need to realize that PHC is not only physical health treatment, that it is just one third of the requirements: that education and conscientization are essential elements too. The Doctor's role should be one of a catalyst, his role in society should be outside the village too. Doctors should be politically aware, and use that in the case of the general elections, not to favor any candidate, but to help people look critically at the process...[56]

Traditional Medicine

Traditional medicine is another subject of particular interest to NGOs. A growing number of small Thai NGOs are encouraging community self-reliance through the revival of traditional medical practices based on Ayuraveda, the teachings of "knowledge of life." These teachings cover two facets of the indigenous health system: the folk tradition with its knowledge of popular remedies and the scientific focus on principles and conscious application.[57]

Although still limited in scope, these NGO efforts to resuscitate traditional health care knowledge and practices are significant not only because of the direct benefits for the community—more effective (in many cases) and cheaper remedies for common ailments—but also because of the linkage with culture. Following years of propaganda by the government and commercial agents, people have come to believe that traditional medicine "..is old fashioned, unreliable...and dangerous." In effect, this set of attitudes severed one more link with indigenous culture.[58]

The NGO approach on traditional medicine initially focused on information gathering, thus helping to rebuild the foundation of medicinal folk wisdom. The process of talking with older members of the community and recording practices and skills has by itself the salutary effect of making villagers aware of the value of their own traditions.

The next stage involved the dissemination of information and knowledge pertaining to traditional medicine through publications aimed principally at community leaders, particularly monks. In addition, a number of community projects involving research on medicinal plants and the actual manufacturing and exchange of traditional medicines were initiated in the early 1980s.

One illustrative case is the village of Huey Hin, Chachoengsao Province in the Central Region not far from Bangkok. This is the home of Khun Vibul, a community leader who collects and distributes information about medicinal plants and traditional health practices. Khun Vibul maintains an exemplary traditional "pharmacy" and an extensive herb garden that contains over 200 varieties of medicinal plants. In fact, his community is now engaged in a small but expanding village network for the exchange of herbs that are required in the preparation of natural medicines. By design, herbs are exchanged and not sold because: "If our exchange is based on money, the rare plants will certainly become extinct rapidly from our village."[59]

In the long run, it is anticipated that small production units such as the one in Huey Hin village, will be representative of a type of village-level industry that avoids the negative consequences of modern factories. However, in addition to the economic benefits, there will be even more important consequences affecting all aspects of village life.

For example, by reducing dependence on modern medicine and by integrating traditional with modern medical knowledge in district hospitals and health clinics, people will be less alienated from their traditional values, their history and from each other. Furthermore, socially and culturally their communities will be less penetrated and exploited by outsiders: traders and middlemen, in particular, will also be reduced.

Overall, the work done by Thai health-oriented NGOs is illustrative of the "power" NGOs are able to generate, largely with resources already available in the communities. Performing primarily as catalysts, these private organizations generate community awareness, provide information, and coordinate and engender learning processes that lead in new directions, offering effective alternatives to largely government-fostered mainstream development.

According to Rosana Tositrakul, co-ordinator of a project on traditional medicine and self-reliance:

> Our experience in the past six years has provided some encouragement that if local traditions of health care—which still exist in rural communities all over the country, though in a weakened state—are well strengthened, people can become completely self-reliant in their primary health care needs.[60]

Thai NGOs in Profile

Considering the presence of social, political and related constraints, Thai society has succeeded in the short period of roughly two decades in generating a surprising number of small but dynamic non-governmental development organizations which supplement and strengthen the efforts of the public development sector with their alternative development concepts, approaches and field projects.[61]

As individual organizations, Thai NGOs typically are small and grass-roots-oriented. On the average, their staff size is less than 10 persons. Yearly budgets typically range from 700,000 to 1,000,000 baht ($28,000–40,000) and the smaller NGOs have budgets between 200,000 and 300,000 baht ($8,000–12,000). Their principal human resource is increasingly professional and highly committed people, generally from a middle class background, who share explicit humanitarian values.

These NGO leaders are assisted by well-educated volunteers, who see their work as separate from mainstream development. Their thinking and underlying philosophy are systemic and holistic in scope, with corresponding emphases on self-reliance, peoples' participation and indigenous culture, particularly Buddhist teachings.

As repeatedly emphasized, these indigenous organizations see themselves to a large extent as responses to the shortcomings, generally caused by large bureaucracies of the public development sector. Consequently, the private organizations have remained intent on avoiding traditional bureaucratic constraints and maximizing organizational independence and flexibility. This is one reason why only a small number of local NGOs are registered with the government. Demanding financial rules and related registration requirements also tend to discourage official affiliation.

In Thailand, private non-profit activities could be organized either as associations or as foundations, the main distinction being that the latter is required to have a certain amount of endowment fund. There are now over 2,000 foundations and 4,000 associations registered all over the country.[62]

The shortage of financial and material resources—particularly in comparison with government agencies—is another characteristic of Thai NGOs that remains one of most troublesome issues for the entire NGO community. Being dependent on foreign financial support (principally from European, North American and Australian NGOs) affects the Thai NGO community in many ways. As long as indigenous organizations are financially dependent, their development activities will also be constrained. Fortunately, a continuing dialogue at all levels—local, national and international—between representatives from the recipient and donor agencies addresses the need for equity and partnership, issues which will be taken up in the following chapter.

Additional Characteristics

Thai development NGOs tend to be established either by professionals focusing on a particular area of expertise, e.g., primary health care or human rights, or they are set up by field workers who operate at the local level and focus on village institutions.[63] However, regardless of who the leaders are, as a rule the organizations tend to avoid political associations, i.e., specific affiliation with political parties and related movements.

In terms of their broad functions, Thai NGOs generally seek to (1) improve living conditions for the underprivileged through heightened public awareness, new and creative approaches to social development, and increased public participation; (2) promote and work in accordance with democratic values, including people's participation, justice, etc.; (3) build and strengthen community institutions; (4) educate the public about social problems; (5) take direct action to alleviate hardships (relief and welfare); and (6) to work for a stronger NGO movement.[64]

One observer categorized the functions of Thai NGOs under three types: one, the prophetic function—presenting a vision of a better, more just order; two, the "supplement" function—NGOs replacing government agencies by performing some of their functions; and three, the modeling function—serving as laboratories, relying on their capacity to experiment and to innovate.[65]

On the debit side of the ledger, there are also liabilities generated by factionalism, expressed, for example, in the not uncommon phenomena of cliques (coalescing generally around personalities and/or lead organizations), organizational rivalries, and program duplication, due to insufficient coordination and seemingly limited capacity to cooperate.

Finally, as part of their ongoing experimentation in alternative development, NGOs tend to experience an undercurrent of continued questioning of their own role:

> Are they simply experiments to be emulated if and when they 'get it right', and if so, is it right to use people as guinea pigs? Are they to be seen purely in terms of the results they achieve locally, and if so do they represent a realistic use of resources, given the small scale of most projects? Can NGDOs be represented as a movement? To what extent should NGDOs become involved in official schemes?[66]

These questions point to many issues that have yet to be resolved. They are also a reminder that a general consensus on concepts, approaches and strategies is still lacking.

To summarize, the following conclusions reached by the DETEC/CIDA Seminar on "Rural Development in Thailand" accurately describe the current status of the Thai development community:

First, their flexibility allows for more effective approaches to the "human factor" at the grass-roots level. This refers particularly to their success in obtaining village cooperation and participation.

Secondly, despite their evident strengths, local NGOs have been underutilized, mainly because of the government's mistrust or, at best, a patronizingly permissive attitude.

Thirdly, Thai NGOs still lack experience in dealing with complex development problems and issues. Finally, as indicated, they lack adequate funding and sufficient staff.[67]

Chapter 6

NETWORKS: THE NEXT PHASE IN THAI NGO DEVELOPMENT

…with or without official blessing, there is no question as to the growing importance of private non-profit organizations in the field of development. In terms of development resources, human and material, these NGOs are like a mere drop of water. This is quite obvious. And anyhow resources that would go into such private channels are bound to be very limited. But the real significance and impact to one's mind, lies in their potential inspiration not only for people at the grass-roots, but also for those few concerned intellectuals within academic establishments themselves.

Saneh Chamarik

Third Generation NGOs

While most Thai NGOs continue to struggle in an effort to consolidate and strengthen their organizations, a small number of progressive Thai development organizations are moving towards a more advanced, mature organizational phase, coordinating their activities through national and international networks.

These local agencies benefited from the experience of the older, first and second generation development foreign NGOs.[1] They have incorporated lessons learned and attempted to minimize problems inherent in the early stages of organizational development.

Led by prominent Thai academics with credentials in community and/or rural development, third generation NGOs successfully tapped the resources of outside donor agencies, both public and private, to underwrite the establishment of a new agenda in Thai development. Without doubt, these NGOs share the problems of traditional development agencies, such as inadequate human and material resources, factionalism, lack of cooperation, as well as the limits imposed by the social, economic and political climate in Thailand.

However, by consciously choosing to become professional catalysts of development, as opposed to functioning principally as operatives of welfare, relief or traditional development projects, they responded to a major need at the present stage of Thai development.

The primary responsibilities of third generation NGOs, as indicated earlier, include communication, consultation, facilitation, as well as outreach, involving all members of the development community (government agencies, international organizations and private sector institutions). In effect, networking and a new professionalism are key objectives of this new breed of private development agencies.

Power, Culture and Alternative Development

Third generation Thai NGOs can accept power defined as "…the ability to change a future state through an act of decision." They would also agree that "Development itself might well be defined in terms of building the power of a society, i.e., …increasing its ability to change its future as an act of choice."[2] Furthermore, from a normative perspective, agreement can be found as well on the following position:

> Truly humane development requires human growth in the sense of people becoming freer human beings, liberated from their own sense of powerlessness and dependency.[3]

As a result of this new awareness of power, third generation NGOs are no longer as overwhelmed by or in awe of formal state authority. Against the backdrop of nearly three decades of largely unsuccessful public development programs on the one hand and a record of increasingly effective community development on the other, and based on the combined efforts of local communities and private development agencies, a shared perspective of power is gaining currency with empowerment of the people as the goal.

Empowerment entails helping local communities to help themselves by capitalizing on existing resources—human and material—particularly indigenous values and culture. The message is "alternative development," asserting that development efforts based on the values of outsiders, to the partial or even total exclusion of local norms and experiences, does not constitute development. Alternative development does not accommodate manipulation and exploitation disguised as development.[4]

For example, protagonists of the socio-cultural approach ask rhetorically: "Is it not yet time that the people should be [the] 'subject' of their own development and fate, not in theory but in practice; that they be the 'owners' of their health and sickness, their work and products, their means and technology, and finally, their own culture?"[5] Their analysis of the current state of affairs in the countryside reflects the reality of life for most people in Thailand:

118

......villagers in many villages have now come to the awareness that the only way to survive and to go against the main current of today's new way of life is to awaken interest in their cultural values. They have to be linked once again to their own history. Once there is historical awareness, the appreciation of cultural values comes alive. One's potential and strength are discovered. Faith in life is regained.[6]

In our society, the outstanding impact of the past development that we recognize well is the vast gap between urban and rural societies. Nowadays, urban society has exploited and sucked the economic wealth from the villages in order to sustain its prosperity, while village society has been left behind with poverty and insufficiency.[7]

The moral-based way of thinking of villagers has been changed gradually by the domination, and incursion of [the] outside capitalist economy. Development work is an important means to serve people in analyzing their realities and facing their problems, in order that they can be led to seek an appropriate strategy of development alternatives.[8]

Alternative development thus emphasizes indigenous culture, folk wisdom and traditional technologies as the crucial building blocks of self-reliant development. This prescription is based on the fact that no one can develop someone else. In sum, alternative development faces up to the fact that the so-called developing world has to do the job on its own, though without denying the need and the validity of outside assistance. But the terms and the methods of the aid are different.

The following definition of development, with its emphasis on positive and qualitative change, highlights the essence of alternative development:

The concern of culture as an element of 'change' leads us into a definition of ...development, [as] a process of 'positive change' in the quality and level of human existence. Development is essentially a socio-economic process of change aimed at raising the standard of living, the quality of life and human dignity.[9]

This then is the direction in which leading indigenous development NGOs are headed after critically examining past practices and mindsets and following a careful reassessment of the relationship between power, culture and development. As previously documented, non-governmental organizations are well equipped to assume positions of leadership as innovators and catalysts, helping people to help themselves.

Partnerships

Partnership, in this context, refers to new, evolving relationships among Thai NGOs, as well as with their foreign counterparts. It is an inclusive term that covers a variety of functions and responsibilities, e.g., cooperation, coordination, collaboration, communication, consultation, facilitation, outreach, and integration. In effect, organizational ties, which are generally shaped by personal relationships, are the components of new NGO networks with the potential for substantive power realignments. As communication channels are opened and information flow is facilitated, the impact of the NGO community on Thai development policies, grows.

In order to assess the nature and scope of these new relationships—particularly with regard to the contributions of the leading third generation NGOs—a general survey of networking activities is necessary.

At the international level, Thai NGOs are linked to two major, multilateral organizations—the Asian Cultural Forum on Development (ACFOD-1977), based in Bangkok; and the Asian Regional Exchange for New Alternatives (ARENA), with headquarters in Hong Kong. Both organizations are multilateral membership networks and forums for the promotion of appropriate Asian development alternatives through communication and the exchange of ideas and experiences.

The stated objectives of ACFOD are: "To coordinate exchanges of experiences and conclusions among individuals and organizations working in development in various countries of Asia, in order to seek development approaches fitting Asian realities. To build friendship and understanding among countries with different cultures."[10]

Particular activities supported by ACFOD include support for small-scale fishermen and establishment of ties among workers, rice farmers, women and development workers in the various Asian countries. ACFOD is funded largely by donations from several European NGOs.[11]

ARENA is also "a non-governmental regional organization established for the purpose of functioning as a forum on Asian development concerns, and promoting cooperation and exchange among people in Asia committed to human progress and development.[12]

The principal contribution of these international, regional bodies to the Thai development community has been the strengthening of progressive core organizations in their own pursuit of alternative development strategies. These organizations have also been effective in strengthening the spirit of solidarity among internationally-minded NGOs.

A list of the most important Thai NGO development catalysts includes: the Catholic Council of Thailand for Development (CCTD, founded in 1973), funding principally from European NGOs; the Justice and Peace Commission for Development (JPCD, 1977), 80% funding from abroad; the Rural Reconstruction Alumni and Friends Association (RRAFA, 1983); the SVITA Foundation (1980), 80% funding from abroad; the Thai Development Support Committee (TDSC, 1982), 80% funding from abroad; the Thai Foundation for the Development of

Human Resources in Rural Areas (Thai DHRRA, 1979), 64% funding from abroad; the Thai NGO Committee on Agrarian Reform and Rural Development (WCARRD, 1980), 100% funding from abroad; and finally the Thai Volunteer Service (TVS, 1980), 66% funding from abroad.

None of the above organizations function without foreign NGO financial support. Clearly, non-governmental organizations in Europe, North America, Australia, and elsewhere were instrumental in nurturing and subsequently strengthening the efforts of indigenous NGOs in Thailand and encouraging them to experiment with non-traditional approaches. A primary example is provided by CEBEMO, the Dutch government-funded donor agency, which has and continues to play a major role in the evolution of many Thai NGOs.

Beginning in 1987 in an effort to escape the negative consequences of traditional donor-recipient relationships, CEBEMO's study section began to explore alternative financing models that permit equitable partnership. These efforts are summarized in an informal discussion paper entitled: "Tentative Framework for a Dialogue between CEBEMO and its main Third World Partners on Sharing of Responsibilities and new Forms of Cooperation."[13] This dialogue continues with Thai NGOs in the form of a regular exchange of views.

Private donor agencies abroad have been in the forefront of lending support to emerging indigenous private voluntary organizations in an effort to change the roles and levels of involvement of foreign-based development NGOs working in Third World countries. However, more recently, foreign governments, particularly in Europe, Canada, Australia, Japan and in the United States, also broadened their funding formulas to include indigenous development organizations, provided certain conditions are met.

For example, CIDA, the Canadian Government's development agency, through its IPVO instrumentality, the Local Development Assistance Program (LDAP), assumed an early leadership role, pioneering in effect, working relationships between the foreign donor agency and its partners. Again, many of the core Thai NGOs that are functioning increasingly as development catalysts are past or present members of the LDAP 'family'. LDAP recently experienced a transformation of its own, changing its status to a registered foundation with a Thai board of directors. This important change is the logical outcome of LDAP's extensive work with the Thai development community.

On the initiative of the government's National Economic and Social Development Board (NESDB) and with financial support from CIDA, an NGO Coordinating Committee on Rural Development (NGO-CORD) was established in 1985. Working at the national level in cooperation with affiliated regional NGO coordinating committees, improved coordination and communication is expected between the Thai NGO community and the government.

POWER AND CULTURE

Although it is still too early to assess the work of the committees, the government's motives in promoting these coordinating bodies have been questioned. Consequently, support from the Thai NGO community has been less than unanimous and enthusiastic.

There are also a considerable number of consortia-type NGO coordinating committees, most of which date from the early 1980s. This list includes the following organizations: the Coordinating Committee for Primary Health of Thai NGOs (CCPN, 1983), 100% NGO funding from abroad; the Coordinating Committee of Thai NGOs on Human Rights (1983), 100% local funding; the Coordinating Group for Religion in Society (CGRS, 1976), 90% NGO funding from abroad; the NGO Coordinating Committee on Slums (1986); the Rural Development Documentation Center (RUDOC, 1986), 90% NGO funding from abroad; the Slum Study Group (1982), 95% NGO funding from abroad; the Thai Development Support Committee (TDSC), 80% NGO funding from abroad; the Thai Inter-Religious Commission for Development (TICD, 1979); the Thai NGO Committee on Agrarian Reform and Rural Development (WCARRD, 1980), 100% funding from abroad; and the Thai Volunteer Service (TVS, 1980), 66% funding from abroad.

The recent proliferation of Thai NGO coordinating committees is in response to the long-felt need for improvements in communications as well as cooperation among members of the indigenous development community. However, coordination remains a major issue in Thai development and it will be the subject of further analysis through the remainder of this chapter.

To summarize the various partnerships between Thai NGOs differ in nature, scope and significance. They range from formal and informal communications to close cooperation in programming and financing, from the international to the local level.

Prominent features include continuing financial dependency on foreign NGOs (which all parties concerned are attempting to handle in a more equitable manner); strong support for alternative development strategies; an emerging sense of community and direction, particularly among individual NGO leaders and their organizations; and finally, an emerging network of confident (albeit still dependent) indigenous development organizations, experimenting with people-centered, catalytic development strategies.

The Research and Development Institute (RDI)

The following case studies will illustrate key facets of the contemporary Thai development community, including rapid change, perceptive leadership, and emerging professionalism in NGO circles. Attention will be focused on a new cross-section of Thai development organizations: the Research and Development

Institute of Khon Kaen University (RDI); the Thai Volunteer Service (TVS), which is associated with the Social Science Research Institute of Chulalongkorn University; the Center for Culture and Development (CCD) in Khon Kaen; and the Thai Institute for Rural Development (THIRD), which works under the umbrella of the Village Foundation (VF). These organizations are rather atypical and merit attention because of their previous or current roles in national and/or international development.

Strictly speaking, RDI is not an NGO but an arm of Khon Kaen University. It is included here because of its previous role and strong influence on Thai development affairs. RDI was known for its commitment to and support of Thailand's development community, especially the non-governmental development organizations. Within the short span of six years (the Institute began to function officially in 1982), RDI established a most impressive track record, in effect, setting the standard for research and field work in Thai rural development.

Based on the findings of a feasibility study for RDI, published in 1983, which identified lack of coordination and integration as foremost problems of Thai rural development, the Institute was established "to promote and support development activities in the Northeast Region" through (1) "Net-working among development agencies..local organizations…and among developing villages;" (2) conduct research on rural development; (3) provide feedback to government agencies; and (4) generate relevant development information for local communities.[14]

> From this study, [referring to the feasibility report] it was discovered that the most serious problem of rural development in Thailand is a lack of coordination. Such lack of coordination occurs at every level of operation. Laterally, it occurred among those implementing projects in the field at the local level as well as among planners in various government departments, agencies and organizations. Vertically, there was lack of coordination, and in some cases there were even misunderstandings, between field workers and administrators, implementors and planners, and all of them with researchers. As a consequence of such lack of coordination, planners have insufficient data of the local situation for planning purposes. Research findings are found to be of impractical use for implementors, or do not respond to the needs of local communities. Local communities and field workers have no information of the sources of available services, or are unable to make contacts and use of those services. Development field workers in each location have no knowledge of what the others are doing. There exists no channel or forum through which experiences and lessons can be exchanged. Mistakes in development tactics, strategies, approaches, and implementation process, keep on recurring in one place or another.
>
> In order to make itself useful to the development of the Northeast Region, RDI, has to fill this gap.[15]

Headed by by Dr. Akin Rabibhadana, the Director and well-known Thai professor with close ties to Thammasat University, RDI quickly attracted extensive funding from public and private sources. CIDA, USAID, the Asia Foundation and the Ford Foundation were among the early donor agencies. Subsequent support for research and consulting activities has also been provided by the German Friedrich Ebert Stiftung, Stiftung Volkswagenwerk and various international agencies.

In pursuit of its overall mission—coordination and integration in the Thai development community—RDI is part of a national and international network that maintains academic ties (research activities, conferences, seminars and workshops), organizational channels (institutional linkages ranging from universities and donor agencies to NGOs and local community organizations), and informational services (including collecting, processing and disseminating data, documents and related information).

It is the Institute's declared policy "to create linkages with outside organizations engaged in development work in the Region, and developing communities in the Northeast...", on which the following activities are based:

- Identifying and Collecting Data for Networking
- Coordinating among Non-government Organizations
- Coordinating between Village Organizations, Implementing Agencies and Academicians
- Networking among Developing Villages, and Villages with Resource Centers
- Producing Media for Technology Transfer[16]

All of RDI's program activities are implemented within a conceptual and philosophical framework that is supportive of qualitative development, emphasizing indigenous culture, self-reliance and participatory development. The Institute, for example, surveyed and published data on active development NGOs and projects (particularly, village level activities) in the Northeast; established contact between villages through resource persons, regarding traditional village technologies and skills (e.g., integrated farming, sericulture, and traditional health care); held conferences for non-governmental organizations (on GO/NGO coordination and the role of NGOs); organized seminars and lectures in villages for local leaders, development workers and other interested parties (on rural development, local culture, the role of universities in development and folk wisdom).

In 1986 RDI experimented with a new transfer program for indigenous technologies, involving the exchange of a selected number of farmers from neighboring provinces, "...to be apprentices to fish farms," with the result that appropriate fish-raising techniques are now disseminated among a growing number of farmers in the target and neighboring villages.

Working with and through NGOs as well as government and donor agencies, RDI has earned a reputation for excellence. Aside from concrete results, such as the technology exchange program, equally or perhaps more important from the standpoint of networking, are the less tangible contributions made to the Thai development community.

Because of its diverse activities—ranging from high level, international conferences, interdisciplinary-oriented field research on rural development and training courses for development workers, to project consulting and evaluation—carried out by a relatively small staff of approximately 40 people, RDI has contributed significantly to a growing institutionalization of formal and informal relationships within Thailand's development community.

The resulting expansion and consolidation of communication channels for the exchange of ideas, experiences and lessons in rural development is an important factor in the rapid evolution of third generation development NGOs. RDI has actively promoted a climate in development circles that is hospitable to change, thus inviting alternative approaches to development. It should also be pointed out that this change process has been fostered without alienating public sector development agencies at home or abroad.

In the future RDI proposes (1) to focus on a comparative research program examining the "applicability, effectiveness, and problems of different approaches to rural/community development..." and (2) to promote, with the aid of revolving funds, the creation of village centers for development, creating a multiplier effect for indigenous culture and technology.[17]

The Thai Volunteer Service (TVS)

Jon Ungphakorn, the Director of the Thai Volunteer Service, commenting on the challenges faced by Thai NGOs, listed five sets of interrelated problems: lack of stability, recognition, and public support; lack of experienced man-power; inadequate NGO self-development and learning through experience; lack of common direction; and problems concerning the political climate.[18] The Thai Volunteer Service came into being against the backdrop of such issues. Its history reflects recent changes in the Thai NGO community.

At the outset, in the late 1970s, Khunying Ambhorn Meesook, a founding member and the current Chairperson of TVS, expressed interest in the concept of indigenous development volunteers, similar to U.S. Peace Corps Volunteers (which was originally proposed by Peter Pond, the son of a U.S. Ambassador to Thailand). At that time Khunying Ambhorn conducted a series of development seminars, where the original idea grew into a proposal for the creation of the Thai Volunteer Service. With the assistance of Mr. Pond, funds for a feasibility study were obtained from the Ford Foundation.

Based on the findings and recommendations of this study, the Thai Volunteer Service was established, using 40,000 baht ($1,600) left over from the grant as seed money. Beginning with 19 founding member NGOs, TVS evolved into a 36 member

NGO consortium, with a full-time staff (including the Director and Deputy Director) of 16 and an annual budget of approximately 3 million baht ($120,000).[19] TVS was granted foundation status in 1987.

Although TVS shares some goals with Khon Kaen University's Research and Development Institute, for example, seeking closer cooperation among NGOs, sharing of experiences and searching for a common direction in development work, the scope of TVS activities is much narrower and the emphases are different.

While the volunteer program was and remains central to the services provided to its members and the entire NGO community, training, information, communication (aimed specifically at the public at large and governmental agencies) and especially coordination are now part of the TVS priority list. In effect, the organization's professional responsibilities evolved through the recruiting and training of development workers to include cooperation, coordination and conflict resolution among Thai NGOs.

The TVS development philosophy is very similar to RDI's orientation. According to its Directory:

> It is the firm belief of TVS that in order to achieve a just and peaceful society in Thailand, the large number of deprived and disadvantaged members of society must be allowed to develop their full potentials, and become fully involved at all levels in the development of society.
>
> It follows that community and social development work must focus on opening up opportunities for the deprived sections of society to achieve a fuller understanding of their situation and to develop their collective abilities to tackle their problems and develop their communities in their own way. Only through the active involvement of the poorer sections of society in working collectively to improve their quality of life can problems of hardship and poverty be successfully tackled and major achievements towards social justice and prosperity be made.[20]

Accordingly, TVS has three main objectives: (1) cooperation and coordination among NGOs, (2) greater efficiency of NGOs and their staffs, and (3) search for appropriate development strategies.[21]

An important aspect of the first objective, which sets TVS apart from many other development NGOs, is the explicit inclusion of government agencies in its efforts to promote cooperation and coordination within the NGO community. According to Professor Jon "…co-operation with the government will be the best way to develop society."[22]

As a result of its policy to explore all potential avenues for better communication and cooperation between public and private development agencies, TVS and especially its Director played a key role in the discussions, meetings and NGO conferences leading up to the establishment of the national and regional NGO Coordinating Committees on Rural Development (NGO-CORD) discussed earlier.

Returning once more to the comparison between RDI and TVS, aside from size and program scope, clearly another major difference lies in the fact that the former is not an NGO, as pointed out earlier, but an institute (albeit independently funded) of Khon Kaen University, while the latter, although with similar university affiliation (through Chulalongkorn University's Social Research Institute), is a registered foundation, functioning as an NGO consortium or umbrella organization.

However, upon closer examination—particularly from the perspective of the interests and needs of the Thai development community as a whole—these distinctions become less important. As the following discussion will illustrate, TVS, in its own right, has also been instrumental in shaping the character and the direction of the Thai development community in the short span of seven years through its declared development philosophy (steadfastly supporting alternative development) and its comprehensive networking activities.

With reference to the importance of informal personal relations in the Thai context, it is apparent that organizational effectiveness to a large extent is a function of horizontal and vertical linkages. These linkages are particularly important at the leadership level, where they translate into power. The wider the network of personal ties and the closer the relations among associates, the higher will be the potential for cooperation, common goals and conflict resolution.

In this context, it is helpful to recall an earlier discussion on the history of the Thai NGO community, which included a brief analysis of the Thai Rural Reconstruction Movement (TRRM), the first professional community development NGO in Thailand. Particularly relevant here is the fact that TRRM was founded by Dr. Puey Ungphakorn, the father of Jon Ungphakorn. The main legacy of the Foundation (stressing integrated community development and self-help), however, was the large number of trained development workers, many of whom were instrumental in setting up other development NGOs.

It will also be recalled that another historical development contributed significantly to the current make-up and orientation of the Thai NGO community. The democratic movement between 1973 and 1976 produced a large number of committed student activists who after a period of political suppression, assumed leadership positions in the NGO community. Both Jon Ungphakorn and Khun Pumtham Wechayachai, the Deputy Director of TVS, as well as other members of their staff and many of the TVS-trained volunteers came out of this movement. According to Professor Jon:

The common focus of the movement was centered on poverty and repression in Thailand; and how to create a more equal and just society. At that time however, most activities within this movement were of a political nature. Following the military takeover of 1976 and the subsequent relaxations concerning political rights in 1978, many intellectuals influenced by the former democratic movement turned to development work as a potential long-term force for social change. This resulted in the emergence of a large number of development NGOs during the early 1980s and such NGOs have been growing in strength and numbers up to the present time. At their core are a number of university teachers, middle-level civil servants and young professionals in various fields; who mainly form the governing committees of such NGOs. For their activities, these NGOs mainly rely on young graduates as their full-time staff.[23]

Thus TVS, is the combined product of the two movements, the pioneering work of Dr. Puey Ungphakorn and TRRM followed by the legacy of the democratic movement of the '70s. This background helps to explain the potentially pivotal position of the Thai Volunteer Service.

Although the TVS organizational network differs in nature and scope from RDI, both organizations serve as consultancies and receive funding form LDAP, CIDA's local NGO instrumentality. Other international ties include funding from NGOs in Europe and Australia. TVS, like many other Thai NGOs, is concerned about these dependencies and is actively engaged in a search for alternative models leading to true partnerships between foreign and indigenous private development organizations.[24]

Another measure of the TVS-coordinated NGO network—its nature, both in terms of quality and scope—are its member organizations, their approaches and development programs. A case in point is the Duang Prateep Foundation (DPF), which is funded principally from domestic contributions, devoting all of its efforts to help alleviate the plight of Bangkok's slum population. Led and given international prominence by Prateep Ungsongtham, given the sobriquet "slum angel" by the press, DPF emerged as the prototype catalytic community development organization. It is committed to the principle of self-reliance, concentrating its activities on communicating, advising, consulting, coordinating, and mediating.[25]

Khun Sompong Patpui, a member of the Foundation's Executive Board, sees three major roles for development NGOs working in the urban crowded communities: providing services, coordinating and cooperating.

Services should be in the nature of relief, and therefore, temporary in nature. Coordination and cooperation, on the other hand should be given constant attention. Sompong speaks of coordination as "thinking with the people to find ways to develop their communities, to find ways to solve the basic community problems, to find proper channels to contact public or private agencies to help them. The NGOs will not provide material support themselves."

Similarly, cooperation should be a process and "a means to strengthen the community organizations and to raise the social awareness of the people." He adds:

It is expected that community activities stimulated by NGO coordination and cooperation will eventually have continuity, be self-generated and can be expanded. They should not be activities for their own sake or for the realization of NGOs' own objectives, but they should be means for development of community organizations so that they can solve their own problems.[26]

Addressing the relationship between the Duang Prateep Foundation and TVS, Khun Sompong pointed out that DPF has little interest in the TVS volunteer program because the Foundation prefers to hire its own staff. The required qualifications are more readily found in older, more experienced development workers, compared to young college graduates.

Still, DPF is a strong supporter of TVS precisely because of its coordinating and networking capacity. Sompong described TVS as an "effective coordinating device—a point of contact—and a sounding board for Thai NGOs."[27]

The Foundation also makes use of the staff training programs offered by TVS to its members and the NGO community as a whole. Again, a principal by-product of these educational activities is reflected in the resulting staff contacts, which facilitate regular personal and organizational relations.

Overall, Khun Sompong echoed the sentiments of other TVS members, indicating that TVS enjoys the support of a sizable sector of the Thai NGO community.

To summarize, the Thai Volunteer Service is not only a professional, non-profit recruiting and training agency for Thai development workers, it is also a center for NGO coordination and cooperation. By the same token, it must be pointed out that the TVS record does not enjoy universal acclaim in the Thai NGO community. Criticism frequently concentrates on the nature and the alleged lack of effective training provided by TVS to its volunteers.

These divergences in opinion frequently are indicative of deeper personal and/ or organizational rifts that continue to characterize the Thai NGO community. The following discussion will cast additional light on the dynamic forces at work in the Thai development community and their competition for influence.

Grass-roots Action: The Center for Culture and Development (CCD)

Third generation NGOs are not limited to the national or international level, as demonstrated by the Center for Culture and Development (CCD), a young Thai organization working in the Northeast. In fact, CCD is the prototype of local development organizations engaged in building community power (e.g., the ability to bargain with forces outside the village from a position of independence) by means of action research and intermediary services. Organizations of this type are also referred to as "Self-Help Promotion Institutions" (SHPIs).[28]

The story of CCD began in 1981 with a group of young, mainly university-educated development professionals who responded to the need for alternative development, rejecting the standard, top-down, bureaucratic approach, characteristic of most government and many NGO development programs. Instead, on the basis of their experience, they felt that control over the development process had to be returned to the villagers—placing the farmer and his community at the center of all development activities.[29]

In 1983, the Northeast Community Development Workers Group, an informal discussion forum which had expanded its membership quickly from 19 to 50, served as the forerunner of CCD. However, initial attempts to turn the Development Workers Group into an organization promoting the socio-cultural or holistic approach failed because of the lack of resources. None of the development workers were in a position to volunteer as staff members due to existing commitments.

Finally, in 1985 CCD did come into existence when a core group of individuals, headed by Apichart Tongyou, decided that the situation in the Northeast villages required sustained action in order to stem increasing poverty and the demise of the peoples' traditional way of life. With a small amount of seed money, 100,000 baht ($4,000) made available through CEBEMO, CCD's skeleton staff set out to expand its contacts in numerous villages, covering as many as four provinces.

The next step involved setting directions and determining priorities. This was accomplished with the aid of a number of well-known academics in Bangkok, who shared their expertise on the history and culture of the Isan (Northeastern) people and their own development experience with the CCD leadership. Most of them subsequently accepted positions on the Center's Advisory Board.

As additional financial support became available from LDAP in 1986, CCD quickly implemented its plan, setting up five major units, each serving the central goal of the new organization—empowerment, helping village communities to regain control over their lives. Each section reflects the holistic philosophy of CCD's founders, addressing particular community needs through concrete action, initiated and led by the community.[30]

The first group within CCD focuses on Traditional Doctors and Medicine. Two CCD volunteers, joined by four villagers, help communities to become part of a network of traditional and modern doctors, clinics and hospitals. The idea is to fuse the clinical knowledge of modern medicine with the traditional know-how of natural remedies and medicinal practices. This program supports a mobile clinic that concentrates on 14 target villages. The traditional doctor group is backed up also by a pharmacy of medicinal plants, which is located at CCD's staff headquarters, outside the city of Khon Kaen.

Village Leaders and Adult Institutions is the second working group within CCD. This is a unique program concerned with the retrieval of knowledge pertaining to practices and institutions in traditional village life, with special emphasis on the role of leadership. The primary purpose of the information gathered from discussions with village elders is to share knowledge about all aspects of past village life—highlighting both positive and negative aspects—in order to lay the foundation for a new "vision." According to Apichart, this vision results from a process in which villagers, "who had forgotten to listen to themselves," begin to recover their identity and their dignity.

CCD volunteers assist village communities in their quest for a new sense of direction and carefully considered sets of goals by immersing themselves in the collective learning process. They do not presume to have the answers (a major difference from most government and many NGO development workers), but assist with information and analysis. For example, farmers encountering particular problems, e.g., with the marketing of their crops, can rely on CCD volunteers to help them explore available options and sources of information.

Most importantly, the CCD staff will encourage community leaders to think through the consequences of each proposed solution, goal or objective. If better roads are called for, to cite one example, the farmers will be asked who benefits and who loses, in an attempt to assess the long-term impact.

The third group, the Small Farmer Network, is also a success story. This program promotes integrated agriculture as the main alternative to government-sponsored, agro-business cash crop production. Encouraging farmers to "put their eggs in more than one basket," i.e., growing a variety of crops and raising small animals principally for home consumption, holds out one solution to the growing debt crisis in Thai farming communities.

The Network distinguishes between three groups of farmers: those who have successfully made the transition to integrated agriculture; others who are giving up cash crops, but have not yet reached the turning point; and those farmers who are interested and want to know more about integrated farming.

Spread out over several provinces, 200 families in more than 20 villages belong to the Small Farmers Network. As many as 400 families have successfully adopted this type of subsistence farming, thus reducing their dependence on external inputs such as fertilizer, pesticides, machinery, and bank loans.

Provided that drought and other adverse environmental conditions do not exacerbate the problems faced by these farmers, they are now in a position to lead a more balanced life in tune with the values and traditions of the Thai village. On average, depending on the skill of the CCD worker, villages will reach this turning point within two or three years.

The Network facilitates exchange visits by farmers from the three groups, thus allowing farmers to compare experiences and to learn from each other directly. This type of grass-roots networking has proved so effective that none of the farmers have dropped out, and each year the number of villagers who wish to become members increases.[31]

The Interreligous Group for Social Development, the fourth section in CCD, seeks to revitalize the role of the temple in the life of the villagers. Working principally with the abbot and village monks, the Center utilizes a small budget of 60,000 baht ($2,400) to assist in the establishment of a number of different types of development projects, ranging from rice banks to co-op farms and stores, to production activities for local consumption. The important feature of these development efforts is their close link to Buddhist teachings and the leadership provided by the monks.

Finally, the Traditional Wisdom Center serves as a multi-faceted resource to the CCD village communities and other interested parties. The primary purpose of this unique establishment is to be of practical use to the farmer. In this capacity, the Wisdom Center functions as an unconventional library, collecting information— e.g., recorded interviews with village elders, slides, pictures, and videos—on subjects of special importance to the villagers, including how to raise specific crops, animals and how to acquire specific skills, such as blacksmithing.

The Center works on the assumption that traditional wisdom is a basic resource which should be central to any strategy of empowerment. Probing and disseminating religious values and practices as well as time tested technologies, thus is a major responsibility of CCD.

There are several points regarding the work of this unique Thai NGO which merit special attention. First of all, CCD does not fit standard NGO categories. Despite the emphasis on concrete results, CCD is not an operational NGO, nor is it a pure catalyst for development.

Similarly, although its activities are focused on the grass-roots, the Center maintains extensive ties at the regional, national and even at the international level. CCD in effect is a "hybrid" NGO which combines all these facets, allowing it to perform in operational, promotional and catalytic modes, drawing on both indigenous and external resources (both quantitative and qualitative in nature), through extensive personal and highly informal networks.

Thirdly, the role of personality in this type of organization appears to be particularly crucial. Practically all facets of the organization—its origin, philosophy and programs are the result of the commitment, the vision and the energy of core groups of individuals who share long-standing relations as friends and colleagues. Their aversion to formal, bureaucratic behavior is also a measure of the importance of personal relationships—be it within the organization itself or in the village context.

Khun Apichart, commenting on his role as co-founder and current member of the CCD Executive Board, helps to illustrate this point. To him, being a development professional is an all-encompassing responsibility, with extensive demands on his private sphere and life style. As an early protagonist of the socio-cultural or holistic school of thought in Thai development circles, he is intent on sharing the life of the villagers as much as possible. Thus, although he does not travel as much throughout the provinces as he used to, he seems always ready to go where he is needed. Because of his long involvement in Northeast development, he is well-known throughout the region and he is also very much in demand as a speaker and facilitator.[32]

Khun Apichart might be described as a person with considerable political acumen, applying his skills in a non-governmental context. Believing, as he does, that one can deal effectively with all development actors—including government officials—as long as one capitalizes on person to person relationships, the key to the success of CCD becomes more apparent. On the other hand, his reputation as social activist, community organizer and popular development worker is not always a winning formula in the eyes of conservative and suspicious government officials.

Clearly, the emphasis on personal relationships combined with the belief in the native intelligence and traditional values of the Thai villager, as illustrated by Apichart serves as the basis for an extensive but informal network that centers on the village.

Cooperation and coordination are also important in this loosely structured system, as long as it serves a concrete purpose. From Apichart's perspective, many prominent regionally and nationally oriented NGOs, which exist principally for coordination purposes, are of little value because "there is only talk and no action."[33]

On the other hand, he approves of a growing number of small regional organizations that are neither well-known nor listed in any NGO directory, but have their roots in the local communities and are intent on coordinating their work through informal channels.

Another recurrent element in Apichart's NGO lexicon is the idea of solidarity, which he applies not only to the relationship between organizations like CCD and the villagers, but also to the interaction between domestic and foreign NGOs.

Fundamentally, partnership is the key to healthy relations between development actors. Equality and mutual respect, particularly where donor and recipient organizations are concerned, are imperative. Beyond these norms, however, in keeping with the holistic philosophy, the specific role of an NGO domestic or foreign—should be a function of expertise, organizational flexibility and staff resources. In principle, Apichart sees nothing wrong for foreign NGOs to be engaged in grass-roots development work.

Finally, as already indicated, one of the most interesting features of CCD is the role of community-designed and formulated "visions." This concept is integral to the socio-cultural approach and it is also connected with the emphasis on personality. Apichart informally defines the concept with reference to "the need to be homogeneous entities, yardstick, and standards."[34]

In the process of determining its own 'vision', a community has an opportunity to assess the past, the present situation and its goals for the future. This amounts to community-centered, bottom-up planning, 'owned' and controlled by the people, with minimum external control.

POWER AND CULTURE

'Vision' symbolizes alternative development offered by the socio-cultural philosophy. Because this alternative derives from the culture of the people, it is realistic. Culture is pervasive, and the traditional values are still alive in rural Thailand. In essence, this is Apichart's response to the challenge presented by the vast resources of the public sector, compared to limited material benefits NGOs have to offer.

Traveling in rural Thailand, he finds that many people implicitly accept the holistic development philosophy. "There are a lot of people thinking about this." He sees an expanding network of like-minded persons. In his view, "non-appropriate development will die" as the people will regain their power.[35]

Toward A New Professionalism

NGOs are set apart from other organizations by voluntarism, humanitarian ideals, personal commitment and sacrifice. These norms are the traditional sources of strength for the private non-profit sector. They are also the foundation for the comparative advantage claimed on behalf of the NGO community.

These assets are no longer sufficient. Good will and good intentions alone do not win the war against poverty. International development is now big business for all development agencies, be they public, private or non-profit in nature. As a result expertise in such fields as finance, accounting, business and personnel management and many other professions is essential.

In the past NGOs tended to be less concerned with "professionalism." They considered the business end of their organizations not as important as the implementation of projects. As a rule, this is no longer the case. Most northern non-profit development agencies made the transition some years ago in order to remain viable. However, a natural aversion to bureaucracy and centralization remains. NGOs want to get on with the job of development; they are conditioned to husband limited resources.

More recently, in response to the negative impact of bureaucracy, size and centralization and the neglect of the human dimension in development, a new type of professionalism has emerged. The term "new professionalism" goes beyond improvements in conventional management skills. The emphasis here is on values, as a reaction to the negative impact of overspecialization, false priorities and misguided approaches. The new development professionals define their responsibilities in terms of reversals, i.e., giving preference to rural people, the poor and the powerless over urban, influential and rich elites. According to Chambers:

The new professionalism that is sought will, then, reverse tendencies to exclusive and increasing specialization. There will always be a case for highly trained professional competence and for rigorous research. Nothing here should be construed as an attack on that. But many of the better chances for the poor lie elsewhere, and can be found and seized through wider and more open-minded observation, discussion, learning and analysis than that of any one discipline, profession or department. Narrowness among outsiders is a luxury poor people should not be asked to afford. Professionals should neither confine themselves to their own disciplinary territory nor fear to trespass in that of others. If they are to see the gaps and help the rural poor to exploit them, outsider professionals have to be explorers and multi-disciplinarians.[36]

This effort to combine expertise with commitment and advocacy grows out of the experience of more than 30 years of failed development programs.[37] Considering that the new development professionals are still in the minority, their challenge to the establishment—the large number of development experts with a vested interest in the existing aid system—might be construed as quixotic in nature were it not for another important consideration.

The new professionalism includes a reassessment of the functions performed by development agencies, going beyond traditional relief and development projects, stressing the need for catalytic roles. Recalling David Korten's typology, this role differentiation corresponds to the evolution of first, second and third generation NGOs.

Third generation or strategic NGOs are evolving as the brokers of international development for a number of reasons. Perhaps one of the most important considerations in this context is the realistic assessment that the resource base for development must shift from external to domestic and local sources.

Another important factor is the growing number of indigenous NGOs and community-based, so-called Peoples' Organizations. Many of these grass-roots movements reflect a greater sense of awareness of external forces. These new Self-Help Organizations (SHOs) are able to assume primary relief and development responsibilities, but they require external assistance in the form of advice, information, know-how, contacts, etc. In short they need the services which catalytic NGOs are able to provide.

Major NGOs in the South thus face a dual challenge. They need to acquire conventional management expertise, in order to function as effective partners of other development agencies, especially of donor organizations. Building on this foundation, the next step involves the gradual development of catalytic capabilities to enhance their overall effectiveness. As indicated, this means avoiding the pitfalls inherent in institutionalization, organizational growth, expanding budgets and staff that account for many failed development programs.

The Thai Institute for Rural Development (THIRD)

In Thailand, as the earlier discussions indicate, third generation or catalytic development organizations are still a new phenomenon. The three preceding case studies—the Research and Development Institute (RDI) at Khon Kaen University, the Thai Volunteer Service (TVS) and the Center for Culture and Development (CCD)—are representative of a core group of indigenous development NGOs, which vary considerably in terms of their particular responsibilities and level of operation, but also share a degree of maturity and professional sophistication which allows them to be classified as potential or evolving catalytic organizations.

The most recent, explicit development in this context is the establishment of two new organizations, the Thai Institute for Rural Development (THIRD) and the Village Foundation (VF), which was registered with the Thai government early in 1988. The Institute functions under the auspices of the Foundation. As stated in the original proposal, the principal functions of THIRD are:

1. Promotion. The promotion of alternative rural development requires staff resources personally concerned with the problems of the villagers. In addition, the staff needs an overall perspective on the development movement.

2. Coordination. Contacts must be established between NGOs, GOs, academics and related parties from the grass-roots to the international level.

3. Support. The support function includes the identification of donor agencies, limited direct support through small-scale grants for specific projects, access to information, conducting research, media services, and staff training.

These two new organizations and their organizational components are premised on the lessons learned in other Third World (mainly Asian) countries, with careful attention given to the historical context of Thai development.

Background

Before describing and analyzing these new organizations in greater detail, a review of their background, including organizational forerunners and leadership is necessary. Several closely interrelated factors provide the context that has shaped all members of the Thai development community. Thailand's political history, the country's socio-cultural system, its development record over the past forty years and the belated but rapid evolution of local NGOs are particularly relevant.

The emerging patterns in development concepts and approaches have not been homogeneous, but most Thai NGOs suffer from familiar shortcomings. Due to insufficient human and material resources, most development NGOs struggle to maintain largely conventional types of programs. Others, for example RDI and TVS, achieved exceptional recognition and legitimacy through close working relationships with governmental and private agencies at home and abroad.

The rural development NGOs are in a separate category. They stand out because of their close, explicit identification with the rural poor, as illustrated by the socio-cultural approach of the Center for Culture and Development (CCD). This is the intellectual and experiential environment from which catalytic development NGOs in Thailand emerged.

The Village Institution Promotion (VI)

Village Institution Promotion (VIP) was established in 1986, specifically "to promote the socio-cultural approach in rural community development and to be a catalyst in rural development issues at all levels."[38] VIP was established by Dr. Seri Phongphit, former Thammasat University Professor of Philosophy and prominent leader of the Thai NGO community. The decision to establish VIP was the first step that in 1988 led to creation of the Foundation (VIPF) and the Institute (THIRD). Together, these initiatives contributed to a new direction in Thai NGO affairs.

Prior to the founding of VIP, Dr. Seri was the de facto Secretary General of the Catholic Council of Thailand for Development (CCTD), co-founder and vice-chairman of the Thai Interreligous Commission for Development (TICD), as well as board member of the Coordinating Group for Religion and Society (CGRS). He is also a close associate of the Center for Culture and Development in Khon Kaen.

Dr. Seri is representative of the new development professional. His impressive background and experience—Catholic priest, professor of philosophy and NGO leader—combined with deep roots in Buddhist culture and Thai society, provide Dr. Seri with a unique vantage point from which to assess the lessons of development. The following conclusions are derived from his research:

1. NGOs are not the only appropriate development agents. Peoples' Organizations or Self-Help Organizations are the newest members of the development community, working at the grass-roots level.

2. "Local resources are not lacking." Empirical data show that local communities are capable of sustained self-reliance with little or no external inputs. Furthermore, it is also evident that material support is at best part of the answer to the problems of poverty and indebtedness.

3. Action with concrete results is vital to effective development. "Learning by doing" is the motto of interaction between experienced individuals and communities. The role of external assistance is to facilitate the process of cross-fertilization.

4. Development needs to be holistic. Model communities, based on integrated agriculture, the return to traditional values and Buddhist principles, have been able to re-establish balance in the lives of individuals and communities.

5. Communities are capable of taking charge of their own affairs. There is no longer room for the hubris of outsiders, which casts villagers in the role of humble subjects, learning from the experts. Instead, development workers have to adopt new attitudes, permitting them to learn from the villagers, before they can render catalytic type of assistance.[39]

POWER AND CULTURE

Similarly, addressing the issue of coordination and cooperation among NGOs, Dr. Seri pinpoints weaknesses in the Thai NGO community, which the new strategic organizations are designed to modify:

> Jealousies and competition render the grouping according to issues impossible. The grouping (clique) happens more 'naturally' through personal relationship, friendship and common interest. This fact derives from the very structure of NGOs. Most of the NGO workers reject bureaucracy and institutionalized systems. They feel themselves more free working in an 'informal' organization, in which they long for the prevailing ideal and spirit. The idealistic attitude of these NGO workers results often [in disappointment] and causes frustration, conflicts and intolerance …..Many NGOs have to spend much of their time to solve these problems.[40]

Seri sees networking as an effective antidote to the divisive tendencies inherent in the Thai development community. A system which maintains communication and ready interaction between individuals, groups and organizations, starting from existing ties of friendship, previous professional associations, reinforced by formal, yet flexible institutional structures, such as VIPF and THIRD, is called for.

The underlying strategy and the rationale for the new development NGOs are also reflected in Dr. Seri's philosophy and analysis of rural development. According to his assessment, there are three currents: (1) state-run development programs, (2) the private business sector, and (3) the village.

The government and the capitalistic economy work hand-in-hand at the expense of the rural communities. One of the results of this situation is the search for development alternatives.

> Many groups in the society have been searching for alternatives. Farmers are more and more aware of their situation. Intellectuals, academics, some government officials, NGO workers, monks, doctors, and other professionals and community leaders belong to this growing movement. The main actors are the villagers. People-centered development is the policy. The common goal is self-reliance of rural communities. New awareness is growing.[41]

Finally, the new institutions are a direct response to Seri's overall perception of the current needs of Thai development. He reiterates that government development policies are destroying the autonomy of the rural community that cultural values still exist, and that they must be renewed.

He is also convinced that religion and religious leaders have essential roles to play in the development process that local resources, both human and material, are not lacking and that as a result of concrete experiences in alternative rural development, a new learning process is taking place.[42]

This is the context in which Village Institution Promotion, with the financial support of CEBEMO, has successfully pursued an alternative course of development. Its agenda concentrates on networking—the strengthening of existing and the development of new NGO contacts at all levels.

VIP is also concerned with resource identification—seeking out resources among NGOs, academic institutions, within the rural communities, and in the government and private sectors. Small rural NGOs may look to VIP for limited financial support—for example seed money to community leaders, NGO workers and individuals who are promoting the socio-cultural approach.

Finally, VIP's educational and liaison functions are reflected in the following activities: seminars, workshops, publications and liaison for rural communities, promoting personal contacts at the village level.[43]

The Rural Development Documentation Center (RUDOC)

On the premise that documentation is an aspect of power which has not been fully developed in support of grass roots movements, a small group of development professionals with extensive experience in rural development decided to establish a new organization that would be instrumental in filling this void. The Rural Development Documentation Center (RUDOC), headed by Surachet Vetchapitak, came formally into existence early in 1986, with financial support from LDAP and European NGOs.[44]

Working in close coordination with VIP, RUDOC's long-term objectives are to provide Thai NGOs with a documentation center "focused on rural development;" the "exchange, analysis and synthesis of experience of NGO workers and villagers;" and the dissemination of the collected information on the widest possible basis.[45] "It aims at information flow from the grass-roots to the NGOs, GOs, intellectuals, the public and vice versa."[46]

Over the past two years, RUDOC established itself as a professional organization, serving a growing number of development NGOs throughout Thailand. In this short period of time the Center acquired a reputation for high standards and a strong commitment to rural communities.

With three full time workers, plus one volunteer and an annual budget of approximately 80,000 baht ($3,200), RUDOC maintains an expanding documentation system, conducts village case studies, publishes books and magazines, provides training for NGO staffs, and actively promotes nation-wide networking among rural development NGOs.

The rapidly expanding documentation system—covering both Thai and English language materials—is at the heart of the Center's programs. More than 1,000 documents—selected articles, reports and research data—are catalogued under the OASIS manual reference system. English language documents—mainly a small, but growing collection of articles translated from Thai—are already computerized for immediate access.

RUDOC's documentation facility does not compare with Thammasat University's Rural Development Data Center which serves principally government agencies, providing base data on the entire rural sector (including nearly all 52,000 villages).

RUDOC has a different clientele. Its services are oriented to the needs of development workers and village communities. Consequently, much of its material is specialized and not readily available elsewhere, making the Center a very valuable resource for NGO workers, academic researchers, students and other people concerned with rural development.

Research activities are closely related to RUDOC's documentation function. They include case studies and project monitoring reports, which are increasingly important because they provide critical benchmarks regarding the changing status of Thai rural communities. They feature interviews with villagers and development workers, providing data for comprehensive analyses. For example, the debt problem of Thai farmers has been a major research focus. With the cooperation of two villages—Huey Hin and Kurang Village—and the financial support of a European NGO, RUDOC produced a series of important documents that address the root causes of indebtedness in Thailand's rural areas, as well as the alternatives available to individual farmers. The papers have been published by RUDOC in Thai and English language editions.

These studies have significantly contributed to RUDOC's reputation as a catalyst in Thai rural development. It is apparent that alternative approaches to development—focusing on indigenous culture, traditional technology, folk wisdom, self-help, local autonomy, and empowerment of the rural people—are gaining visibility not only among rural NGOs, but also among government and international agencies. The evidence for this growing reputation is provided by the steady increase in publicity, inquiries, consultancies, monitoring requests, and various working relationships with official Canadian, U.S. and Australian development agencies, as well as sustained financial support from major European NGOs.

RUDOC's dissemination program ranges from its Thai and English language magazine—*Community Development Magazine* (Thai) and *RUDOC News*—to pocket books, monographs, posters, slides and lectures. For example, the poster campaign on the "Rice Route"—explaining to villagers what happens to their product from the moment it is sold to the point where it is consumed in Thailand or abroad—is an innovative approach to educating and conscientizing the farmer.

Many of RUDOC's programs perform indirect services to the rural communities. This is particularly true for its staff training programs. Annually a series of seminars, training sessions and extended workshops on topics ranging from relevant documentation techniques for rural NGOs to computer application are part of its NGO curriculum. As these programs have become known, the number of applicants has steadily exceeded available space. Whenever possible, separate funding is sought for these training activities in order to keep tuition as low as possible.

Finally, one of the most important catalytic functions performed by RUDOC is networking, which increasingly requires a larger share of the organization's human resources. In the interest of greater coordination and improved cooperation among NGOs and other development agencies, especially government organizations, RUDOC has contributed significantly to the ongoing process of building and expanding various NGO networks—at all levels from the grass-roots to international regional organizations, e.g., ACFOD and ARENA. These activities are extremely costly in terms of time because most of the networking in its early stages has to be done through visits, meetings, and personal contacts.

Given these extensive, closely interrelated functions and considering the constraints of limited human and material resources, the question arises how these tasks can be accomplished while high standards are maintained. As in the case of VIP, a partial answer is found in the enormous energy and dedication of its staff.

Khun Surachet, RUDOC's Director, is a prominent example. Following his activist days in the student movement during the 1970s at Chulalongkorn University, Surachet worked as a trade unionist and as a journalist. From 1980 to 1985 he was a staff member of the Catholic Council of Thailand for Development (CCTD), serving as editor of the Thai Development Magazine and the English language *CCTD Newsletter*.

From the time he assumed the directorship of RUDOC in 1986 to the creation of the Village Institution Promotion Foundation (VIPF) and the Thai Institute for Rural Development (THIRD), under which RUDOC is now reorganized, Khun Surachet has provided the organization with forward-looking leadership—setting goals, obtaining financial support and continuously seeking to improve the services provided by his organization. For example, in the 1986 RUDOC Progress Report, under the heading "Self-Evaluation and Reflection," he stated:

Giving consultation on documentation systems and techniques to other organizations is a way to raise funds for RUDOC. But raising funds this way consumes a lot of time. We are not going to run a business. The question is how to make it balance or be able to integrate it with other work. Sometimes we must give first priority to people organizations although they cannot pay for our services. However, we hope that the training on documentation techniques for Thai NGOs will help decrease consultation work.

Most of RUDOC's activities support villagers indirectly…We must create more activities which support villagers' movements directly….We forecast that, in the near future, villagers will need the 'supportive role' of NGOs, rather than the 'working role'.[47]

Capitalizing on his academic background in communications, his extensive NGO experience, plus his computer expertise, Surachet has given close attention to

RUDOC's principal activities as part of an integrated plan to advance the interests of Thailand's rural communities. Viewing his work as much as an avocation as a vocation, he devotes many hours traveling throughout the country, visiting communities, interviewing villagers and development workers, consulting with or monitoring NGO projects, attending meetings and or making presentations at seminars or workshops.

He has written extensively, based on his research in the rural communities. Surachet is also known for his networking skills, which he has demonstrated at all levels, from local NGO groupings to the international regional level.

To summarize, the key to the success of both organizations, VIP/RUDOC—and their reputation among rural NGOs as leading catalysts in Thai development—lies in the quality of their leadership and staff work.

Conditioned in part by the Thai socio-cultural setting, the tendency for organizations to mirror individual leadership is an asset because it projects sought-after qualities. However, strong personal leadership may over time also create constraining dependencies if the necessary precautions are not taken.

A Learning Organization for People-Centered Development (THIRD)

The new Thai Institute for Rural Development (THIRD), which combines both the Village Institution Promotion (VIP) Project and the Rural Development Documentation Center (RUDOC) under the auspices of the new Village Institution Promotion Foundation (VIPF), represents an important organizational development that will affect the future of the Thai NGO community.

The Institute and the Foundation represent an ambitious undertaking in the new professionalism, aiming at nothing less than a gradual re-orientation of Thai development. Against the backdrop of almost a decade of intensive engagement with Thai NGO affairs, this strategy involved taking stock of the historical record, incorporating lessons learned at home and abroad, and adopting concrete measures in the interest of qualitative development.

This concerted effort to create favorable conditions for a new generation of indigenous NGOs—catalytic or strategic development organizations—(as intentionally implied by the acronym THIRD) is an exercise in power to the extent that a change in the equation of forces faced by Thailand's rural poor is sought.

Although Thailand, according to Dr. Seri, is clearly not among the poorest countries in the world, the gap between rich and poor widens every year. Today more Thai people suffer under the yoke of poverty than before. People are growing more and more dependent, losing their autonomy and self-reliance, due to centralized power.

The failure of externally imposed development programs, caused largely by disregarding the values, the wishes, the interests and the wisdom of individuals and communities, is now acknowledged even by the government. This record includes education and economic policies which produced large numbers of unemployed people, modern hospitals dispensing services which only the rich can afford, confusion and alienation among local leaders and their followers, plus the loss of values and a traditional life style that once generated self-respect through self-reliance.[48]

> However, nobody can stop time and changes. Nobody can go back to the past. But is it [not] possible to be to some extent also 'autonomous' in the changing society of today? …many individuals and rural communities have already succeeded…
>
> Resources are not lacking in the rural areas, human or material. The question is how to develop these resources. The simple answer should be: let [the people] be themselves; let them be subject to their development; give them back their power, their decision, their education, their health, their government, their values, their self-respect, [their] self-confidence.
>
> If the people should become the subject of their development they could only base it on their values. They will find the way to adapt themselves. But this does not mean that nobody should bother about the villagers anymore. They need help and assistance from outsiders. But they should encourage the villagers towards self-reliance and autonomy as much as possible; they should respect their potential and their wisdom; they should provide them with conditions to become aware of the changing society and to develop their existing resources.[49]

THIRD represents a particular organizational response to this perception of the historical development and current status of Thai society. It is the result of a learning process, which contrasts with the traditional blueprint approach to development programming with its emphasis on central decision-making and planning, projects, timelines, budgets, specialists, etc. Instead, the learning process approach values flexibility, leadership and action within a decentralized context. Thus the corresponding learning organization has the ability to "embrace error," to "plan with people" and to "link knowledge building with action."[50]

The following rationale illustrates the fit between THIRD and the prototype of a "learning organization:" Although VIP and RUDOC became quickly known in development circles, they discovered that access, which is essential for the performance of their catalytic functions, to key political institutions, including parliament and political parties, as well as organizations in the business sector, eluded them. Subsequently, the lesson drawn from this experience was to opt for institutionalization and professionalism.

> The respect and recognition from all these sectors [can] be obtained only if VIP/RUDOC [are able to develop] "a new development professionalism based on alternative values and

offering a variety of alternative technologies, organizational forms, and management and research methods appropriate to people-centered development."[51]

The reorganization of VIP/RUDOC under the Thai Institute for Rural Development (THIRD) and the Foundation (VIPF), without changing the original functions of VIP and RUDOC, did produce important changes: (1) program expansion, (2) new types of linkages with foreign NGOs, (3) improved managerial capacity, and (4) a larger organization.

There are other new components associated with VIP and RUDOC in the fields of finance, media work, and research. Aside from a projected Revolving Fund for Self-reliance (RFS), a program called Partnership for a Decentralized Development and Investment (PADDI) is of particular significance. The Revolving Fund, generated by financial contributions from foreign and domestic NGOs as well as a Thai commercial bank, supports community development.

Similarly, PADDI is designed (1) "to facilitate cooperation of as many parties as possible to assist local development initiatives," (2) to generate "financial resources from local, national and international levels," (3) to "facilitate technical assistance," and (4) to "promote regional, national and international partnerships of similar groups, organizations, and enterprises."[52]

The Foundation and the Institute are governed by their respective boards, which are composed of prominent Thai academics, physicians, former government officials, members of Parliament, and NGO professionals. In addition, the Foundation is advised by a Board of Consultants, which includes village leaders, Thai officials and academics. The funding programs are each supervised and administered by special boards and a full-time staff. The projected budget for all organizational components, covering the 1988/90 biennium, is projected in the range of 24 million baht ($960,000).

From the beginning THIRD made its impact felt not only on NGOs and other members of the development community at home, but also in NGO circles abroad. Looking ahead, (provided there are no major political or economic changes) there are a number of factors which potentially enhance the chances of success for THIRD and similar strategic organizations in Thailand.

The list of supporting factors includes broad-based and growing support at the grass-roots level, an extensive network of community development professionals, imaginative, and energetic leadership, a clearer sense of direction and better understanding of alternative development, increased acceptance of catalytic development organizations, a commitment to the new development professionalism, academic, organizational and financial support provided by foreign NGOs, financial support from domestic commercial sources and legitimacy derived from recognition and approval by the government.

However, there are also constraints which need to be reckoned with. First and foremost, heading this list is pervasive lack of coordination and factionalism among Thai NGOs and the history of suspicion between the private non-profit and the governmental sectors. These are two major obstacles that THIRD will not be able to avoid. For instance, it is still unclear how other key NGOs will respond to the presence of potentially competing development organizations. Also, numerous issues will have to be addressed dealing with the redistribution of power as a result of new organizational and financial arrangements.

But by far the biggest questions are raised by Thai society itself and the dynamics of modernization. Recalling the parameters of development in Thailand (discussed in Chapter 4), one is reminded that alternative development has yet to be fully understood by the people before wide-spread public support can be generated.

Even more significant are the dynamic forces set into motion some thirty years ago, under the heading of modernization and industrialization. In fact, Thai society—including the most populous sector, the rural population—has been changed in fundamental ways. Whether these changes will still be amenable to the future envisioned by the leaders of THIRD is a troublesome question.

All things considered, this discussion points in the direction of gradual modifications in existing policies and programs, making allowance also for a growing presence of strategic or third generation Thai NGOs.

Khun Vibul Khemchalerm, Head Huay Hin Village, Chaseongsao Province—applying Buddhism to development through integrated agriculture.

Chapter 7

BUDDHIST DEVELOPMENT: AN ALTERNATIVE MODEL?

It is almost laughable simply to speak of solving the problems of hunger, illiteracy, and illness, because these are not the real problems at all; they are only symptoms. The fundamental problem is the lack of religion *sasana* and moral principles *siladhamma* in modern society.

Bhikkhu Buddhadasa

Religion, one of three pillars in Thai society—together with Nation and King—contributes to continuity, stability and consensus. Despite rapid change brought about by the modernization of Thai society, "Buddhism is the most important symbol of and primary base for a feeling of national and cultural identification."[1]

The symbiotic relationship between religion and culture in Thai society has the potential for an alternative development model that may reach beyond the borders of the Kingdom. The analysis of this subject begins with an overview of Buddhist principles and their implications for development before examining the religion-culture-power nexus.

There are several points, aside from the main theme of power and culture in development, which will be stressed throughout the discussion: First, while the Buddhist development paradigm is not likely to replace secular models of development, it has already affected their interpretation. Second, it will be shown that Buddhist influence on Thai development derives from religious and lay sources, making for a distinct comparative advantage. Third, the growing visibility of Buddhist development activities results largely from the confluence of two simultaneously expanding movements, the community of development monks and the rapidly expanding local NGOs working principally in the rural areas.

Buddhist Ideals

In order to see the relationship between Buddhism and national development and its potential for significant change, some familiarity with the broad outlines of

POWER AND CULTURE

Buddhist teachings is necessary. Leaving aside sectarian differences—represented by prominent but controversial movements such as Santi Asoka and Dhammakaya—what are the constants in the Buddhist *Weltanschauung*, and how do they apply to the human condition and the natural environment?

Taking as a guide Bhikkhu Buddhadasa, one of Thailand's most revered (and highly controversial, in the view of some observers) monks and influential thinkers as our guide, we begin with two fundamental truths: the impermanence of life (anicca) and the pervasiveness of suffering (dukkha); followed by the negation of self, craving being the source of all evil; loving kindness and compassion (metta-karuna); and the ultimate state of release or freedom (nibbana/nirvana). The interrelatedness and circular nature of these concepts is explained as follows:

> Our self-centeredness which blinds us to the true nature of things promotes personal suffering (dukka), and in preventing us from acting compassionately (karuna) contributes directly to the arising social ills: [and according to Buddhadasa] 'In modern society there is no compassion, because people have become selfish and are attached to the idea of a self and what belongs to it. They are ignoring God's wish that we love one another, that is, that we consider the good of society before we think of our own personal gain.'[2]

The teachings of Buddha call for non-attachment, "…a mind free from preoccupation with materialism." Attachment in all its manifestations causes only suffering and unhappiness. A second principle, the inter-relatedness of life that equates with nature is a state of normalcy.[3]

Closely related is the Buddhist ethic of sufficiency or moderation—the "morality of nature"—which leads to a "community of restraint." According to Buddhadasa such a community, which he calls Dhammic Socialism, corresponds to the natural state of things. Thus, Dhammic Socialism "may be said to characterize the original moral condition of individuals and society."[4] In order to maintain the balance of this natural state, the good of the whole must be accepted as a constant:

> In a society that puts the interests of any one individual above those of the community, social problems cannot be effectively addressed because the context of the problems is the way society operates as a whole.[5]

Also, the principle of restraint and generosity, in conjunction with a simple life style—adequate food, clothing, housing and medicine (the optimal way to live)—are the natural concomitants of a truly Buddhist society, as are mutual respect and loving kindness, seeking peace and condemning war, respect for life and the environment.[6]

These noble underpinnings of the ideal Buddhist society stand in stark contrast to contemporary reality. In Buddhadasa's words:

We have entered a brutal, selfish age. Human beings have devastated nature until some kinds of plants and animals have become extinct because of the tremendous upsurge of anti-social thought and behavior.[7]

Implications for Development

Balance or the middle way is a major theme in Buddhist teachings. Recognizing the frailties of human nature and thus the difficulties in overcoming greed, hatred and other evils, Buddhists are taught to avoid extremes. Applied to development this means:

...the end result of development is that man should know the natural golden mean of action, the Middle Way, gaining that full insight into the nature of life which brings one to life's goal which is freedom.[8]

Sulak Sivaraksa, a well-known social critic, lay spokesman for Buddhism and an authority on development issues, categorically rejects narrow definitions of development. From a Buddhist view, no matter how the subject is defined or approached, it always comes down to man and the world; furthermore, he argues religion, like politics, cannot be kept out of development.[9]

The fundamental difference between Buddhist and secular models of development, according to Sulak, lies in the distinction between quantitative and qualitative development. Because quality is difficult to measure, we tend to focus on quantitative aspects. For economists, development becomes a matter of:

...currency and things, thus fostering greed. Politicians see development in terms of increased power thus fostering ill-will. Both then work together hand in glove and measure the results in terms of quantity, thus fostering ignorance and completing the Buddhist triad of evils. So we can say that the error in development lies in making quantity the goal, in continually trying to measure results in terms of materialism and modernity. It is evident that our world is caught up in a cycle. Especially in quantitative development, the further it goes, the more problems appear, often faster than they can be solved...[10]

In effect, the technocrats are afraid to stop things because they fear that everything will come to a grinding halt, and most importantly "they want to maintain the status of the rich."[11]

Buddhist Analysis of Underdevelopment in Thailand

Buddhist critics of mainstream development pinpoint external pressures as the root causes of underdevelopment. They blame modernization and rapid change for the transformation of Thai society with its widening gap between the rich and the poor, social alienation, environmental destruction and other ills.

> The further development has proceeded the more it has resulted in the rich becoming richer while the poor become poorer, and the rich are still not happier. Nature and the environment are deteriorating day-by-day. Animal life and other natural resources are increasingly wasted for selfish purposes...[12]

Development has also taken its toll in Thai religion and culture. According to Donald Swearer:

> The effects of Thailand's development in the past thirty years have badly eroded the significance and meaning of traditional symbols, institutions, and cultural values. Traditional Thai Buddhism—its beliefs, practices and institutions—has lost its centrality in some sectors of Thai life, especially among the educated elites.[13]

However, the impact of modernization is most evident in the rural people and the urban poor. Based on his intimate knowledge of Thai society and his personal experience with the people in the North and the Northeast, William Klausner noted:

> The rural and urban upcountry population is subject to escalating tensions created by social and economic changes that are occurring too abruptly. It is increasingly difficult to cope psychologically as less dependence on traditional 'supports' including the Sangha is now the norm.[14]

This line of thought leads to the conclusion that development as practiced under government and international agency auspices for the past forty years is at the center of the development *problematique*. The presumption is that in the pre-development days Thai people lived relatively balanced and harmonious lives. This desirable state of affairs, according to the argument, underwent fundamental changes with the introduction of modernization and industrialization. In short, the Western concept of development is viewed as the main cause of underdevelopment.

For example, two noted contemporary Thai thinkers, Dr. Prawase Wasi and Dr. Preecha Piampongsarn, blame capitalism for changing the "structure of farmers" lives from self-reliance to cash crop farming, which has resulted in economic dependency, bankruptcy and the breakdown of their rural communities."[15] In the words of the Governor of Bangkok Chamlong Srimuang:

> Our ancestors were not cash-crop oriented. With an integrated farm where they planted rice, vegetables and fruit, as well as raise cattle, they could survive, while the additional

150

gains were distributed through the community. And there were no such things as debt and severe need among farmers.[16]

Buddhist Solutions to Underdevelopment

What then is the Buddhist response to these complex issues? Specifically, how do the advocates of Buddhist development propose to address the problems of mass poverty, unemployment, and underemployment, malnutrition, lack of health care and education?

Mindful of the current turmoil in Thailand and the lack of clear vision among the people and the government, Buddhadasa and other Buddhist leaders offer solutions based on seemingly simple concepts, which are however, most complex in their application. Buddhist alternative development presents intrinsically a political challenge; namely, how to counteract and ultimately replace conventional power. Referring to poverty as a case in point, according to Buddhadasa:

The problem of poverty is a result of our getting off track. Even the current problems of illiteracy and ignorance of good health practices arise from our going in the wrong direction.... Greed, then is at the heart of scarcity and poverty.

If we were to put our religious principles into practice, even the problems of global shortages would disappear....If we were to use the earth's resources according to the laws of Nature and within its limits, we would not need to use as much as we do now.

The kind of morality that feeds our desires for luxurious living, however, makes living in a *prakati* [state of normalcy] way difficult, because it gives rise to *kilesa* [craving and mental impurities]. It costs much less—or nothing at all—to practice the kind of morality that leads to *nibbana*, because it can solve the problems that lie within. It does not require billions for development projects.

Ariyasiladhamma is the morality that can bring peace and happiness without investing a great deal of money or going to considerable trouble. Is this not the kind of morality we should want? What then, holds us back from wanting it? In the first and most fundamental sense, we do not realize what we are doing: we want what we should not want, and we do not want what we should want. We go blindly along seeking satisfaction in physical or material pleasures. We even desire things that will bring us trouble and anxiety. We say we want *siladhamma*, but in our hearts we long for the satisfactions of eating well and living well.[17]

Clearly this is the language of religion. Although some politicians in their more philosophical moments might agree, it is indeed a rare occasion to hear these sentiments expressed in political circles. One major exception is Bangkok Governor Chamlong Srimuang, a devout Buddhist and member of the Santi Asoka Buddhist sect, who preaches and personally practices a fundamentally Buddhist way of life. Speaking at a forum, he said:

> Eat little, use little, but work hard and share with society. That's the key. Some people in society are already practicing this. But we need to have more people of this kind. So let's help create more of this breed and seriously put the idea to practice...[18]

Thinking also of the need for political action, Sulak asks rhetorically: "When our own ancient religion provides so many solutions to our problems, why should we continue so tamely and blindly to follow the Westerners?"[19] His solution lies in cutting the umbilical cord which ties developing countries, like Thailand, to external donors. He argues that self-reliance and self-sufficiency, based on the traditional Buddhist way of life, is the only realistic response to the syndrome of underdevelopment and lack of freedom.

> The solution can only come when the poorer country realizes it is being taken advantage of and finds a way to cut its dependence at the points where it is at a disadvantage. What is called aid or development funds is a means whereby the aiding country can gain stronger control and bring the developing country even more under its influence. It may cause material hardship at first for a small country to cut itself off from a large one, but it will bring freedom in the long run and can truly remedy poverty.[20]

The place to start is with "Conscientization, or teaching one to know one's own situation," seeking change within the individual and in society at large. Referring to Gandhi as the foremost practitioner of this approach, he points to the following features: The village with its culture is the focal point of Gandhi's method. The objective is to promote the well-being of the community without destroying its culture. Production methods that do not require machinery are emphasized. As the village becomes more self-sufficient, levels of participation and the scope of decision making will increase.[21]

Sulak sums up his view of Buddhist development by citing Dr. Puey Ungphakorn's criteria: peace, worthy development goals, well-planned development procedures, and power—carefully used and properly checked.[22]

Religion, Culture and Power

There are some 300,000 monks and novices in Thailand, living in approximately 30,000 *wats* that are spread out among 52,000 villages and a handful of large urban centers.[23] Thailand remains a rural society, with more than 70% of the population living in the countryside, despite the fact that the agricultural contribution to the GNP has steadily declined.

Presently, and in the foreseeable future, Thai national development is thus circumscribed by a predominantly rural society, with cultural values and social norms increasingly subjected to the corrosive influence of modernization. Western development is fostered by and largely for an urban middle class and a wealthy elite.

In conventional terms of power, there is no contest between the world of the villager and that of the urbanite. The relationship is decidedly lopsided. Yet, if one takes a broader view of power that is not limited to material resources, especially a view disregarding economic and military factors, but also includes "spiritual sources," e.g. culture and religious values, a different equation emerges.

Recognizing that Buddhism is believed to be in the early stages of a renaissance (indicated by the growing interest in religious teaching; that Buddhism is synonymous with Thai society, thus drawing on the weight of tradition; that the spiritual power of religion is strongest at the village level; that the economic, social, and related problems faced by the villagers have reached a crisis stage; and considering that today rural people are better informed of the forces which have caused their present predicaments), the combination of these factors lends credence to a scenario which provides an alternative to the current, purely secular approach.

The alternative model of development concentrates on the village where the *wat* once again emerges as a center of power. This power is based on the combination of religious teachings, cultural norms and traditions, and a new concept of secular involvement by the Sangha (the community of monks). In the past monks and abbots held the keys to the villagers' political universe. Speaking of the monk's position in the village, a knowledgeable government official said:

They are respected, trusted, and regarded as neutral by the villagers. What they request or recommend, the villagers always follow and obey. Their development work, though sometimes following no fixed principles, is effective and economical.'[24]

And comparing the influence of the monk with other village leaders, Somboon observed in an earlier study:

These three village leaders, the abbot, the village headman, and the school headmaster derive their positions and prestige from different sources. These are respectively religion, government and knowledge. Among them there appear to be latent tensions; they may clash as soon as one of them thinks that another is operating in his own particular sphere of competence. However, it is suggested that the influence of the abbot in terms of villagers' support tends to be far greater than that of the village headman and the headmaster.... The village headmanship tends to be the least effective in the village power structure, especially when the abbot shows an active interest in village affairs, in which case the position of the abbot tends to carry most weight.

POWER AND CULTURE

Thus it is the Sangha which is ultimately the most influential institution in the village, and the abbot the person who wields the greatest motivational power.[25]

"Motivational power," derived principally from spiritual sources, combined with a renewed emphasis on traditional values and culture represent the dynamic elements of the alternative Buddhist development paradigm. Consequently new definitions of politics and government have emerged. For example, according to Bhikkhu Buddhadasa, politics is:

...a strategy for addressing the problems that arise from increasing numbers of people living together....Ideally, then, politics is a moral system for addressing the problems arising from the need for social cooperation...

True politics is a struggle against misunderstanding, wrongview, craving after defilements and the like. ... All over the world politics has become a means to take advantage of others, and politicians speak only for their own advantage. This poisons the real meaning of politics.[26]

Similarly, governance, according to Buddhadasa:

...can be thought of as a means of running the village, the town, the nation, or even the world. Governance thus means solving the problems that arise in relationship to large aggregates of people.[27]

Thus, the nexus of religion, culture and power serves as the foundation for an alternative development model that is put to the test in Thailand. The Sangha ("an aggregation or group") and Buddhism, "the religion of the people" (Buddha means one who knows, one who is awake, one who is enlightened), thus are key forces promoting the alternative development strategy.[28]

Attempting to find creative alternatives to those types of culture that have produced suffering in Western societies, namely the "industrial, consumer and success cultures,"[29] the Buddhist message presents a clear ideological challenge to both liberal democracy and communism. This challenge is expressed most clearly and directly in Buddhadasa's discussion of Dhammic Socialism. Referring to the destructive capabilities of the capitalist and marxist systems, he says:

When people have fallen to such a level how can we say that they are human beings...Each side has enough support to eliminate the other, and yet they contend that they will solve the world's problems. This is like cleaning something that is dirty with dirty water, or conquering evil with evil.[30]

In this view, a key fault of both Marxism and liberal democracy is seeking to correct the fundamental problem of inequality through force and power, a strategy which in fact only promotes craving and greed. Donald Swearer concludes:

> His [Buddhadasa's] vision serves as a critique of Western political theories of capitalism and communism, and provides the basic principles for a political philosophy with the potential to guide not only Thailand in the coming years, but all societies struggling to create a just and equitable social, political and economic order.[31]

Speaking of this "religio-political philosophy," he goes on to say:

> ...in general Buddhist socialism can be characterized as an attempt to integrate a sense of cultural national identity represented by Buddhism as an organized religion and a spiritual value into the political and economic structures and programs of the modern West.
>
> Bhikkhu Buddhadasa's interpretation of dhammic socialism is one of the few attempts on the part of an original Theravada Buddhist thinker to propose a political philosophy for his time generated out of an Asian belief system within an Asian context.[32]

By the same token, it must also be emphasized the Buddhist strategy for alternative development, unlike its secular counterparts, is not confrontational in nature, as stated by Bhikkhu Buddhadasa:

> It is my hope that in the end people everywhere might work together in harmony, no matter what their nationality, language, or religion might be.[33]

The Role of the Sangha in Thailand's National Development

Although Buddhism is deeply embedded in Thai society and culture and thus directly related to Thailand's national development, the relationship between religion and development is complex and controversial.

The recent record of the Sangha's involvement with national development work in Thailand dates from the early 1960s when the government explicitly enlisted the help of the Buddhist hierarchy in its struggle against communist subversion. Against the background of an ongoing debate questioning in principle any secular engagement on the part of Buddhist monks, two principal Sangha development programs—"Dhamma Carik," which brought the combined assistance of monks and government officials to the hilltribes and the "Dhammathud" program, focusing on citizenship training and various development-related activities—were established under the auspices of the two major Buddhist Universities, Mahachulalongkorn and Mahamakutra. These programs were financed largely by foreign foundations.

POWER AND CULTURE

Out of this period of ambiguous and frequently uneasy relations with a security-conscious government subsequently emerged an independent movement of monks attempting to address the development needs of rural Thailand. Dating back to the early 1970s but not publicly recognized until ten years later, this new movement, generally referred to as 'the developing monks' or *phra nak pattana*, came into existence. The one factor crucial to its emergence was the simultaneous increase in activity on the part of indigenous secular development organizations, the Thai rural development NGOs.

As a result of the seminal political events in the early and mid-1970s in Thai history, a great deal of vital energy came to be concentrated on the nascent Thai NGO sector. Those liberal forces that had been pushed underground by a repressive military regime eventually found themselves collaborating on social, cultural and general development affairs. It was precisely this infusion of new ideas, idealism and energy which benefited individual monks who began to set out on their own, helping their village communities to help themselves. Monks were among the early participants in NGO-sponsored workshops, providing them with a sense of direction and skill in development affairs.

Nation, Religion and King

In accordance with tradition and backed up by law, Buddhism in Thailand is tied to and controlled by the state, with the King as the titular head of the ecclesiastic order. Quoting from the *Annual Report* of the Department of Religious Affairs, "It is also held that 'Nation, Religion and King' are bonds of unity of the Thai nation; that national security and the stability of religion (Buddhism) must not be separated."[34]

As a result of this reciprocal, tri-partite relationship, several government agencies share responsibility for supporting and guiding the Sangha and its affairs. The major state agencies concerned with religious matters are the Department of Religious Affairs, Ministry of Education; the Department of Local Government Administration, Ministry of Interior; and the Department of Medical Services, Ministry of Public Health.

Most formal aspects of the monk's life, e.g. identity papers, titles, honoraria (for those in administrative positions), etc. are prescribed by the state. In the area of administration, particularly since the adoption of the Sangha Act of 1962, under the Sarit government (which in effect abolished all democratic features of Sangha organization):

> ...the organization of the Sangha and its administrative structure parallels the administrative structure of the government and is closely integrated into that of the civil government ...the Sangha is effectively incorporated into the governmental structure at the higher and administrative levels in such a manner that the government

can exercise effective control over Sangha policy and procedure at the higher administrative levels.[35]

Fears of communist insurgency in conjunction with ethnic and regional problems were the motivations behind national development, modernization and the enlistment of the Sangha by the government in its early development efforts. Security concerns were paramount.

Thus, the rural development programmes became the main policy of the government from the 1960s onwards, with the aim of raising rural standards of living, and so meeting the challenge of potential insurrection.[36]

Sangha-Government Development Programs

The early Sangha development programs were strictly top-down in design and execution. The institutional setting for these government-approved activities was provided by the two national Buddhist universities, Mahachulalongkorn and Mahamakutra.

Beginning with the early to mid-1960s these universities established new academic programs and new faculties "to define and develop a constructive service role for the Universities and assure that these institutions maintained their relevance to the social as well as religious needs of society."[37] More specifically, the changes were intended to improve the caliber of religious education, to encourage monk graduates to take more interest in community development, and "to promote unity among the Thai people and thus help to promote national and religious security."[38]

Since these changes in academic programs were regarded as an overall effort to upgrade the Buddhist Universities, financial support was made available by The Asia Foundation and the International Monetary Fund for Social and Economic Studies.

Coincident with the strengthening and redirection of Buddhist higher education, two development programs were formally initiated in 1964 and 1965 respectively, the Dhammic Ambassador (Dhammathud) and Dhammic Hilltribe (Dhamma Carik) Programs.

On the whole the monk graduates assigned to these programs were expected to be actively engaged in education, propagation of Buddhism, and social welfare. Furthermore, it was understood that the monks were to function also as "intermediaries and co-ordinators between government officials and villagers."[39]

Under the auspices of the Dhammic Ambassador Program, the Sangha, in cooperation with the Department of Religious Affairs, sent more than 1,000 monks to travel throughout the country "…giving sermons which incorporate citizenship training, and modern hygiene and sanitation practices, as well as moral and religious teaching." It was hoped that this program would both strengthen people's faith and assist them with their material needs.[40]

Staying in the provinces for one year at a time, the monks were assigned to work closely with local ecclesiastic officials, assisting them in the implementation of various government development programs. Aside from the inevitable friction between the local clergy and the new graduate monks, the main problems were insufficient financial support, lack of cooperation from government officials at the district level and hostile communists.[41]

In 1964, in response to renewed insurrectionist activities, these co-operative programs, as well as all of the government's development programs were supplemented by the establishment of the Accelerated Rural Development Programme (ARD), which was to serve as the government's overall development coordinating mechanism, providing also technical assistance as well as needed equipment. Subsequently, ARD concentrated on infrastructure, particularly the construction of roads.[42]

> The main objective of the ARD programme is not only to promote the villagers' welfare, but also to 'win the hearts and minds' of these people.[43]

The Dhamma Carik Program operated under the joint sponsorship of the Sangha and the Public Welfare Department, sending monks and government officials to the hilltribes. Motivated principally by security concerns, the project sought to integrate these ethnic minorities into the main stream of Thai society by building bonds of loyalty to the Thai nation and through their conversion to Buddhism.

Another category of Buddhist-sponsored development activity was carried out by the Sangha Education and Development Centers, beginning in the mid-1960s and early 1970s. Established initially by a small number of monk graduates, these centers provided leadership training programs offered to monks, abbots and lay persons, as well as seminars on technical subjects, including community development programming. They were thus instrumental in promoting both Sangha and government development objectives. By the early '70s the centers had spread to practically all provinces in Thailand's Northeast and North.[44]

Even more significantly, the centers became the operational base for more enterprising individual monks, who expanded their realm of activity, by initiating "…specific development projects at the village level in such areas as vocational and adult education, village library development, agriculture and water resources development, home economics, sanitation and preventive medicine."[45]

Another influential Sangha instrumentality with development overtones was the Center for the Education of Sangha Private Schools, Wat Phra Singh, Chiang Mai. "For more than a decade this Center has played a dynamic leadership role in encouraging a greater community service orientation on part of approximately 50 Sangha administered private schools throughout the country." The curriculum includes training courses for teachers in rural non-formal education, vocational training, and development programs.[46]

It should also be noted that funding for all the above programs has come principally from foreign foundations, except for intermittent indirect support, e.g. lecturers and equipment, provided by the government. On the whole, contributions by the private and public sectors were minimal.

Critical Issues

Given the Sangha's traditional loyalty to the state, which in itself is a product of the reciprocal relationship between Buddhism and Thai society (Buddha personally instructed his followers in their responsibilities towards the society which supports them), monks were thought of as natural allies by the government in the nation-building process:

> For these reasons the various Thai governments have always been highly conscious of the potential role that the Sangha can play in policies of national development and integration, and of the fact that the Sangha may be employed to develop a system of political legitimacy and to aid in mobilizing the villagers for political ends. It is not surprising therefore that the Sangha's active role in government programmes is systematically organized and institutionalized.[47]

However despite these seemingly strong ties, the relationship entails complex issues. For one thing, there is the persistent question whether Buddhist teachings permit monks to engage in purely secular matters, physical activities, and financial dealings.

Conservative critics within and outside the Sangha maintain that there are inherent incompatibilities between Buddhism and purely worldly responsibilities. In their view, monks are restricted to religious roles, alone through which the cause of development must be fostered. The following excerpt from *Political Buddhism in Southeast Asia* reflects these sentiments:

> Yet this kind of active involvement in nation-building and modernization is an innovation in Thai Buddhist history, and almost contrary to the traditional idea that the monks should remain apart from mundane affairs, practicing the holy life and striving for Nirvana and in that way contributing to the merit and welfare of the society. ...the evidence [in reference to two surveys] is that both junior and learned monks were opposed to the idea that the monks should take part in the government's politically defined programmes, with the exception of helping to build hospitals and development education....But this point of view of the junior monks is overshadowed by the determination of members of the Sangha at the higher level.[48]

POWER AND CULTURE

On the other hand, William Klausner, sharing the majority view, puts the matter this way:

The creative tension and conflict between the worldly developmental and religious roles of the Sangha have been the subject of some controversy...There has been a growing consensus that the two roles are not incompatible but rather complementary. Sangha leadership, both in the capital and in the provinces, has increasingly committed itself to developing institutional mechanisms which will enable the rural Sangha to gain greater technical competence and skill in rural development related activities and, thus assist it to better fulfill its traditional community service responsibilities.[49]

Klausner and others present a long list of reasons to justify why the Sangha should be and in fact is involved in development tasks. They stress, for instance a number of secular roles, which monks have traditionally performed in the villages of Thailand. The list includes the time-honored role as arbitrators in village affairs, the use of the temple as a depository for valuables (including cash), and the use of the *wat* as a hostel for travellers and thus a village social center. In the past the wat has also looked out for the physical well-being of the village community .

...bhikkhus do not divorce themselves from the everyday life of their followers. On the contrary, they involve themselves in the community's life and use their knowledge and prestige to alleviate problems that are of the very fabric of village secular life.[50]

There are additional reasons to support secular involvement by the monks, for example, the lack of knowledge and expertise on the part of villagers, the frequent absence of government services, and the "silent opinion of the villagers." Klausner refers also to "psychological pressures" on the monks to participate in community affairs.[51]

Although not expressed overtly, the villagers feel that, by virtue of this close and intimate relationship, the bhikkhus should not divorce themselves from the everyday life of the village.[52]

Furthermore, the intimate personal ties of the monks to the village community need to be taken into account. Frequently the monk comes from the village where he now serves. Chances are, that he has relatives nearby. Further, he knows the hardships of the farmer's life.

The Wat and the bhikkhus have become so intimately tied into the whole fabric of village life that the Wat itself is the naturally chosen physical site for village activities of a widely divergent nature.

> …the bhikkhus play a secular role both defined for them and by them. Thus, there is agreement on the advisability of the bhikkhus' actively participating in certain secular aspects of village life while, of course, carefully abiding by the rules of discipline.[53]

Finally, leaving the issue of secular activities performed by the Sangha aside, there remains the question of whether the Sangha is the most appropriate vehicle to carry the government's message and to assist in the implementation of its development work. Conversely, it has been argued that in the long run it may be contrary to the interests of the Sangha to be too closely tied to the political arena.

These questions need to be viewed within the context of the dominant attitudes of the villagers in order to make a valid assessment. It is no secret in Thailand that villagers generally believe in keeping their distance from government officials.

In terms of the government's own interests, which concentrate on three principal objectives—promoting self-help at the village level, democracy and national consciousness—the following considerations cast doubt on the overall effectiveness of most if not all, government-sponsored Sangha development programs.

It has been generally confirmed that villagers tend to fear government agents more than the communists, that the monks' propagation efforts were superfluous, and where the Buddhist faith needed strengthening, the limited efforts of itinerant monks were insufficient, that Thais consider merit making principally an individual concern, which tends to limit the scope of this activity, and, finally, with reference to Thai Muslims, many of these programs were, by definition, counterproductive.[54]

In general, from the standpoint of effective development programs, the rule of thumb is that those projects which are imposed from the outside, under whatever auspices, tend to be doomed from the start.

Secondly, based on his first extensive study, which focuses on joint Sangha-government development programs, Somboon Suksamran also concluded that these efforts failed to "increase the influence of religious norms on Thai behavior." In fact, he goes on to say that the Sangha itself has been hurt by this type of collaboration.[55]

Once again, considering the basis for this conclusion, in the villagers' mind politics is a matter of power and decision-making in the distant capital. This involves individuals and programs at various levels, but they are all removed from the farmer's immediate purview. He feels essentially powerless and exposed to distant forces affecting his life. "In other words, politics belongs to the wider world, the world of people who have power, from which ordinary people like themselves should remain detached."[56]

Politicization of the monks' activities can only hurt their image and their prestige. "If the manipulation of primary traditional rules for political ends becomes too obvious, Buddhism and the Sangha may cease to provide a major source of legitimacy."[57]

POWER AND CULTURE

For all of these reasons it would appear, then, that the presupposition that the monks are the best agents for national development and integration, with consequent political modernization, seems unjustified. On the contrary, the use of Buddhism and the Sangha to serve political ends,…may in fact bring undesirable consequences for the Sangha's position and for Buddhism.[58]

The Development Monks

In his introduction to *A Buddhist Approach to Development: The case of the 'Development Monks' in Thailand* (1986), Somboon characterizes this movement as follows:

> Within the last few years, movements comprised of both religious and lay members have been developing and complementing alternative models of development. One of the most innovative movements has involved monks who voluntarily organized themselves for development tasks in villages throughout the country. Although each monk or group of monks has its own style, strategy and concept of development, the groups share a common goal: to relieve the suffering of human beings and reveal to them the path to happiness, in both worldly and spiritual terms.[59]

As indicated, the official Sangha Education and Development Centers, set up in the mid-1960s, served indirectly as the origin of a new movement, which became later known as *phra nak pattana*. In the early 1970s, on the initiative of individual monks, a growing number of community development activities, which went beyond the Sangha programs, took root and subsequently were strengthened through NGO support. These projects, which did not fully come to the attention of outsiders until recently, focused on vocational and adult education, agriculture, water resources, sanitation, and related development concerns.

The main difference between the work of the development monks and previous undertakings lies in their independence from the authority of the government and the Sangha. Their guiding concepts are quality of life, self-reliance, self-respect and respect for traditional culture.[60]

More specifically, the development concept of the monks represents a composite of the following ideas and values:

- Relieving human suffering
- Improving the quality of life through self-reliance, self-respect and reliance on local resources
- The middle path: a blend of material and spiritual values (search for balance)
- Rejection of a common development model
- Flexibility and accommodation

- The need for peoples' participation
- Viewing development as a continuing process
- Confining the government's role in development to seeking cooperation and coordination for its own programs
- Emphasizing the importance of compromise and adjustment in the operation of development projects

Development monks are committed to improve the material and spiritual dimensions of village life, emphasizing the importance of community initiative. Their strategy is "…to make rural people understand the roots of their problems and then co-operate willingly with each other to remedy their own sufferings."[61] Additional aspects of their strategy include an emphasis on long-term, interrelated development programs and readiness to cooperate with other development agencies.

The background of the development monks also provides insight into their approach to rural development in Thailand. The majority of the development monks are between 35-45 years old; they entered the monkhood motivated by tradition and in search of education; they are geographically mobile; however, they tend to be indigenous to the region where they are working; most of them have administrative experience; they come from peasant stock; their early life experiences are identical to those of the villagers; they all have compulsory primary education and passed various levels of religious education; they are experienced in development work; and they share a common motivation to be involved in development work.[62]

Given this background and considering the appalling pockets of poverty and ignorance in the rural areas, it is easy to see why these monks believe that their place is in the village and that the development process has to start there. This premise also points to one of the main differences between monks and government officials: monks live in the village and are committed to its people; the official does not and he cares most about position and promotion.[63]

Somboon points out that "…the development programs of the development monks seek to complete the entire circle of development, i.e., to achieve both material and spiritual well-being, with villagers participation on a continuing basis."[64]

The Importance of Culture

There is another major difference between development monks and government development workers in the monks' view, "material development should not be achieved at the expense of local traditions, culture and social life of the people."[65] In fact, the strong position taken by the monks with respect to the importance of traditional values, knowledge and cultural wisdom must be considered the principal key to the success of many of their development activities and programs. Effective development is a function of strategies that are compatible with the moral base of society combined with programs that do not undermine the moral base of society.

> In the case of Thailand…development efforts over the past three decades have not been fully successful because the moral base of society has not been given serious consideration.
>
> By contrast, development monks have constructed their concepts and strategies in harmony with the moral base of Thai rural society. Traditional cultural values, deeply rooted in Buddhism, are naturally and carefully inculcated as integral parts of the Sangha's development process.[66]

Illustrative of the government's tendency to be oblivious to the cultural dimension of development is the long-standing rural job creation program. Designed to alleviate unemployment during the agricultural off-season, large amounts of money have been pumped over the years into the rural sector, paying wages for temporary labor, generally in conjunction with infrastructure projects.[67] Observing the impact of this large public works job program, monks found that one of the results of a cash economy is a basic change in values. Villagers became increasingly more materialistic and selfish. Long standing traditions of mutual help were significantly weakened. In response, development monks explicitly incorporate cultural awareness into their own development activities to the extent of reviving traditional practices, such as friendship bonds (young people publicly declaring their life-long friendship) and children showing respect to their parents.

The monks blame the weakening of the cultural base of society on the modernization process and the introduction of the cash economy. The government, in its zeal to modernize rural society, is held primarily responsible for this state of affairs. The government's attitude towards culture, viewing culture principally as a hindrance in the development process, further compounds the problem.

> Thus, the attitudes of development monks and most government officials toward local culture and tradition are different. The development monks consider culture and tradition as a potential force for development, while government officials view tradition and culture more negatively.[68]

The Sangha-NGO Connection

The interface between religion and the NGO community in Thailand is significant because it strengthens the foundation for an alternative development paradigm based on Buddhist principles. Comparable to two small rivers joining to produce a much stronger current, Thai development professionals, representing nearly all sectors (academia, trade unions, the media, community development workers, and even some government officials), are joining hands with a growing number of progressive abbots and monks, who work closely with villagers on many development projects.

The historical circumstances—particularly the fateful political events of the 1970s—that make this confluence of religion and secular development possible, have already been sketched. The question now is, exactly what do these groups have in common and how do they collaborate?

Although the personal background of the individuals concerned—i.e. monks on the one hand and urban middle class academics on the other—often are very different, there can be little doubt about their shared values, beliefs, attitudes, development strategies, approaches and overall goals.

For example, the preceding discussion of the role of culture placed into the Thai NGO context points to a tacit alliance among abbots, monks and lay development workers, underscoring the belief that development devoid of its cultural base is doomed to fail. This shared commitment to common values is not just a fortuitous coincidence, rather it is a measure of the regenerative power of Thai Buddhist culture. The coming together of the religious and secular constituencies, joining hands with the people in the villages, represents a key element in a new power equation.

Similarly, monks and Thai NGOs are in agreement on the main outlines of the development strategy. Already familiar with the key features of the NGO model—including the emphasis on popular participation, self-respect and self-reliance, and catalytic roles for outside development agents—it is not difficult to identify other areas of agreement.

Finally, there are overlapping concerns and mutual interest regarding professionalism and politics. Although Thai NGOs themselves are still engaged in building and solidifying their own organizational base and managerial skills, they are prepared to lend support of this type to the development monks.

Also, with reference to the political arena, Thai NGOs have accumulated practical experience and increasingly have access to the universities, government offices, political parties, as well as to other traditional centers of power. Combined with the revered position of the Sangha in all sectors of Thai society, a potentially powerful coalition is in the making.

Characteristics of Buddhist Development

The similarities between indigenous NGOs and their Buddhist counterparts also extend to the project areas that they address. The development monks are active in agriculture, education vocational training, co-operative self-help programs (rice- and buffalo banks as well as co-operative stores), sanitation and health care, community services, and socio-cultural issues including preservation of traditional values and Buddhism.

POWER AND CULTURE

Furthermore, compared to government-sponsored development activities, both NGO and Buddhist projects share the following features:

- Voluntarism
  The principal motivation is social and moral obligation. In the case of the development monks the sense of accountability to the community is reinforced by sharing the life of the villagers. By way of contrast, a villager notes that government officials…
  …do not put their hearts into the work. They do it and get it out of their way because it is their duty. They do not care to improve the result if it is not successful. Instead, they would put all the blame on the villagers. They just don't have Metta [loving kindness and compassion].[69]
- Qualitative as opposed to quantitative development
- Development from the inside and from the bottom up
  The individual, the group and the local community are the starting points of Buddhist development.

The Sangha model of development, represented by the movement of development monks, has a number of constraints that limit its scope and impact on national development. For instance, the relationship between the Sangha and the government in development affairs, has been characterized by ambiguity from the start. Gains for either party through cooperative programs may readily turn into liabilities. Similarly, the independence of development monks from overt government control is both an advantage and a limitation. Working on their own, individual monks are more effective on a case by case basis. However, by the same token, they also lack the backing of a national Sangha development plan.

Most Buddhist inspired development activities depend on a single individual for motivation and guidance, they do not only stand alone, but they tend to be very small. Financial constraints and lack of outside support are chronic problems often reducing projects to operate hand-to-mouth.

Perhaps even more important, the villagers' understanding of key development principles—self-reliance, self-respect, etc. often is not very profound. They have been conditioned to think more along authoritarian lines and putting their faith in client-patron relations.

There is also the tendency on the part of monks to pursue a soft approach of loving kindness and compassion, thus perpetuating underdevelopment. However…

Despite all these constraints on the Sangha's approach to development, the development monks' concepts and strategies have great potential for contributing to Thai rural society.[70]

This line of thought is based on the socio-political effects of the Sangha approach, which include increased self-confidence on the part of villagers, strengthened ties

166

between the monks and laymen, revived prestige and position for the Sangha within rural society, better village participation in their own development, possible compromise between Western and traditional values and attitudes, enhanced group solidarity, political awareness and consciousness, and broadened horizons for the rural communities through better access to socio-political information.

The following statement appropriately sums up the discussion of this chapter:

Whatever the limitations placed on monks' involvement in community development activities in terms of doctrine, discipline, public opinion, it is evident that there is still a constructive role to be played at the village level. This role is being played with increasing confidence and technical competence by village monks.[71]

Steps in the preparation of herbal medicines by development workers and villagers under Khun Vibul's supervision.

Chapter 8

BUDDHIST POWER: ALTERNATIVE DEVELOPMENT IN ACTION

> This extensive overlapping of culture and development is now widely accepted and taken for granted.
>
> UNESCO *News* (1988)

In pursuit of the main inquiry of this study—to explore the NGO struggle against underdevelopment and poverty in Thailand with particular reference to the concepts of power and culture—this final chapter examines implicitly the parameters of an alternative Thai development model. This means returning to the subject of Buddhism in development, against the background of major trends in international development and another perspective on the relationship between culture and development.

Trends in World Development

The parameters of international development which have determined the players and the rules for the past forty years, are reflected in the principal phases of development thought. The first phase (1945-1960s), according to Keith Griffin, may be described as the "Brave New World;" the second phase (1960s-1980s) as the "Golden Age of Global Expansion;" and the third phase (1980s) may be considered a "Rude Awakening."

The optimistic, 'can-do' outlook of the early post-war era put its faith in economic growth, capital formation, planning, industrialization and foreign aid as the right way to go about the development business. The public sector was the mover and shaker in this scheme, relegating all other actors to the periphery of the development community.[1]

The "Golden Age" came to take growth for granted, along with significant shifts in emphasis: Now attention focused on issues of poverty and equity with the corresponding concern for the development of human capital, calling for expansion in education and manpower planning. Agriculture and the informal sector in Third

POWER AND CULTURE

World economies were also part of the ongoing reassessment. This then is the period (the 1960s and 1970s) when NGOs move beyond relief to long-term activities.

The "Rude Awakening" of the 1980s, the lost decade for many developing societies, shook fundamental assumptions about the role of the state and the entire international aid dispensing apparatus. A severely battered growth doctrine made room for sweeping economic reform, fostering, as it were, a Darwinian environment of the survival of the fittest.

Increasingly dependent on their own resources, new organizations at the grass-roots level set up diverse programs in health, nutrition, education, family planning and similar fields, prioritizing opportunities for women and human rights issues. These activities differed sharply from the mainstream, government-sponsored programs by stressing quality over quantity, popular participation, self-reliance, and the importance of tradition and indigenous culture.

What came as a "Rude Awakening" to the business-as-usual development community provided new opportunities for the rapidly expanding private, non-profit agencies, particularly for Third World NGOs. This is also the takeoff point for what the Club of Rome calls the "Barefoot Revolution," involving literally thousands of grassroots organizations in a spirit of self-reliance, capitalizing on local material and human resources in a new effort to stem the tide of poverty.[2]

Thai society, as shown, is very much in the forefront of this "Barefoot Revolution," contributing to the evolution of an alternative development paradigm, with its socio-cultural, Buddhist approach. In this context, the emphasis of the remaining discussion will be on the actual work of the development monks, documenting the potential of Thai Buddhism as a major factor in Thailand's future development.

The case materials drawn on for this analysis are representative of the diversity in approach and conditions that characterizes Buddhist development work. The intent is to examine both, the development activities carried out directly under the auspices of monks and abbots as well as the indirect influence of Buddhism in local development programs initiated and conducted by lay people.

Development to What End?

This question once again brings into focus the relation between culture, power and development. The search for a meaningful answer cuts through misinformation and confusion profusely generated by "Developmentalism"—the mainstream ideology of development with its nearly singular focus on materialism and quantification. With reference to Thailand, this question also leads back to the actual contributions of Buddhism to development.

A recent thought-provoking paper entitled "Development For What? Or, Which Culture Are We Serving?," written by Joseph van Arendonk, sets the stage for this discussion.

Briefly, Arendonk argues that development is principally about culture—"the whole range of thinking, doing, and being that is transmitted by means of symbols. As such, it includes reference to all the distinctive achievements—language, industry, art, science, law, moral codes, religion—that characterize a social group or society." Because there is a powerful trend towards one global culture, all societies are challenged by the dominant values of the industrialized Western world, specifically, rationalism, individualism, secularism and utilitarianism.

As is clearly evident from the historical record of the 20th century, these values generated a growing sense of alienation, conditions of anxiety and fear. In the past, man addressed his inherent vulnerability with transcendence and communality, which pertains to the ability "to break through the boundaries of one's ego" in the search for community. Referring to the examples set by the Gandhian experiment, Nyerere's communalism and the Sarvodaya Movement, the author continues:

In everyday life, transcendence-communality is constantly exhibited in volunteerism of all sorts and by good parents or good teachers providing a temporary moral environment for themselves and the children, away from the direct influence of a bewildering, cold society that is beyond their control.[3]

As for the main point, while these qualities—transcendence and communality—have always been at the heart of philosophy and religion (both East and West), they are excluded from modern life, science and technology and thus they are banned also from development. Qualitative, human development must be premised on these fundamental values.

Development that humanizes rather than dehumanizes this can no longer be left to wishful thinking. Many dilemmas and paradoxes in present-day development are there because of the mindless way we do development, that is, without regard for what is genuinely most important to us or to what gives life meaning.[4]

This mindless approach to development accounts precisely for the debilitating dualism that characterizes most underdeveloped societies. P.R.Dubhashi could well be describing the situation in Thailand when he writes:

...development connotes a qualitative and structural change. The structure of an underdeveloped country is characterized by a 'dual economy' and a 'dual society.' While there are manifestations of development in a few metropolitan centres in the shape of modern industrial and commercial establishments, the bulk of the country, the vast hinterland of rural areas, is underdeveloped in every sense of the term. Life there could be described, if not as nasty, brutish and short, certainly as short, poor and isolated. Thus metropolitan centres are only enclaves in vast areas of darkness and backwardness. As against this a developed country is characterized by the homogeneous development of social and economic life in all parts of the country.[5]

Dr. Likhit Dhiravegin, a Thammasat University political scientist, asks rhetorically: "What good will it do if material inventions and high-rise edifices are only to be had at the expense of a sense of community?"

> Already many of us may feel that we hardly know our neighbors, let alone a sense of good neighborhood. In a nutshell, is a society marked by material prosperity amidst cultural and humanistic poverty the ideal target for planners?[6]

Accepting, for the moment, the premises of Arendonk's argument, the answer to this "common dilemma in development" cannot be found in money and material things because they only compound the problem; we must of necessity incorporate the values of transcendence and communality in the new effort of rethinking and redoing development.

With these values as part of the agenda for an alternative development paradigm, a number of things begin to happen; for instance, the donor/recipient relationship will take on new dimensions. So-called poor nations, whose people have demonstrated a remarkable ability to survive under the most abysmal physical circumstances, base their concept of success on a wealth in tradition, culture, and religious beliefs. This non-material wealth qualifies them as donors in their own right.

Similarly, poverty, the family, freedom, work, and related concepts, assume new meaning once placed in the context of societies not yet destroyed by "development." Thus, one can appreciate why the messages of grassroots organizations, e.g., in the case of local Thai NGOs, strike a responsive cord. In fact, the growing awareness that development has not only failed but threatens to strike at the very sources of strength in Third World countries is part of the dynamic that drives the "Barefoot Revolution."

> Now, with the governments having shown their weaknesses in development efforts, the civil society through the NGOs are acquiring space. What guarantee is there that they will do better when doing better, in my view, would necessitate some good grasp of the problems and dilemmas mentioned above? Are NGOs attuned to these problems? NGOs are close to the grass roots, but so were the church and the state in the early stages of development. Will bureaucratization pose a threat as it did to the church and the state?[7]

According to Arendonk we are at the crossroads, left with two choices: "development for increased anxiety and vulnerability with its culture of the ugly mixed with the beautiful; and, the other, development toward man's dream of brotherly love with all its promise of beauty."[8]

Buddhist Power in Development

The questions raised by Arendonk represent the challenge faced by NGOs everywhere: will they be able to avoid the pitfalls of materialism, bureaucracy and power? The answer, to be sure, will be shaped by "the dominant power correlations" at home and abroad. But, the answer will also lie in part with culture and religion, the trumpcards of Buddhist power.

For these reasons, it is absolutely essential to reexamine Buddhism in development—examining actual case studies of how Buddhism and development have come together to work together in villages all over Thailand. The first two case studies are based on data collected during field trips of mine in Northern Thailand to Wat Bupparam (Abbot Phrakru Mongkolsilawong) and to the Foundation for Education and Development of Rural Areas at Wat Pa Daraphirom (Abbot Thepkhawi).

The other case studies are based on the field work of Dr. Seri Phongphit and Khun Surachet Vetchapitak. They focus on several villages where monks and lay leaders are applying Buddhist principles to day-to-day development tasks.

Wat Bupparam

Wat Bupparam is located in the Center of Chiangmai, Thailand's principal northern city. Despite its urban setting, the temple's development work, directed by the amiable abbot, Phrakru Mongkolsilawong, is almost entirely rural in its orientation.[9]

This *wat*, like many others throughout the country, has been the recipient of extensive funds from The Asia Foundation as part of its overall program in support of Buddhist educational and specifically development-oriented activities. In this case, support from the Foundation was applied towards the start-up costs of village schools. Previously the Abbot benefited directly from the assistance provided by the Foundation to the Buddhist Universities in Bangkok, where he was trained.

I visited Wat Bupparam to learn more about the Abbot's approach to development and to observe various programs in action.

Experienced in government-sponsored Sangha development programs, Phrakru Mongkolsilawong began his work in the Chiangmai area more than ten years ago. Since that time, he estimates some 75 temples in the Northern region of Thailand have started their own development programs.

The abbot's pragmatic approach to development not only compels him to be involved in program administration, but also to accept assistance from practically any available source, public or private. Since some of the original tasks of the monks, particularly education, have been assumed by the state, he feels it is incumbent on the Sangha to "keep up with the times" without jeopardizing indigenous values and wisdom. He sees educating monks in the art of village communication, rather than having them just stay at the *wat*, as one of his major responsibilities. In his view, it in no way contravenes against religious teachings for monks to help villagers to improve the quality of their lives. To underscore this point, he presented pictures of himself and other monks standing next to villagers working in the fields.

Although the abbot has no theoretical objections to cooperating with civil servants and government agencies, he did mention "too much bureaucracy" as a clear and definite problem in this context. In his experience, government offices tend to be very slow. None of the projects he initiated have formal government connections.

There is a definite Buddhist model of development in the abbot's view. This model derives its relevance, as well as its strength and gentle tenacity, from the religious wisdom that guides monks in their lives. As indicated above, active engagement by Buddhist monks in development affairs is rapidly spreading. More and more monks in virftually every region of the country are waking up and responding to this need.

During the day-long visit to main development projects, originally set up by the abbot, I recorded the following observations:

"Our first stop [Khun Solot Sirisai, my research assistant accompanied me] was at a typical village school with two young teachers and some 40 children, most of whom were sleeping as we arrived. The children appeared to be healthy and well cared for. Having interrupted their nap, they quickly sprang into action, gathering around the visiting "farangs" [Thai expression for foreigners]. The abbot, smiling all the while, talked with the young women in a relaxed mood. We left the school grounds after this brief visit to the cheers and good-bys of the children and the teachers, with the impression of having visited a modest, but well-run country school."

Additional information provided by the abbot indicated that this and similar schools in other districts were started with seed capital, ranging from 2000–5000 Baht ($80–200) per school, provided by The Asia Foundation and funds raised by the communities themselves. Furthermore, The Asia Foundation funds were treated as loans to be repaid."

The next stop, not far from the school, was a small house along the roadside, where two young women were weaving. The abbot explained that weaving was promoted by the Wat as part of a sizable cottage industry program. Later on in the day, we witnessed this activity on a larger scale, where more than 20 women worked on looms in a spacious building, which served also as storage area and store for the traditional silk and cotton materials produced by the women. The abbot helped set up the marketing system, which includes a roadside store for handicrafts produced by the villagers. The income generated from the sale of the cloth partially supports the women and their families."

Further on, the abbot asked the driver to turn off the main road and to take us to a piece of property, approximately 30 rai, that had been purchased by the Wat with funds once

174

again made available by The Asia Foundation to be used as common land for agricultural purposes. On the initiative of a nearby village, this land was placed under the care of several landless families who were considered trustworthy. Now, several years later, this sizable plot had been turned into a productive orchard (mainly mango and banana trees), and areas used for the cultivation of tobacco, chilies, eggplant, etc. The abbot considers this particular project a demonstration site."

We also visited a small community where several Thai women were busily sewing hilltribe clothing, items which are frequently found in tourist shops. Again, we were told that this is another part of the cottage industry program."

The remainder of the day involved a stopover at a village cooperative store and an unplanned but revealing rest stop. At the coopstore we were treated to an all-purpose herbal medicine. We learned that, despite some problems created by a few dissatisfied villagers (mainly in connection with a conflict of interest involving middlemen), the store was financially sound and on the whole successful. To be sure, the enterprise was of the most modest kind. Items on the shelves were limited to basic household necessities. But, more significantly, the store, run by a family, gave the impression of a friendly place where people came to visit and chat. For example, as we arrived, various villagers gathered around to welcome the abbot and his guests. Water was served and an animated conversation ensued. It was obvious that the abbot was a most welcome visitor here."

Before returning to Chiangmai we stopped at a popular open-air restaurant where the abbot was received with open arms. This establishment, connected with a nursery, was the home of a man now dead, who had been widely recognized for his exemplary agricultural station."

As we enjoyed a large fresh salad, the abbot engaged in a lively conversation, first with the man's wife, and then with the assistant sheriff of the district who happened to be present. As it turned out, this was very much a political gathering. The sheriff in effect asked for the abbot's assistance in taking care of some problems in a village. In return he offered to lend his support to one of the new projects planned by the abbot."

This gathering was particularly interesting because it showed the interaction and close cooperation between a monk and a representative of the state. Working together informally on a personal basis, they brought their respective power to bear on each other's needs."

Observing the abbot in this situation was akin to witnessing a highly skilled politician getting his way. Of course, the abbot's source of power did not derive from secular authority, but was based on his personal charisma and his religious status."

Finally, another anecdotal occurrence is indicative of the abbot's methods in generating support for his development activities. In the course of the initial interview at the abbot's quarters in the temple grounds, a teacher from a vocational school in Chiangmai came to offer food to the monks. In the ensuing brief conversation, the abbot asked her to consider volunteering some of her time to teach villagers how to sew. Presumably she accepted his suggestion."[10]

Wat Pa Daraphirom: The Foundation for Education and Development of Rural Areas

One of the differences between Wat Pa Daraphirom and the development activities of Wat Bupparam lies in the more restricted role preferred by the abbot, Phra Thepkhawi. His involvement in development work was limited to program planning, initiation and administration, as opposed to direct operational activities. In fact, the existence of a separate Foundation underscores this point.[11]

Wat Pa Daraphirom is also located in the city of Chiangmai. Its principal development activities are concentrated in seven surrounding villages. In addition, the temple grounds provide facilities for an extensive vocational program. Most of the Foundation's training activities promote weaving, pottery, sewing and related traditional crafts.

In the villages the Foundation supports a diverse range of projects, including revolving funds, credit unions, pre-school programs, buffalo and rice banks, leadership training, libraries, health activities, tree planting, irrigation systems, cooperative stores, etc. There are also special projects, such as capital investment (buying agricultural equipment and vehicles), and specialized, advanced courses in engineering, development and religion and tradition.

> "On our arrival at the wat, we were welcomed by the abbot, who accompanied us on a tour of the temple's vocational training facilities, following a brief discussion in his office.
>
> The abbot made clear that, in principle, monks should contribute to development by concentrating on religious affairs, delegating secular matters to the care of lay advisors. We spent the remainder of our visit in the company of Khun Achareechai Rujavichai, Field Coordinator for the Foundation, who patiently answered our questions and volunteered his own views regarding the work of the Foundation."
>
> Trained as an agricultural specialist at Kasetsart University, Khun Achareechai worked for 12 years on integrated rural development projects in Northern Thailand, funded by the Friedrich Naumann Stiftung (FNS). He assumed his present position in 1984."
>
> Khun Achareechai supervises a staff of 11, including 6 field representatives (4 trained by the Thai Volunteer Service—TVS). The Friedrich Naumann Stiftung funds the salaries of the staff, most of whom are permanently stationed in the villages."[12]

Although the Foundation is a secular institution, administered by lay people, our discussion with Khun Achareechai reflected the pervasive Buddhist spirit that guides the work of the staff. We were referred to a concise four-page document on the "Principles and Administration" of the Foundation, which states under the heading "Way of Thinking and Inspiration for Its Formation":

> The Foundation for Education and Development of Rural Areas was founded through the faith and dedication of one group of Buddhists, with Phra Thepkhawee as the Committee

176

Chairman. They established the Foundation to support work in rural development because they realized that most villagers lacked the opportunity for education. This led to a lack of knowledge and leadership. Villagers could not adjust their work to progressive changes. This resulted in their very poor standard of living.

Due to these problems, the group sought approval to establish [the Foundation]. The main aim is to develop people in poor rural areas by giving them the abilities to help themselves and others. The Foundation emphasizes spiritual development combined with economic development, which includes the four basic necessities for maintaining life.

The document continues by listing four general objectives: to encourage agriculture, education, religion and to develop local areas. Elaborating on each objective, one reads, for example, in connection with the promotion of agriculture:

It emphasizes developing people in their occupation. It encourages cooperation in solving one's own problems and those of the local area, with Foundation program to help where needed. [*sic*]

With reference to the promotion of religion:

The first and second principles [agriculture and education] are solutions for material problems. The third principle [religion] is a solution for the spiritual problem. The Foundation emphasizes the Buddha's teachings which bring about behavior which will develop one's occupation, solve the problems of poverty and society. These teachings include:
- to increase diligence
- to strive towards frugality
- to practice doing good
- to encourage local unity.

These can be summarized as 'diligence, frugality, self-sacrifice and unity.'

The commentary regarding the development of local areas [the fourth principle objective] is also significant:

The word 'local' refers to the topography of the land, the people, and the good traditions. Development following the first three principles works towards progress in local development.

Finally, by way of commenting on what the Foundation hopes to accomplish in the long run, the following list of anticipated results is provided:

1. Members will gain knowledge about their occupation and will better know how to help themselves.
2. Members will receive training in the methods of credit unions in order to have funds for future work.

3. Members will work together to help each other.
4. Members will better understand the value of time and life.
5. Members will understand religious values.[13]

Given the wide scope of the Foundation's programs, what are its most challenging problems? Responding to this question, Khun Achareechai spoke of the lack of control over the market, the attempt to return agricultural practices gradually to traditional technologies and finally, occasional "misunderstandings" between field workers and villagers.

Elaborating on these points, he expressed his personal development philosophy, emphasizing the need for village self-sufficiency, more emphasis on tradition by way of undoing some of the damage done by previous modernization programs (although, he underscored, that he is not opposed to modernization per se), and for villagers to take charge of their own development affairs through direct participation.

The example set by the Foundation's programs, its approach to development and the apparent receptivity of the villagers (judging from the feedback provided by other staff members and villagers enrolled in the vocational training programs at the Wat) suggests that the indirect approach of Abbot Phra Thepkhawee is a viable alternative to active involvement by monks in day-to-day development work. Extensive follow-up research, comparing the situation at the village level, would be required to allow a more conclusive assessment."[14]

Summing up, the development activities of Wat Bupparam and Wat Daraphirom offer a sampling of the range of Buddhist development programs and approaches found in Northern Thailand. It is apparent that these activities, as far as their operational facets are concerned, are not significantly different from other NGO projects. They cover essentially the same development areas, ranging from education and training, to nutrition and financial matters. All of the programs rely to various degrees on lay workers and they share essentially the same long-term goals and objectives.

Thus, aside from different emphases, the main distinction between Buddhist and NGO development programs is the spiritual dimension. Although the religious authority brought to bear by monks in the development context should not be taken for granted (too many Buddhist projects, like their secular counterparts have failed), it does constitute a major potential source of power, which can only be approximated in secular development programs through close association with the Buddhist development movement.

The Village of Suan Poh

Phra Kru Visit Nandakan is an old monk, the abbot of Suan Poh temple. In his early 70s, the abbot spends most of his time in the temple, giving advice to individuals and groups, and travels to other village temples in the district to preach.

Dr. Seri Phongphit describes how this monk singlehandly changed the life of entire communities in Thailand's Northeast:

He was ordained a monk 50 years ago. The people in Roi-et and the nearby provinces know him as the Inventor Monk of Suan Poh. Twenty five years ago he invented a truck using a second-hand pump, motor spare parts and wood. Up to now he has produced over 10 trucks of this kind, some motorcycles and other things with a motor. He is best known as a development monk, who has played a significant role in Suan Poh community development during the past 30 years.

The village, Suan Poh, Seri explains, consists of about 240 families or 1000 people and is located in Roi-et province, one of Thailand's most depressed areas. In 1986, after 30 years of development activity under the guidance of the amazing abbot, Suan Poh was given an award as the best development village in Roi-et province.

This accomplishment was the result of many small projects and activities, all of which contributed in some way to improve the quality of life for the people. The projects initiated over the past thirty years include various group activities (e.g. young agriculturist and housewives groups), savings institutions (rice bank and Sacca Group), plus cooperatives and a health care center.

In the abbot's own words:

I have initiated all these projects in our village, but I let the villagers administer themselves through committees. I intervene only when there are problems they cannot solve themselves. I still propose new ideas and help them learn to be democratic but each project committee will handle everything. The villagers come to the temple only for general assembly. I want them to learn to do things themselves first. The final decisions are taken in the general assembly. I ask the villagers to prepare for the assembly discussing everything in detail among themselves first.

I often have to emphasize the point that they should decide to do things for the benefit of the majority. No decision should be made because they are afraid of somebody or because they respect somebody when they think that decision is unreasonable. I told them that they should not do things like politicians or members of parliament. This is the learning process of democracy....They should have critical minds.

Development has to be human first. I do not think that to help the villagers increase their income is automatically development. If that income does not contribute to all other aspects, it may be harmful. When I initiated the rice bank in our village, I thought of using it to help the villagers get rid of their vices. (Some villagers are fond of drinking and gambling and would sell their rice for money for bad purposes.) At the same time we had rice also for poor people. When we got the money from the province to build a barn and make a rice bank proper, the authorities doubted whether we would succeed, because of negative experiences in many other places. I assured them that if the barn was set up in the temple grounds, it would go all right as we monks would help. If the rice bank is set up only for its own purpose, it will not go far. It has to be linked with all the other activities. It has to be based on religion. Without a religious foundation it will not work as the villagers will quarrel sooner or later and will come to a dead end.

There is a small piece of public land of about 2 hectares in our village, where, every year the villagers work together growing rice. The yield is used for public purposes within the community—some years for the school, some years for the centre or for the temple. During the past few years, those who worked in this rice field were given also a part as most of them are poor and have no land. Besides this common rice-growing project, the villagers help one another also during ordinary rice growing season and on other particular occasions as in the past. We now try to renew that spirit.

My development ideal is Buddhist. I teach the people to practice Dhamma while working. Both have to go together. I teach also while working…

Development is possible only if we start to do things. It is not a theory. It is like Buddhism. You don't know what Buddhism is as long as you learn it only through books. You have to practice it. My six principles for development are: diligence, improvement, change, modification, self-reliance and solidarity.

I started my work in this community with the young because I thought that it was the best way to gather people together. The young did not have much to do and they liked being together. We have to pay a great deal of attention to young people, to think of the future and make a long term plan. I teach Dhamma at the school in our village every day and every summer about 50 young people are ordained novices, of whom some 5 or 6 remain longer. During Buddhist lent there are about 20 monks living in our temple. These are things that may be very normal and traditional. Yet, I think it is precisely here that we prepare people for our community in the future. We need human development first.

And commenting on the present situation in the village:

I would say it has improved a lot although the land is still dry and poor. Up to now we have succeeded in solving many problems together. The people have learned to spend their money carefully, to save and to help one another. Most of them have stopped drinking and gambling. There is no drinking and gambling during public festivities in the village, or in the temple. No cinema, no theater or entertainment in our temple grounds. I have planted trees here. There is no more room for such activities. I leave some space only for parking.

I had and still have many things in my mind that I would like to do. I took things easy and sometimes they came about unexpectedly. I don't know how I managed to do them, although I am sure that we can manage a lot if we are committed to Dhamma. I have been applying Buddha's principles in all my social and development activities. They involve commitment and sacrifice. I always started to do things first. I sometimes stayed working all day long in the sun until the villagers saw and understood I was doing that for them. I teach them by example first.[15]

The abbot of Suan Poh personifies development. Teaching by example, as he says, for the past thirty years he has been "doing" development through the direct and hands-on application of Buddhist principles to the basic needs of the people in his care.

From the standpoint of power and culture in the struggle against poverty, Phra Kru Visit Nandakan is indeed a most influential person, deriving his strength from the realm of religion and traditional values. Relying on a very personal, direct approach and the power of persuasion, based on personal examples, the abbot is Buddhist power in action.

Wat Samakki (Temple of Unity)

Monks have responsibility of teaching Lord Buddha's Dhamma, yet they should also know something about making cement tanks or about agriculture so as to act favorably and fruitfully for villagers.

These are the words of Phra Nan Suttasilo, the Abbot of Wat Samakki. His story is told by Khun Surachet Vetchapitak, Director of RUDOC, who has visited development monks and their communities throughout Thailand to learn more about Buddhist development.

Summarizing the main points about development under the guidance of the Abbot of the Temple of Unity, the first telling observation is that he was born in the village. As mentioned, this fact is not unusual, but it is a significant factor in explaining the extraordinary strong ties between the monk and his village.

Phra Nan Suttasilo has been working with his own hands on behalf of the villagers ever since he became Abbot of Wat Samakki in 1959. In those days, he recounts, he along with other monks and novices began building a road with hoes and spades, until they were later joined by some villagers. Once the road was half completed he decided to approach the provincial administration for assistance, which was promptly granted through the Accelerated Rural Development (ARD) Department.

The practice to seek out assistance from other organizations is one of the hallmarks of the abbot's approach to development. On another occasion he personally went to see the provincial Irrigation Department when the canals dried up. Again he succeeded in getting the government's cooperation and remedial action was taken. In 1978 he contacted the regional office of the Girls Guide Association of Thailand, asking their assistance in securing cheaper fertilizer for the villagers. Once again, he was successful.

POWER AND CULTURE

His own projects include a rice and a fertilizer bank, a co-operative shop, a mushroom growing hut and extensive religious programs presented at the village temple. His primary concern is the spiritual dimension of development. It is for this reason that he has been working very hard to turn the temple once again into "a refuge for villagers' life."

His efforts are paying off also because of his high regard for tradition. For example, the abbot established, "Nakrachapmit," a friendship-enriching group in which villagers assist each other in the rice fields, a tradition which had fallen into disregard.[16]

Wat Takorai and Wat Yokkrabat

Drawing on the experience of two other temples and their abbots, Khun Surachet highlights several features of their development programs. In the case of Wat Takorai, which is situated in the sub-district of Ban Hua near Buriram, Abbot Boon Mo Piyathammo attracted considerable attention from the authorities as well as from some of his more conservative villagers who saw some of his development ideas as communist inspired. Generally these were projects based on communal activities, including agricultural production.

> In every new thing, we monks are likely to risk misunderstanding, contempt and carping. But we feel happy, because we are sincere. They can say anything they want to. Time will prove it. Some even said 'I was a communist and a mob mobilizer. Sometimes I would like to say that it was good to be a communist if they could help us.'[17]

Another feature of the abbot's approach is to rely on groups as instruments of development: "Setting up a group is a way to check their behavior. Everybody will care more for others and learn from one another."

Further explaining his personal development philosophy, he notes:

> Development is the responsibility of monks. Is development equal to improvement? We should improve everything bad….If I commit some moral offense, it's only for the sake of people around me. What about those who sit in two or three storied buildings with air conditioners and TV sets, their offense must be more serious than ours? If we do good, we should not pay attention to what people say about us. We should always be sincere in our heart.[18]

Finally, he cites the example of Wat Yokkrabat and its Abbot Phrakru Sakorn Sangvorakit, who is also a firm believer in direct action and personal involvement by monks. After introducing his villagers to the familiar rice banks and related activities, the abbot remains concerned that there are not enough development monks:

It's good that people realize that monks are important. If not, monks will become like ordinary standing statues or shrines for which people will come and offer some food and candles when they want to make merit. We should make ourselves more useful to people and the community as much as we can.[19]

The Thod Pha Pa Ceremony

In an essay on Thai culture, Duangkamol Chansuriyawong explains: "Thod Pha Pa is an ancient Buddhist ceremony created by lay people to offer material support for the religious community."[20]

This old religious ceremony has been revived and adapted to Thailand's contemporary development needs. In essence, Pha Pa is a community-wide self-help method, inspired by the Buddhist principle of merit making. The Buddhist practice of "making merit" is tied to the law of Karma, expressing the belief that the fate of an individual in this and future lives is a function of one's good and bad deeds. To make merit, such as offering alms to monks, is an ancient and widely practiced tradition in Thailand.

With the adaptation of Pha Pa to contemporary development needs, the community seeks donations—food, medicine, clothing, etc.—which are presented during a lengthy ceremony to the monks, who in turn offer the donations to those for whom they are intended.

The significance of this approach goes beyond the self-help principle, which is its premise. Pha Pa establishes close links between the donors and the recipients, as the following case materials will illustrate. Furthermore, Pha Pa also has a strong spiritual dimension, which is its driving force. Finally, inherently a religious act, Pha Pa enhances the role of the monks and the image of the Sangha. In short, the revival of this traditional ceremony symbolizes the joining of hands of ordinary people and monks, serving each other in the name of Buddha and through the furtherance of development.

Ban Hua Seuh, following the account by Duangkamol, is a remote village in Chiangmai Province suffering from the all too familiar problems: lack of water, insufficient land, and thus not enough rice to eat for the whole year. Some 25 households are entirely without any farmland of their own. The root cause of these problems is a combination of population pressure and man-caused environmental destruction including encroachment on forests and the ensuant consequences.

The village used to be known as "the thief village" because some people resorted to theft in order to survive. An attempt to set up a cooperative store ended with a big loss. People were forced to borrow rice every year at interest rates of 100%. The village reached the point where a decision was made to take matters into their own hands by setting up first one and then four additional groups, consisting of ten households each. Based on the self-help principle, each group maintained a rice bank system allowing families to borrow rice, charging 50% interest.

POWER AND CULTURE

The system worked. After several rice-growing seasons and having extended this approach to fertilizer, the first group accumulated a savings account of 28,000 Baht ($1,220). The groups that followed were also successful. Buffalo banks, with the initial support of an outside NGO, were set up at a later point.

The biggest challenge arose with the organization of two additional groups composed of the villagers without land. By working the land of others, men could earn two buckets of rice per day or 50 Baht ($2), and women received only one and one half buckets or 30 Baht ($1.20), which was not enough to sustain their families.

After consulting with development workers, the decision was made to organize a Pha Pa Kao (rice) ceremony involving large numbers of people from several provinces and Bangkok. "Everyone collected rice or money from his friends or his relatives to give to the poor during the ceremony."

The day of the big event, people from all over gathered at Ban Hua Seuh for this festive occasion. The ceremony, which lasted most of the day, consisted of a village cultural celebration (traditional musical instruments were played), followed after lunch by the religious ceremony, where 130 buckets of rice were presented.

During the morning, several speakers reflected on the meaning and the significance of the event. They emphasized that:

> This act of helping others is from the old Thai culture that we have learned from our ancestors. Rice that is given is virtue rice. We must never forget this. This merit-making and charity make us all (both the giver and the receiver) to be very happy.[21]

It is too early to assess the long-term impact of this particular Pha Pa Kao. After all, the rice donated to the poor did not change the fact that they do not own land. However, as Duangkamol points out, the spirit and the new community bonds created by the event constitute a major accomplishment by themselves. Furthermore, Pha Pa may provide the basis for new initiatives based on the self-help principle.

The Medicine Man of Chachoengsao

This is the story of village headman *Phoo Yai* Vibul Khemchalerm of Ban Huay Hin in Chachoengsao Province, about 60 km east of Bangkok in Thailand's Central Region. The experience of this remarkable Thai farmer highlights the personal dimension of Buddhist development. It proves the viability of what may be termed a "do-it-yourself" approach to development based on Buddhist teachings.[22]

"As we turned off the road to Khun Vibul's house at the outskirts of the village, we were immediately surrounded by greenery—tall trees and plants seemingly everywhere. We had picked a good day to visit because the Vibul family and several villagers were preparing one of their herbal medicines, an oil-based preparation which is widely sought after in the region for its healing qualities when applied to skin infections."[23]

184

Drawing on previous interviews with Khun Vibul, his own writings, as well as my discussion with him, the following background information is essential to an understanding of the 'Vibul phenomenon.' Vibul in fact represents two success stories. His initial accomplishments came as a big-time entrepreneur, working as a middleman in agricultural commodities. He became rich by playing the system. Taking the government's advise, he invested in cassava, borrowing money and eventually buying land to start his own farm. Meanwhile Khun Vibul acquired a taste for the comfortable life.

> My life changed. I liked luxuries, eating in expensive restaurants, driving a nice car. My business did not continue that well for a long time. Since 1970 I became more and more in debt. I changed from cassava to cotton and made a good profit. In 1979 cotton went down. I started to organize farmers to bargain over the price of cotton and rice with the local and finally also with the central government.
>
> The farmer's group did not succeed in keeping united. It was the government's Bank of Agriculture and Cooperatives that ruined that unity.
>
> The struggle kept on going. We were always promised by the government that we would get better prices. No guarantee was materialized. It was always just a promise.
>
> I realized that there was no hope any more. We struggled in vain. We still had to eat expensive rice from mills.[24]

This was the turning point for Vibul. After a great deal of soul searching, he sold all of his land except for 1.5 hectares to pay off his debts and turned to traditional, integrated subsistence agriculture, leaving the market system behind. He said: "I used to depend on the (commercial) system, but now I can see the difference very clearly. In Buddhist terms, start now and then you will know the truth."[25] His exceedingly difficult decision to abandon a comfortable life style and to go "back to the roots," as it were, was more than opting for an alternative, simpler, and traditional Thai way of life. It was a reaffirmation of his Buddhist faith. Henceforth, Buddhist principles served as his guide.

> I do not reject modern culture. I buy clothes only when I really need them. This is the Buddhist way of thinking, namely, not to acquire things in order to upgrade one's status or in order to be praised by others, but just to prevent the cold. Since we cannot make cloth ourselves, we should use it modestly.
>
> The real problem is the 'Kilesa' (desire). It is not possible to satisfy all the desires we have. Development is not successful because it serves Kilesa. We think with development we can achieve perfection. It is an illusion. We can never achieve 'perfection' of life with what we call 'development.'
>
> We usually take development only by its economic aspects. We think that the main problem is that people have not enough to eat; therefore we have to help the people to

increase their income. The real point is not the fact that the people have not enough to eat, but that they have too many desires and do anything in order to earn money and to buy what they want.[26]

There are two important points to note in Khun Vibul's application of Buddhism, a personal element and the importance of thinking small.

As in previous cases involving individual monks, Vibul also believes in the power of setting personal examples, to be followed by others of their own free will. However, this is only possible after an internal conversion—a personal commitment to Buddhism—has taken place. Development, in this sense is a personal journey; development starts from the inside. The second point pertains to the issue of scale and follows from the importance assigned to individual action. According to Vibul:

I think we need not to think of too wide a scale. Think first of ourselves. I tried hard to ask myself whether I could live without running after Kilesa. It is more realistic to start in such a way then think, 'what can I do so that the whole village can also make this decision.' If I can prove that we can make it, the people will see by themselves and decide themselves. I do not think that we should think first of the whole village, the whole society. We need not put the whole world on our shoulders. The people have to see and believe it themselves.[27]

Is this not a contradiction? Doesn't Buddhism, as pointed out earlier, call for getting rid of "self"? Vibul responds:

If I say that the villagers should solve their own problems, I do not think that they should think only of themselves and be egoistic. They do know that their neighbors also suffer, but they should not wait till everybody moves together at the same time. They should start to do what they believe will solve their problems. They should learn from the past and make decisions themselves.[28]

This pragmatic motive—getting started rather than waiting carries democratic undertones. There is also the related element of freedom in Vibul's thoughts on development:

I found that once I changed may life to a small scale of production, I felt more free. I became myself.

I believe that once we are free, we will be more self-confident and have the courage to make decisions and to do many things that we could not do before. That is real self-reliance. This is the courage to believe that we can survive by being autonomous. We have to be self-reliant in order to live freely.[29]

186

Finally, several other key values reflect directly or indirectly the close ties between Vibul's road to development and Buddhism. First, morality or virtue is writ large in his thinking. For instance, referring to the villagers, he said: "They should realize that if they live with more virtue their lives will be better." Elaborating, with reference to the onslaught and corrosive effect of modernity:

It is almost impossible today to resist temptation to consume that the mass media offer in their commercials, but we still have a chance. I do not mean that we have to mobilize the people to resist at the national level. The bargaining power is small. We have to resist within ourselves. Good values are being destroyed. We must fight back within ourselves....Moral standard is for me a means in itself."[30]

Second, the family is assigned a central role in the development process: "We should think of our family as the most important institution which has to be first self-reliant."[31]

Third, Vibul incorporates a genuine love for the environment in his development ideals—living in harmony with nature, as taught by Bhikkhu Buddhadasa—the embodiment of Buddha's teaching. As the title "Medicine Man of Chachoengsao" implies, Khun Vibul is well known for his knowledge of herbs, medicinal plants and traditional healing techniques. His home and his garden, which contains more than four hundred medicinal plants, are living testimony to his faith in nature. "I think of the environment, of peace, of the perfection of my life which cannot be torn into pieces."[32]

Last, there is the importance of tradition and culture. Khun Vibul sees local culture as one of the underpinnings of self-reliance, as well as a method to further Buddhist development.

Relating how he helped to organize a traditional Thai New Year celebration (April 13), which included almost forgotten games, story telling and useful discussions on herbal medicines, among other activities, he confessed how perplexed he was by the popularity of this event. By word of mouth alone, people knew about the planned celebration. When the time came, there was hardly enough room to accommodate everybody.

During the celebration we did not only 'celebrate,' but we had a sort of 'training.' The villagers learned about things they face in their daily life. We had some officials who gave information about local administration and development plans...The highlight was the rite of pouring water on the hands of elders. They did not have such a ceremony since they came to this area some thirty years ago. They were all moved. Some elders could not hold their tears.

We found that the villagers still long for their culture and traditions. They have not forgotten them.[33]

POWER AND CULTURE

A subtle point, still on the subject of culture, is the difference in the concept of time. As *farang* visitors to Ban Huay Hin, one is made conscious of time in the traditional Thai way. People are not driven by clocks. Time is measured in human terms—visiting and chatting with neighbors and friends; people making themselves and other feel comfortable (*sanuk*). In this sense, the extended visit with Khun Vibul made time stand still for us.[34]

Alternative Development: Reflections on the Struggle against Poverty in Thailand

This interpretive analysis of the underlying causes of poverty and underdevelopment and the responses by public, private and non-profit development agencies—particularly the indigenous NGOs (including the Buddhist development movement) in Thailand—point to a meaningful alternative to the mainstream development approaches that have been applied the world over for the past forty years. The question, however, remains, is there a realistic alternative for the Thai people and by implication, for other Third World societies?

Today Thailand progresses along two increasingly diverging paths, thus perpetuating existing divisions between the urban rich and the rural poor, between the privileged few and the exploited majority. This fork in the road of Thai history (for that matter in the history of most underprivileged societies) was not caused, but compounded by "development" when the government accepted in principle the Western concept of development, with the accent on materialism and the industrialization of society.

Development came to be synonymous with progress and modernization. Science, technology, technocracy, bureaucracy, experts, and specialization are among the main criteria for determining the status of a society. In the name of development, the state steadily expanded, centralized and concentrated its control over society. As a result, development became an instrument of state power, a matter of public policy.

Supported by and in close cooperation with foreign elites and their international centers of power, the myth of development became reality. It is perpetuated principally by rhetoric dealing with the needs of the people, especially the plight of the poor.

What is in fact happening to the poor? In Thailand the poor constitute nearly two thirds of the population of 53 million. How are their needs determined? Have they themselves been asked what should be done to address their own problems? Who decides which particular development projects are "good for the people" in the villages? Are villagers given choices? What about traditional values, culture and religious norms—are they taken into account? Who defends the true interests of the people?

The government's record is an open book. It shows what is wrong with "development." True development is not exploitation (economically, socially, culturally, or otherwise); it is not modernization without respect for tradition and culture; it is not destruction of the environment; nor is it the loss of autonomy, independence or self-respect.

To say this is still akin to heresy and the myth of development imposed from above lives on as orthodoxy. However, chinks are showing in the armor of orthodoxy.

> The paralysis of development has modified the perception of the myth and weakened the pressures of developers over our settings, thus allowing us to start remedying the damage done by them to our land and culture. We are now able to smile at the modernizers, who want to 'develop' our ways out of existence and are worried by the reduced budgets. We are now counting our blessings.[35]

The pressure exerted from below by individuals, groups and entire communities resorting to self-help measures, taking charge of their own affairs, has moved beyond the marginal stage, the fringe phenomenon. Governments are now facing the challenge of the "Barefoot Revolution" with its alternative platform for development.

Outlines of an Alternative Model

Despite the cacophony of dissenting voices from below, the multitude of approaches, concepts, strategies and types of organizations, there are, as we have seen, common assumptions, shared principles, objectives and organizational features which characterize the grass-roots movements, not only in Thailand but all over the developing world.

On the premise that development deals in facts and values (reflecting its material and spiritual dimensions) and to the extent that it allows for both modernity and tradition, development becomes of necessity a matter of reversals—or in the words of Robert Chambers, "putting the last first." It follows, therefore, that development cannot be imposed. Individuals, groups or societies cannot be developed by some one else or from the outside. Development is the process of unfolding from the inside out.

Ends do not justify means. The methods are part and parcel of the goal. Thus community participation in decision-making, regardless of the outcome, is valuable in itself. Similarly, autonomy, self-respect, self-reliance, cultural integrity, and independence reflect both the means and the goals of development.

Reversing requires reordering and rethinking of the old ways and priorities, focusing especially on:

POWER AND CULTURE

- Balance: The avoidance of extremes (rich/poor, urban/rural);
- Social justice: securing the rights of the poor, women, children and minorities;
- Equity: assuring the basic needs of all people;
- Cultural autonomy: promoting cultural independence and diversity;
- Environment: re-learning how to live in harmony with nature.

In practice, to seek these reversals means to generate new sources of power:

- The power of culture: Capitalizing on the strength and influence that flows from shared values and tradition.
- The power of religion: Turning spiritual values into benchmarks of development.
- The power of scale: Lending organizational structure and support to the poor (families, groups, organizations).
- The power of example: Allowing successful development activities to be replicated.

On the whole, this is clearly not an agenda that government officials, international development experts and hard-nosed economists and business people would subscribe to. After all, where are the indices, the statistics, the hard facts, the "bottom line" (profit) in culture or religion?

Still, the abbot in Chiangmai, the participants (farmers and guest from the city alike) in the Pha Pa Kao ceremony, the "Medicine Man from Chachoengsao," the rural development workers, the hundreds of small rural NGOs and their supporters—all the people who are part of Thailand's "Barefoot Revolution"—know this power and how it works for them.

As we have seen, sometimes NGOs have succeeded where governments failed. However, this does not suggest that NGOs have "cornered the market." Rather, the situation requires a basic reassessment of the existing division of labor. While it is obviously unrealistic to assume that the conventional system—the vast, interest-riddled international aid establishment—will simply fade into the background and disappear, a new political strategy, dealing in the coin of interests, can succeed.

Such a political approach has not only the advantage of talking to the government in its own language, but it also provides NGOs with bargaining power based on their grassroots support. As we have seen, the tables are turning on the government. In order for their projects to be acceptable in the future, more and more government officials consult with grass-roots organizations (the development monks, individual leaders such as Vibul Khemchalerm and NGOs).

Consequently, the changes in the respective roles of the main actors—government agencies, international organizations, business and multinational corporations, academic experts, international NGOs and the grass-roots or peoples' organizations which, for all practical purposes, are already taking place, must be generally acknowledged, accepted and promoted.

Starting from the bottom, grassroots organizations, being the peoples' voice, should be allowed to strengthen their infrastructure (qualitative staff support) in order to improve their role as practitioners of development.

Urban-based, rural development NGOs, the second tier of the indigenous NGO community, perform largely in a support and liaison capacity. They are the linkages at the regional, national and increasingly at the international level as well. Their professionalism and accomplishments to-date need to be legitimized.

International NGOs and private foreign donor agencies perform in a dual capacity as intermediary aid and development agencies (working increasingly through indigenous counterpart organizations) and as strategic or catalytic organizations. As catalysts, their primary tasks include consulting, coordinating and making connections between different actors.

Finally, governments and international aid organizations, including the major international lending agencies, are warming up to the partnership principle, gradually accepting the fact that the NGO community does have a comparative advantage. This pattern of increasing cooperation between the public sector and the non-governmental agencies at the various levels is evidently one of the consequences brought about by the "Barefoot Revolution."

The struggle against poverty in Thailand will continue to fail if the conventional approaches and the old mindsets are allowed to perpetuate themselves in the interest of the few. On the other hand, given enough political room to maneuver, Thailand does have viable alternatives. As a Buddhist society with deep cultural roots and endowed with the unifying influence of the monarchy, Thailand has a wealth of vitally important resources upon which to draw.

Thus, development that does not destroy the soul of the Thai people in the name of modernization, relies on its own resources. Thailand's preferred future lies in the hands of its people—their religion, their culture and their traditions.

APPENDIX

NGOs Included in the Study:

Adventist Development and Relief Agency (ADRA)
Asian Cultural Forum on Development (ADFOD)
Asian Regional Exchange for New Alternatives (ARENA)
CARE/Thailand
C.C.F. Foundation in Thailand
Center for Culture and Development/Khon Kaen (CCD)
Duang Prateep Foundation
Friedrich-Naumann-Foundation/Thailand
Human Development Center (HDC)
REDD BARNA/Thailand
Research and Development Institute/Khon Kaen (RDI)
Rural Development Documentation Center (RUDOC)
Thai Institute for Rural Development (THIRD)
Thai Volunteer Service (TVS)
The Asia Foundation/Thailand
The Foundation for Education and Development of Rural Areas
Village Institution Promotion (VIP)
World Concern

NOTES

Chapter 1

[1] Sivard 1985:40
[2] Suchart 1987:6
[3] BP 5/6/88
[4] Girling 1981:153
[5] Ibid.: 164
[6] BP 10/29/87
[7] Cf. Chapter 4
[8] Chambers 1983:37
[9] Ibid.:38
[10] Ibid.
[11] Ibid.:43
[12] Jacobs 1971:3-12
[13] Cf. Chapter IV
[14] Hirsch 1986:23
[15] BP 4/5/88:3
[16] BP 11/18/87
[17] Ibid.
[18] Suchart 1987:7
[19] National Statistical Office 1987:192
[20] BP 11/18/87 : 17
[21] BP 11/6/87:4
[22] Hirsch 1986:25
[23] BP 10/29/87
[24] Cf. Chapter IV
[25] BP 10/26/87
[26] Chambers 1983:146-47

Chapter 2

[1] Chambers 1983:9
[2] Ibid.:16
[3] Ibid.:18
[4] Ibid.
[5] Ibid.:19
[6] Ibid.:21

[7] Ibid.:22
[8] Ibid.:22 ff.
[9] Ibid.:75
[10] Ibid.:98
[11] Ibid.: 185
[12] BP 1/21/88
[13] CDD:1-2
[14] CDD:5
[15] Jon n.d.-a:19
[16] Ibid.
[17] Seri 1983:3
[18] White 1987:33
[19] Surachet 1982:5-6
[20] Ibid.
[21] Komson 1983:5
[22] Somsakdi 1982:127
[23] Ibid:123-24
[24] See Morell, Chapter 3, "Traditional Political Institutions and Modern Thai Politics: Bureaucracy, Military and Monarch," pp. 41-73, and also a discussion in Keyes, Thailand: Buddhist Kingdom as Modern Nation States, pp. 144-169.
[25] BP 10/13/87
[26] BP 7/5/87:1
[27] Ibid.
[28] Ibid.
[29] Ibid.
[30] BP 1987:7
[31] Ibid.:17
[32] BP 4/21/87
[33] Ibid.
[34] Ibid.
[35] BP 5/23/87
[36] BP 3/25/87
[37] BP 10/9/87

[38] Ibid.
[39] BP 10/3/87
[40] Ibid.
[41] BP 11/11/87:32
[42] Ibid.
[43] Ibid.
[44] Ibid.
[45] BP 12/2/87
[46] BP 11/11/87
[47] Ibid.
[48] BP 6/17/87
[49] Ibid.
[50] Ibid.
[51] BP 12/2/87
[52] BP 12/6/87
[53] Ibid.
[54] Heim, 1986:49-50.
[55] Ibid.
[56] Ibid.:51-52
[57] BP 4/3/87
[58] Surendra 1987:189 ff.
[59] Cf. Schneider 1988
[60] Saneh :7.
[61] BP 12/15/87
[62] Ibid.
[63] Morell, 16
[64] ibid., 25
[65] ibid., 4

Chapter 3

[1] Chambers 1983:150
[2] BP 11/24/87
[3] BP 11/1/87:14
[4] Ibid.
[5] Ibid.
[6] Chambers 1983:140
[7] Chambers 1983:149
[8] USAID Program Evaluation Paper, "Turning Private Organizations into Development Agencies: Questions for Evaluation" plus "What Ever Happened to Poverty Alleviation?"
[9] Tendler 1982:3
[10] Tendler 1982:3
[11] Ibid.:iv
[12] Ibid.:4
[13] Cf. Sulak 1987-c
[14] Korten 1986:6-8
[15] Tendler 1982:5
[16] RB 1987:6-9
[17] CCF :24
[18] Ibid.:13
[19] Jewson 1984:1
[20] Tendler 1982:80
[21] Bolling 1982:158-59
[22] Tendler 1982:5
[23] The Asia Foundation 1986:71
[24] Ibid.
[25] Ibid.:72
[26] Saneh R. 10/20/86
[27] Ibid.
[28] Cf. Chapters Five and Seven
[29] Tendler 1982:6
[30] Gorman 1984:59
[31] Bolling 1982:190
[32] Ibid.:190
[33] Somsakdi 1981:68
[34] Heim 1986:8
[35] Vanpen 1986:1
[36] Ibid.:2, xv
[37] Ibid.:xvi
[38] Heim 1986:104-05
[39] Scale 1985:4
[40] Ibid.:6-8
[41] Ibid:18
[42] Gorman 1984:57
[43] Bolling 1982:190
[44] Tendler 1982:101
[45] Maier 9/30/86

[46] Tendler 1982:102
[47] Cf.Ibid.:vi.
[48] Ibid.:94-95
[49] Cf. Korten
[50] Tendler 1982:14
[51] Ibid.:56
[52] Ibid.:57
[53] Ibid.:60-61
[54] Korten 1987:1-21

Chapter 4

[1] Chambers 1983:212
[2] Jacobs 1971:28-29
[3] Ibid.:4
[4] Ibid.:47-48
[5] Ibid.:32
[6] Ibid.:55-56
[7] Ibid.:58-59
[8] Ibid.:59
[9] Ibid.:65-66
[10] Heim n.d.:6-7
[11] Cf. the previously cited statements by Bangkok Governor Chamlong Srimuang.
[12] Ibid.:16
[13] Jacobs 1971:15
[14] Ibid.:31
[15] BP 12/22/87
[16] Jacobs 1971:9
[17] Ibid.:10
[18] TVS 1987:13-29
[19] TVS n.d.:12
[20] TVS 1987
[21] Seri 1982:2
[22] Cf. Klausner 1981
[23] Gohlert 1986-a
[24] Cf. Anan 1986
[25] Seri 1982:2
[26] Cf. Seri 1988-b
[27] Anan 1986:1

[28] Ibid.:16-17
[29] Akin/Yupin 1984:1
[30] Ibid.:21-22
[31] Akin/Yupin 1984:13
[32] Ibid.:14
[33] Anan 1986:26
[34] Akin/Yupin 1984:15
[35] Ibid.:14
[36] Ibid.:25
[37] Ibid.:35
[38] Akin/Yupin 1984:19
[39] Ibid.:20
[40] Akin/Yupin, 1984:17
[41] Ibid.:20
[42] Ibid.:40-41
[43] Ibid.:29
[44] Akin/Yupin 1984:17
[45] Chambers 1983:82
[46] Chambers 1983:28-46
[47] Chambers 1983:73
[48] Anan 1986:37
[49] Ibid.:39
[50] Akin/Yupin 1984:9
[51] Ibid.:38-39
[52] Akin/Yupin 1984:19

Chapter 5

[1] ACFOD 1987:8
[2] CCTD Jan.-Feb. 1982:3
[3] Likhit 1986:46-47
[4] Saneh n.d.:5
[5] Werachai 1986:26
[6] Sulak 1987-c:29
[7] Asian Conference on Credit Unions 1961:392
[8] Ibid.:387-88
[9] Ibid.:29
[10] Sulak 1987-c:29
[11] Werachai 1986:26
[12] TVS 1987:125

13 TVS 1987:70
14 Sulak 1987-c:30
15 Ibid.
16 Ibid.
17 CCTD Mar/June 1983:10
18 TVS 1987:195
19 Ibid.
20 Sulak 1987-c:30
21 Sompong 1987
22 Saneh n.d.:7
23 Werachai 1986:8
24 TURA 1985: 12.
25 TVS 1987:7-9
26 TURA 1985:12-13
27 Ibid.:17
28 Ibid.:24
29 Ibid.:24
30 Seri 1988-a:24
31 Ibid.:24.
32 TURA 1985:39-40
33 TVS 1987:9-11
34 Chamniern 1981:5-6
35 Hirsch 1986:23
36 Ibid.:24
37 Hirsch 1986:24
38 Jon 1983:2
39 Seri 1982:5
40 Ibid.:5-6
41 ACFOD 1987:10-11
42 Chambers 1983:146
43 TVS 1987:10
44 Prawase 1986:14-16
45 Ibid.:15-16
46 Ibid.:16
47 TURA 1985:34-35
48 Prawase 1986:14-16
49 Chanpen 1986:34
50 Ibid., 34.
51 Ibid.:35
52 Ibid.:36
53 Ibid.:36

54 TDN 1986-a:4
55 Ibid.:31-32
56 Ibid.:32
57 Rosana 1986:17
58 Ibid.:18
59 Ibid.:20
60 Ibid.
61 TURA 1985:26
62 Saneh n.d.:6
63 TVS 1987:9-11
64 Ibid.:9-12
65 Werachai 1986:8-9
66 Hirsch 1986:25
67 TURA 1985:26-27

Chapter 6

1 Cf. the role of the the Catholic Council of Thailand for Development [CCTD]
2 Korton 1987:6
3 Ibid.:29
4 Cf. Sheth 1987
5 Seri 1986:17
6 Ibid.:18
7 Appichart in Seri 1986:69
8 Ibid.:70
9 Colletta 1975:61
10 TVS 1987:39
11 Ibid.
12 Dembo 1988:209
13 CEBEMO 1987
14 Akin 1987:1
15 Akin 1986-b:4
16 Akin 1987:Introduction
17 Akin 1987:14-15
18 Jon, n.d.-a:18 ff.
19 TVS 1987:242-243
20 Ibid.:240
21 TVS 1980:2
22 Jon n.d.-b:25

[23] Jon 1985:4
[24] Jon 1986
[25] Cf. DPF
[26] Sompong 1983:6-7
[27] Sompong 1986
[28] Verhagen 1987:9
[29] Apichart 1988
[30] Ibid.
[31] Ibid.
[32] Ibid.
[33] Ibid.
[34] Ibid.
[35] Ibid.
[36] Chambers 1983:185
[37] Cf. Schneider 1988
[38] Seri 1988-a:28
[39] Ibid.:23-24
[40] Ibid.:25
[41] Seri 1988-b:1
[42] Ibid.:2
[43] Seri 1988-a:28-29
[44] Surachet 1986-b:2
[45] Ibid.:4
[46] Seri 1988-a:30
[47] Surachet 1986:9
[48] Seri 1987:1-3
[49] Ibid.:3
[50] Korten 1980:498
[51] Ibid:30
[52] Seri 1988-c:1-2

Chapter 7

[1] Somboon 1986:8
[2] Swearer 1986:27-29
[3] Ibid.
[4] Swearer 1986:29-33
[5] Buddhadasa in Swearer 1986: 34
[6] Ibid.:37
[7] Ibid.:38

[8] Sulak 1987-d:9
[9] Ibid.:9-10
[10] Ibid.:14-25
[11] Ibid.:25
[12] Ibid.:4
[13] Swearer 1986:23
[14] Klausner 1981:161
[15] BP 9/15/87:34
[16] BP 8/20/87
[17] in Swearer 1986:46-139
[18] BP 8/20/87
[19] Sulak 1987-d:65
[20] Ibid.:51
[21] Ibid.:52-55
[22] Ibid:5
[23] Seri 1988:1
[24] Somboon 1986:31
[25] Somboon 1976:75-76
[26] Swearer 1986:78-80
[27] Ibid.
[28] Ibid.
[29] Rajavaramuni 1987:25
[30] Swearer 1986:31
[31] Ibid 1986: 16
[32] Ibid.:20-39
[33] Ibid.:45
[34] Somboon 1976:6
[35] Ibid:43-45
[36] Ibid.:62
[37] Klausner 1981: 146
[38] Somboon 1976:3-64
[39] Ibid.:87
[40] Klausner 1981:150
[41] Somboon 1976:101
[42] Ibid.:90
[43] Ibid:91
[44] Klausner 1981:146-47
[45] Ibid.:147
[46] Klausner 1981:149
[47] Somboon 1976:63
[48] Ibid.:68-69

49   Klausner 1981:144
50   Ibid.:131
51   Ibid.:145
52   Ibid.:132
53   Ibid.:133-34
54   Somboon 1976:113-15
55   Somboon 1976:113-114
56   Ibid.:119
57   Ibid.:121.
58   Ibid.:116
59   Somboon 1986:1
60   Ibid:2
61   Ibid.:36
62   Ibid.:22-25
63   Ibid.:37
64   Ibid.:41
65   Ibid.:33
66   Ibid.:58
67   Cf. Vanpen 1986
68   Ibid.:52
69   Somboon 1986:56
70   Ibid.:61
71   Klausner 1981:152

14   Gohlert 1987-a
15   Seri 1988-d:107-110
16   Surachet 1982-c
17   Ibid.
18   Ibid.
19   Ibid.:3-5
20   Duangkamol n.d.:3
21   Ibid.:5-6
22   Gohlert 1987-b
23   Ibid.
24   Surachet 1986-a:138-139
25   Shari 1986:13
26   Surachet 1986-a:140-141
27   Ibid.:141
28   Ibid.:141
29   Ibid.:144
30   Ibid.:142, 146
31   Ibid.:144
32   Ibid.:151
33   Ibid.:153-154
34   Gohlert 1987-b
35   Esteva 1988:1

Chapter 8

1   Griffin 1988:1-12
2   Cf. Schneider 1988
3   Arendonk 1988:4
4   Ibid.:7
5   Dubhashi 1988:29-30
6   BP 12/17/87
7   Arendonk 1988:15
8   Ibid. 1988:16
9   Gohlert 1987-a
10   Ibid.
11   Gohlert 1987-a
12   Ibid.
13   The Foundation for Education and Development in Rural Areas: 1986, 1-4

REFERENCES

1. International Development and Non-Governmental Organizations (NGOs)

Alliband, Terry. *Catalysts of Development: Voluntary Agencies in India.* West Hartford, Conn.: Kumarian Press, 1983.

"An Agenda for Action," *Development Dialogue* (1987:1), pp. 88-111.

Arendonk, Joseph van. "Development For What? Or, Which Culture Are We Serving?," SID 19th World Conference, New Delhi: March 25-28, 1988, pp. 16.

Bolling, Landrum R. with Craig Smith. *Private Foreign Aid: U.S. Philanthropy for Relief and Development.* Boulder, CO: Westview Press, 1982.

Brodhead, Tim. "NGOs: In one Year, Out the Other?," *World Development* Vol. 15, Supplement (Autumn 1987), pp. 1-6.

CEBEMO, *Promotion of Autonomous Development.* Report on the Proceedings of the Experts' Consultation. Noordwijk, The Netherlands (October 27-30, 1987).

___________. "Tentative Framework for a Dialogue between Cebemo and its main Third World Partners on Sharing of Responsibilities and new Forms of Cooperation," (September 18, 1987).

Chambers, Robert. *Rural Development: Putting the Last First.* London: Longman, 1983.

Colletta, N.J. "The Use of Indigenous Culture as a Medium for Development: The Indonesian Case," *PRISMA* No. 2 (November 1975), pp. 60-73.

Dembo, David, et. al., eds. *Nothing to Lose but Our Lives: Empowerment to oppose Industrial Hazards in a Transnational World.* New York: New Horizons Press, 1988.

Drabek, Gordon A., "Development Alternatives: The Challenge for NGOs - An Overview of the Issues," *World Development* Vol. 15, Supplement (Autumn 1987), pp. ix - xv.

Dubhashi, P.R. "Development: An Overview," SID 19th World Conference, New Delhi: March 25-28, 1988, pp. 18.

Elliott, Charles. "Some Aspects of Relations Between the North and South in the NGO Sector," *World Development* Vol. 15, Supplement (Autumn 1987), pp. 57-68.

Esteva, Gustavo. "The Old Development Paradigm Now Emerging From NGOs," SID 19th World Conference, New Delhi. (March 25-28, 1988), pp. 4.

Gorman, Robert F., ed. *Private Voluntary Organizations as Agents of Development*. Boulder, CO: Westview Press, 1984.

Griffin, Keith. "Thinking About Development: The Longer View," SID 19th World Conference, New Delhi. (March 25-28, 1988), pp. 12.

Korten, David C. "Community Organization and Rural Development: A Learning Process Approach," *Public Administration Review* (September/October, 1980), pp. 480-509.

__________. "Micro-Policy Reform: The Role of Private Voluntary Development Agencies," National Association of Schools of Public Affairs and Administration (NASPAA), Working Paper No. 12, Revised August 8, 1986, pp. 1-19.

__________. "Strategic Organization for People-Centered Development," *Public Managers Forum* (July/August, 1984), pp. 341-352.

__________. "Third Generation NGO Strategies: A Key to People-Centered Development," Paper presented to NASPAA. (Aug. 21, 1987), pp. 21.

Lappe, Frances Moore. et. al. *Aid as Obstacle: Twenty Questions about Our Foreign Aid and the Hungry*. San Francisco: Institute for Food and Development Policy, 1980.

Maloney, Clarence. "Voluntary Organizations in Development in South Asia," *UFSI Reports (University Field Staff International, Inc.)*, (1987/No. 11 - Asia), pp. 1 - 10.

Minear, Larry. "Reflections on Development Policy: A View from the Private Volunteer Sector, " in Gorman, ed., *Private Voluntary Organizations as Agents of Development*, pp. 13-39.

Moshoeshoe II, His Majesty the King. "Alternative Strategies for Development - A Clarion Call!," *Development Dialogue* (1987:1), pp. 77 - 87.

Nossiter, Bernard D. *The Global Struggle for More: Third World Conflicts with Rich Nations*. New York: Harper and Row, 1987.

Nyoni, Sithembiso. "Indigenous NGOs: Liberation, Self-reliance, and Development," *World Development* Vol. 15, Supplement (Autumn 1987), pp. 51-56.

Rice, Andrew, ed. *The Role of Non-Government Organizations in Development Co-operation*. Paris: Development Centre, OECD, 1983.

Schneider, Bertrand. *The Barefoot Revolution*. London: Intermediate Technology Publications, 1988.

Sewel, John W. and Christine E. Contee, "Foreign Aid and Gramm-Rudman," *Foreign Affairs* Vol. 65, No. 5 (Summer 1987), pp. 1015-1036.

Sheth, D.L. "Alternative Development as Political Practice," *Alternatives* Vol. XII, Number 2 (April 1987), pp. 155-171.

Sivard, Ruth Leger. *World Military and Social Expenditures* 1985. Washington, D.C.: World Priorities, 1985.

Soedjatmoko in David C. Korten, ed. *Community Management: Asian Experiences and Perspectives*. West Hartford, CT.: Kumarian Press, 1986, pp. 19-31.

Sommer, John G. *Beyond Charity: U.S. Voluntary Aid for a Changing Third World*. Washington, D.C.: Overseas Development Council, 1977.

Surrendra, Lawrence. "The Role of Critical Social Science in Asia: Emerging Concerns and the Need for Regional Interaction," *China Report* 23:2 (1987), pp. 189-205.

Tendler, Judith. "Turning Private Organizations into Development Agencies: Questions for Evaluation," USAID Program Evaluation Paper No. 12, 1982.

__________. "What Ever Happened To Poverty Alleviation?," Report Prepared for the Ford Foundation, March 1987.

Tri, Huynh Cao, et. al. *Strategies for Endogenous Development*. New Delhi: Oxford and IBH Publishing Co., 1986.

UNESCO, "World Decade For Cultural Development Launched," *UNESCO News* No. 222 (25 January 1988), pp. 22.

Verhagen, Koenrad. *Self-Help Promotion: A Challenge to the NGO Community*. Amsterdam: Royal Tropical Institute, 1987.

Ward, *F.L.A. Evolving Patterns of NGO Support*. Experts' Consultation on Promotion of Autonomous Development. Noordwijk, The Netherlands. (October 27-30, 1987).

Wignaraja in David C. Korten, ed. *Community Management: Asian Experience and Perspectives*. West Hartford, CT.: Kumarian Press, 1986, pp. xv-xviii.

World Health Organization. "Housing - The Implications for Health: Report of the WHO Consultation," (Geneva, 9-15 June, 1987), pp. 1 - 29.

2. International Development and NGOs in Thailand

Adventist Development and Relief Agency (ADRA). *Interface: The Quarterly Journal of ADRA*. (Fourth Quarter, 1986).

Akin Rabibhadana. RDI Khon Kaen University. Booklet. (March 1987).

__________. et. al. *Report of a Study of CUSO Volunteers: Cultural Adaptation for Work and Living in Thailand*. (August 1986-a).

__________. *Report on October 1982–March 1986 Activities*. RDI. Khon Kaen University, 1986-b.

__________. et. al. *Report on the Process and Impact of the Net Project in Surin, Northeast Thailand*. (March 1985).

__________. *The Transformation of Tambon Yokkrabat, Changwat Samut Sakorn*. n.d..

REFERENCES

Akin Rabibhadana and Yupin Yensuwarin. *Report on the Evaluation of the Work of Redd Barna, Thailand at Khon Kaen.* (June 1984).
__________. et. al. *Development of Self-Managed Primary Health Care Villages.* Report. (December 1986).
__________. et.al. *Evaluation of the Administration [sic] and Management of the Sericulture/Settlement Project.* Report. (March 1983).
Amara Pongsapich, et.al. *Traditional and Changing Thai World Views.* Bangkok: Chulalongkorn University Social Research Institute, 1985.
Amporn Wattanavongs. Interview conducted by the Author. (April 26, 1988).
Anan Ganjanapan. *The Integrated Rural Development Project at Thung Hua Chang and Li, Pamphun Province/Thailand—An Evaluation Report.* (August 1986).
Apichart Tongyou. Interview conducted by the author. (February 17, 1988).

Apichart Tongyou. "Reflections of a Village Development Worker," in David C. Korten, ed., *Community Management.* West Hartford, Conn.: Kumarian Press, 1986, pp. 40-45.
__________. "Village: Autonomous Society," in Seri Phongphit, ed., *Back to the Roots: Village and Self-Reliance in a Thai Context.* Bangkok: RUDOC and VIP, Publishers, 1986, pp.45-87.
Asian Conference of Credit Unions. *A Glimpse into the Asian Credit Union Movement: A Compilation of the Histories of Credit Unions in Six Asian Countries.* Seoul: 1961.
Asian Cultural Forum on Development (ACFOD). *Dependence or Self-Reliance? Alternatives to Grants for Asian NGOs.* Bangkok: ACFOD, 1987.
Bangkok Post, Cimi Suchontan. "A Whiff of Good Thai Fortune Down on the Farm," (December 12, 1987).
__________, "Bank Says Income Gap is Widening," (May 6, 1988), p. 28.
__________, Suporn Pornsrisuk. "Chamlong Warns Youth on the Evil of Selfishness," (October 26, 1987).
__________, "Close Ties with U.S. Affected by Export Rise," (December 2, 1987).
__________, "Dark Inheritance," (December 22, 1987).
__________, "Educating Rural Residents in the Methods of Kitchen Sanitation," (June 25, 1987).
__________, "Expert: Lift Human Resources Standards," (June 17, 1987).
__________, "Expert Sees Need to Develop Exports More," (November 18, 1987), p. 17.
__________, "Finding a New Dimension of Culture in Ourselves," (August 20, 1987).

__________. Sumitr Hemasathol, "Giving Power Back to the People," (November 1, 1987), p. 14.

__________, "Helping Farmers Help Themselves," (November 18, 1987), p. 6.

__________, "'Hunger Remains` in ESCAP Region," (November 24, 1987).

__________, Franz G. Heim, "Implications of Snoh's Rural Development Policy," (April 3, 1987).

__________, "New Economic Thinking Should Draw on Buddhism," (September 15, 1987).

__________, Suporn Pornsrisuk "Noppachak Project for the Development of Rural Youth," (December 15, 1987), p. 33.

__________, "Panelist Says Premier Has Failed in Fiscal Policies," (April 5, 1988), 3.

__________, "Prem and the Peasants," (April 8, 1988).

__________, "Prem: Govt. to Maintain Growth of Economy," (October 29, 1987).

__________, "Small Farmers: The Backbone of Asia and Pacific," (October 9, 1987).

__________, "So Much More than a Paddy Field," (November 6, 1987), p. 4.

__________, "Thailand Finds Own Path to Export Growth," (November 11, 1987).

Bangkok Post, Likhit Dhiravegin, "The House is here to Stay," (January 21, 1988).

__________, "UN Advisor: Thai Economy Strong," (November 11, 1987).

__________, "UNICEF Continues Aid for Slum Improvement," (March 25, 1987).

__________, "What Price Progress?" (December 17, 1987).

__________, "Where's the Spirit of Cooperation?," (April 1987).

__________, "World Bank Staffer Says Beneficiaries Know Best," (October 3, 1987).

Bong Wright, Victor. "Spreading the Word: A One-man Development Organization," *RUDOC News* Vol. 2, No. 2 (Jan. - Mar., 1987), pp. 22-24.

Calavan, Michael M. "Community Management in Rural Northeastern Thailand," in David C. Korten, ed., *Community Management.* West Hartford, Conn.: Kumarian Press, 1986, pp. 93-104.

Canadian Embassy. *Canadian Embassy Mission Administered Fund Program: General Information.* n.d..

Canadian International Development Agency. Country Profile Thailand. Information sheet. (August 1982).

__________. *ASEAN–Canada Development Cooperation Program: An Endeavor in North/South–South/South–South Cooperation* . n.d..

__________. *1983-84 Annual Report.* (December 1984).

REFERENCES

__________. *List of Projects Funded by Local Development Assistance Program FY 1984-85/85-86/86-87/87-88/88-89*. (Appendix 3).

CEBEMO, "Tentative Framework for a Dialogue between CEBEMO and its main Third World Partners on Sharing of Responsibilities and new Forms of Cooperation." Unpublished Report. (September 18, 1987), pp. 14.

CCTD NEWSLETTER, "Interview with Mr. Chalad Buranaphol: 'We have not seriously implemented a development project to its full meaning,'" CCTD NEWSLETTER (Nov. - Dec., 1982).

__________, "Thai Cultures and Rural Development Work," *CCTD Newsletter* (Jan. - Feb., 1982), pp. 2-4.

__________, "Thai Development Support Conference will be held in Bangkok," *CCTD Newsletter* (Mar. - Jun., 1983).

__________, "Urbanization for Whom," (Editorial) *CCTD Newsletter* (Sept. - Oct., 1982), p. 1.

Chakrit Noranitipadungkarn. *Social Development Planning in Thailand with Particular Reference to Local Level Planning*. Bangkok: National Institute of Development Administration (NIDA), Paper Series in Social Development, No. 3, 1984.

Chalad Buranaphol, "Rice Bank Project," *Samgkom Patana* (*Social Development*), (Dec., 1980).

Chamniern Voraratchaiyaphan, "What, Why, and for Whom are We Developing," (Interview) *Social Development* (Oct., 1981).

Chanpen Wiwat, et.al., "Primary Health Care and the People in Thailand," *Thai Development Newsletter* Vol. 4, No. 2, 1986, pp. 33-36.

Chartchai Na Chiangmai. *Social Change, Social Networks, and Political Behavior*. Bangkok: National Institute of Development Administration (NIDA), Paper Series in Social Development, No. 7, 1984.

Christian Childrens' Fund. How CCF Helps Children around the World. Brochure. (1984-1985).

Committee for Coordination of Services to Displaced Persons in Thailand (CCSDPT). The CCSDPT Handbook: Refuge Services in Thailand, (1986 edition).

Community Development Department. Ministry of the Interior. *Introducing Community Development Center, Region 3*. Brochure. n.d..

Duangkamol Chansuriyawong. "Thai Farmers: Don't want to be Farmers," *Alternative World*, Vol. 4, No. 1, 1987, pp. 2-4.

__________. "The Ayurawet College and Borvonivej Traditional Medicine Hospital: The Hope of Thai Traditional Medicine," *Alternative World*, Vol. 2, No. 3 (September 1985), pp. 6-10.

__________. "Thod Pha Pa: A Buddhist Approach to Development Work." n.d.

Duang Prateep Foundation (DPF). *The Duang Prateep Foundation Working for the Children of the Bangkok Slums*. Brochure. n.d., pp. 1-12.

Ead Dee-poon. "Cooperation of NGOs in Southern Southeast," *RUDOC News* Vol.1, No. 2 (Oct. - Dec., 1986), pp. 10-12.

Fieg, John Paul. *Guidelines for Thais and North Americans*. Yarmouth, Maine: Intercultural Press, Inc., 1980.

Forum for Integrated Agricultural Management (FIAM): Annual Report. 1986.

Friedrich Naumann Stiftung. *Friedrich Naumann Foundation in Thailand*. Booklet. n.d..

__________. *Integrated Rural Development Project, Northern Region Agricultural Development Center (NADC): Friedrich Naumann (FNS)*. n.d..

Gohlert, Ernst W. "Alternative Development: The Role of Indigenous Private Voluntary Organizations in Indonesia and Thailand." Manuscript. (January 1988), pp. 28.

__________. Field Data: Ubol - Yasothon, October 6-12, 1986-a.

__________. Field Data: Chiangmai - Mae Chaem, December 2 -7, 1986-b.

__________. Field Data: Chiangmai, March 29 - April 5, 1987-a.

__________. Field Data: Huey Hin, Chachoengsao (Vibul), July 16, 1987-b.

__________. Field Data: Khon Kaen, March 14 - 19, 1987-c.

__________, ed. "Grass Roots Economics for Rice Farmers: NGO-CORD Training Workshop 13-17 November, 1986," *RUDOC News*, Vol. 2, No. 2-3 (April-Sept., 1987-d), pp. 4-13.

__________."Partners in Development: The Role of Non-Governmental Organizations in Thailand's Aid Community," *Scandinavian Journal of Development Alternatives*, Vol. V, No. 4 (December 1986), pp. 95-108.

__________. "'Strategic Organizations` - Development Agencies of the Future," *Scandinavian Journal of Development Alternatives*, Vol. VI, No. 4 (Dec. 1987), pp. 108-121 and *RUDOC News*, Vol. 2, No. 4 (Oct.-Dec., 1987), pp. 1-3.

Girling, John L. S. *Thailand: Society and Politics*. Ithaca, NY: Cornell University Press, 1981.

Grandstaff, Terry B. and Somluckrat W. Grandstaff, "Choice of Rice Technology - A Farmer Perspective," in David C. Korten, ed., *Community Management*. West Hartford, CT.: Kumarian Press, 1986, pp. 51-61.

Heim, Franz G. et. al.. *How to Develop the Small Farming Sector: The Case of Thailand*. Bangkok: Thammasat University, 1986.

__________. "The Structure of Thai Society and the Problems of the Farmers," n.d., pp. 6-29.

REFERENCES

Hirsch, Philip. "Which Route to Rural Prosperity?", *Inside Asia* (April-May 1986), pp. 23-25.

Jacobs, Norman. *Modernization Without Development: Thailand as a Case Study*. New York: Praeger Publishers, 1971.

Jewson, Ruth H. Report of Trip to Thailand. CCF Memorandum. (October 16, 1984).

Jon Ungphakorn. "A Summary of the Situation and Problems of Thai Development NGOs," (Paper presented to the Thai Development Support Conference) n.d.-a, pp. 18-21.

__________. "A View: The Co-Operation between the Government and NGOs in Development," n.d.-b, pp. 24-25.

__________. Interview conducted by the Author. (August 19, 1986).

__________. "Non-Government Organization and Thai Development," *CCTD Newsletter* (Mar. - Jun., 1983), pp. 1-4.

__________."The Role of the Private Sector in regard to the Problem of Poverty in Rural Areas." Unpublished Paper (August 1985).

Keyes, Charles F. *Thailand: Buddhist Kingdom as Modern Nation State*. Bangkok: Editions Duang Karmol, 1989.

Khien Theeravit, et.al. *Research Report on Danish, German, and Japanese Assistance to Agricultural Development in Thailand: A Comparative Study*. Bangkok, Thailand: Institute of Asian Studies, Chulalonkorn University, (January, 1984).

Klausner, William J. *Reflections on Thai Culture*. Bangkok: Suksit Siam, 1981.

Komson Hutapaed, "The Second Meeting of Non-Government Organizations," *CCTD Newsletter* (Mar. - Jun., 1983), pp. 4-6.

Likhit Dhiravegin. *Political Attitudes of the Bureaucratic Elite and Modernization in Thailand*. 1972.

__________. *The Bureaucratic Elite of Thailand: A Study of their Sociological Attributes, Educational Background and Career Advancement Pattern*. Bangkok: Thai Khadi Research Institute, Thammasat University, 1978.

__________. *Nationalism and the State in Thailand*. Bangkok: Krirk College, Monograph Series No. 1, 1985.

Likhit Dhiravegin. *The Postwar Thai Politics*. Bangkok: The Research Center, Faculty of Political Science, Thammasat University, Monograph Series No. 11, 1986.

Maier, Joseph. Interview conducted by the Author. (September 30 and October 14, 1986).

"Man must be treated as Man," *CCTD Newsletter* (Mar. - Apr., 1982), pp. 1-6.

Maniemai Tongsawate and Walter E. J. Tips. *Cooperation between Governmental and Non-Government Organizations in Thailand's Rural*

Development. Bangkok: Asian Institute of Technology (AIT), Division of Human Settlements Development, 1985.

__________ and Ngaosilp Kongkaew. *Directory of Development NGOs in Northeast Thailand.* Draft. (October 1986).

Morrell, David and Chai-anan Samudavanija. *Political Conflict in Thailand.* Cambridge, MA.: Oelgeschlager, Gunn & Hain, Publishers, Inc., 1981.

Murray, Charles A. *A Behavioral Study of Rural Modernization: Social and Economic Changes in Thai Villages.* New York: Praeger, 1977.

National Statistical Office. Office of the Prime Minister. *Statistical Handbook of Thailand 1986-1987.* Bangkok: 1987.

Nivat Chimpalee. "Thai Social Structure and Rural Development (Extract), *CCTD Newsletter* (Jan.- Apr., 1981).

Nitya Pubbakasikor. *CARE International in Thailand: Mission History Report 1979-86.* (October 1986).

Paisan Wisalo (Phra), "One Day in the Life of a Monk," *Thai Development Newsletter* Vol. 5, No. 14, 1987, pp. 18 - 19.

Pasuk Phongpaichit. *From Peasant Girls to Bangkok Masseuses.* Geneva: International Labour Office, 1982.

Phrakru Mongkol Silawong Chaiaman. *The Life of the Buddha and His Teachings.* (Booklet, April 1985).

Pira Sudham. *Siamese Drama and other Stories from Thailand.* Bangkok: Siam Media International Books, 1983.

__________. *People of Esarn.* Bangkok: Siam Media International Books, 1987.

Porter, Doug and Kevin Clark. *Questioning Practice: Non-Government Aid Agencies and project evaluation.* Canberra, Australia: Australian Council for Overseas Aid, 1985.

Prawase Wasi. "Primary Health Care as a Means for Human Emancipation," *Thai Development Newsletter* Vol. 4, No. 2, 1986, pp. 14-16.

Prizzia, Ross. *Thailand in Transition: The Role of Oppositional Forces.* Honolulu: University of Hawaii Press, 1985.

Rajavaramuni (Phra). Translated by Grant A. Olson. *Looking to America to Solve Thailand's Problems.* Bangkok: Sathirakoses Nagapradipa Foundation, 1987.

__________. *Thai Buddhism in the Buddhist World.* Bangkok: Mahachulalongkorn Buddhist University, 1984.

Ravadi Chaipan. "A Discussion on Data Management, Follow-up and Evaluation of Rural Development Project," *RUDOC News* Vol. 2, No. 2 (Jan. - Mar., 1987), pp. 17-21.

Redd Barna/Thailand. *Annual Report 1985.* (1986).

__________. *Annual Report 1986* (1987).

__________. *Annual Report 1987* (1988).

REFERENCES

Rosana Tositrakul. "Primary Health Care and Cultural Movement: A Case Study of the Traditional Medicine in Self-Curing Project [sic], THAI DEVELOPMENT NEWSLETTER Vol. 4, No. 2 (1986), pp. 17-20.

Ruang Sooksawasdi. "Experiences and Lessons learned in Development Work, *RUDOC News* Vol. 1, No. 2 (Oct. Dec., 1986), pp. 5-9.

RUDOC News, "Interview with Mr. Niyom Jittradit: 'Can Farmer Groups really help Farmers?,'" *RUDOC News* Vol. 2, No. 1 (Jan.-Mar., 1987), pp. 3-8.

__________, "Interview with Mr. Chalerm Srikamkae: 'I will do it small and use my own labor,'" *RUDOC News*, Vol. 2, No. 2-3 (April-Sept., 1987), pp. 13-15.

__________, "Interview with Mr. Chit Supa: 'We will continue doing and living like this until we die after debts,'" *RUDOC News*, Vol. 2, No. 2-3 (April-Sept., 1987), pp. 15-18.

__________, "Interview with Mr. Wong Thongmee: 'I do not place much hope on the government anymore,'" *RUDOC News*, Vol. 2, No. 2-3 (April - Sept., 1987), pp. 19-27.

__________, "Interview with Saitarn Intrawong (NGO Worker): 'It's the task of the government to be responsible for the debts of the farmers,'" *RUDOC News*, Vol. 2, Nos. 2-3 (April Sept., 1987), pp. 28 - 34.

Saneh Chamarik. "Roles of Private Grant-Making Foundations: A Thai View." Essay n.d., pp. 5-8.

Saneh Ratchinda. Interview conducted by the author. (October 20, 1986.)

Sanguern Nittayaramphong. "The Co-Operation between Governmental and Non-Governmental Organizations," *Thai Development Newsletter* Vol. 4, No. 2, 1986, pp. 31-32.

Sarote Roskunpanit and E.C. Waters II. *Project Proposal: Mae Chaem Agroforestry FY85 - FY86.* (January 1986).

Scale, Warren. *Moei River Health Project.* Grant Proposal. 1985.

Seri Phongphit. "Another Way of Thai-Japanese Relations," ALTERNATIVE WORLD, Vol. 2, No. 3 (September 1985), pp. 2-5.

__________. *A Way to Development Professionalism.* Bangkok: Thai Institute for Rural Development (THIRD), 1988-a.

__________, ed. *Back to the Roots: Village and Self-Reliance in a Thai Context.* Bangkok: RUDOC and VIP, Publishers, 1986, pp. 13-21.

__________. "Dialogue and Development: A Buddhist-Christian Search for Alternative Model of Development in Thailand," *CCTD Newsletter*, No. 4 (Jul.- - Aug., 1985), pp. 1-8.

__________. "CCTD on the Way to Development," *CCTD Newsletter*(Jan. - Feb., 1983), pp. 1-6.

__________. "Financial Assistance for Rural Development in a Thai Context." Unpublished Paper. 1988-b, pp. 12.

Seri Phongphit. *Partnership for a Decentralized Development and Investment (PADDI).* Bangkok: Thai Institute for Rural Development (THIRD), 1988-c.

__________. "People-Centered Development." Unpublished Paper. 1987, pp. 5.

__________. *Religion in a Changing Society: Buddhism, Reform and the Role of Monks in Community Development in Thailand.* Hongkong: ARENA Press, 1988-d.

__________. "The Quest for Self-Reliance of Thai NGOs," *RUDOC News* Vol. 1, No. 2 (Oct. - Dec., 1986), pp. 1-3.

Shari, Michael. "The Medicine Man of Chachoengsao," *RUDOC News* Vol. 1, No. 2 (Oct. - Dec., 1986), pp. 13-15.

Siffin, William J. *The Thai Bureaucracy: Institutional Change and Development.* Westport, Conn.: Greenwood Press, 1966.

Sippanondha Ketudat. "Existing Relationships between Universities and Government Planning Agencies in Thailand," in Yip Yat Hoong, ed., *Role of the Universities in National Development Planning in Southeast Asia: Proceedings of the Workshop Held in Singapore, 26 - 29 July, 1971.* Singapore: Regional Institute of Higher Education and Development, 1971.

Snit Smuckarn. *Socio-Economic Conditions of Northeastern Thai Villages in Relation to Irrigation Development.* Bangkok: National Institute of Development Administration (NIDA), Paper Series in Social Development, No. 4, 1985.

Social Development, "What's Development?," in *Social Development* (Dec., 1980).

Soedjatmoko, "Political Systems and Development: Reflections on an Asian Research," PRISMA No. 19 (Dec. 1980), pp. 25-38.

Somboon Suksamran. *Political Buddhism in Southeast Asia: The Role of the Sangha in the Modernization of Thailand.* New York: St. Martin's Press, 1976.

__________. *A Buddhist Approach to Development: The Case of Development Monks in Thailand.* Unpublished Report. Bangkok. (April 1986).

Somjai Sirikanokvilai. "Primary Health Care and Community Participation: A Case Study of Noan Kui Village," *Thai Development Newsletter* Vol. 4, No. 2, 1986, pp. 21-26.

Sompong Patpui. Interview conducted by the Author. (December 12, 1986.)

__________. *Slum Development in Bangkok.* Booklet. Bangkok: DPF, 1983, pp.8.

Somsakdi Xuto. *In Retrospect: Views and Comments from Selected Writings.* Bangkok: Social Science Association of Thailand, 1982.

REFERENCES

__________, et. al. *Thailand in the 1980's: Significant Issues, Problems and Prospects*. Bangkok: TURA Institute, 1981.

__________. *Strategies and Measures for the Development of Thailand in the 1980's*. Bangkok: TURA Institute, 1983.

Sopon Pornchokchai. "The Urban Poor Amidst the Change of Bangkok," *CCTD Newsletter* (Sept. - Oct., 1982), pp. 2-5.

Suchart Prasith-rathsint, ed. *Thailand's National Development: Policy and Challenges*. Bangkok: TURA, 1987.

Sulak Sivaraksa. *A Buddhist Vision for Renewing Society* . Bangkok: Tienwan Publishing House, Prt., Ltd., 1986.

__________. "Buddhism and the Socio-Political Setting for the Future Benefit of Mankind," Pridi Banomyong Institute, Occasional Papers, 1987-a, pp. 11.

__________. "Development for Peace," Pridi Banomyong Institute, Occasional Papers, 1987-b, pp. 16.

__________. "Non-Governmental Organizations (NGOs) Involved in Culture and Religion," *Thai Development Newsletter*. 3rd. Quarter, No. 14 (1987-c), pp. 29-33.

__________. *Religion and Development*. Bangkok: Thai Inter- Religious Commission for Development, 1987-d.

__________. "Science, Technology and Spiritual Values: A South-East Asian Approach to Modernization," Pridi Banomyong Institute, Occasional Papers, 1987, pp. 7.

__________. *Siamese Resurgence*. Bangkok: Asian Cultural Forum on Development, 1985.

Surachet Vetchapitak in Seri Phongphit, ed. *Back to the Roots: Village and Self-Reliance in a Thai Context*. Bangkok: RUDOC and VIP, Publishers, 1986-a, pp. 131-154.

__________. "Documentation and Rural Development," *RUDOC News* Vol. 1, No. 1 (Jul - Sept., 1986-b), pp. 1-5.

__________. "Farmer Crisis," *RUDOC News* Vol.2, No. 1 (Jan. - Mar., 1987-a), pp. 1-2.

__________. *Progress Report:* February - December 1986-c. Document. pp. 9.

__________. "Resources and Potential in Development," pp. 22-25.

__________. "Struggle for Survival: Farmers, Debt and NGOs," *RUDOC News* . Vol. 2, No. 2-3 (April-September, 1987-b), pp. 1-3.

__________. "Thai Cultures and Rural Development Work," *CCTD Newsletter* (Jan.-Feb., 1982-a), pp. 1-4.

__________. "Thailand Development Policy," *CCTD Newsletter* (Jan.-Feb., 1985), pp. 2-10.

__________. "The Meeting of the Non-Governmental Organizations," *CCTD Newsletter* (Jan. - Feb., 1982-b), pp. 4-8.

__________. "Wat and Community Development," *CCTD Newsletter* (May-June, 1982-c), pp. 1-6.

Surapol Kanchananchitra, et.al. *The Evaluation Report of the Child and Family Development Project, C.C.F.* (October 1986).

Swearer, Donald K., translt. and ed. Bhikkhu Buddhadasa. *Dhammic Socialism.* Bangkok: Thai Inter-Religious Commission for Development, 1986.

Textor, Robert B. et.al.. *Alternative Sociocultural Futures for Thailand: A Pilot Inquiry Among Academics.* Chiang Mai, Thailand: Chiang Mai University, Faculty of the Social Sciences, 1984.

Thai Development Newsletter, "A Buddhist Road to Development," Vol. 5, No. 14, 1987, pp. 11-13.

Thai Development Newsletter, "Back to Culture and Religion?," Vol. 5, No. 14, 1987, p. 3.

__________, "Back to the Communal Culture: A Solution to the Rural Problems?," Vol. 5, No. 14, 1987, pp. 6-10.

__________, "Briefly Quoted," Vol. 5, No 14, 1987, p. 14.

__________, "Development Work in Muslim Communities," Vol. 5, No. 14, 1987, pp. 42-44.

__________, "Here comes the age of NGOs!", Vol. 4, No. 2, 1986-a, p. 40.

__________, "Introduction to Primary Health Care Issue," Vol. 4, No. 2, 1986-b, pp. 3-4, 31-32.

__________, "NGOs' Campaign Work in a Nutshell," Vol. 5, No. 14, 1987, pp. 41-42.

__________, "NGOs' Help: Better late than never," Vol. 5, No. 14, 1987, pp. 37-39.

__________, "Non Governmental Organizations (NGOs) involved in Culture and Religion," Vol. 5, No. 14, 1987, pp. 29-33.

__________, "Sign of the the Times," Vol. 5, No. 14, 1987, p. 5.

__________, "Tourism Earned 37,321 Million Baht in 1986," Vol. 5, No. 14, 1987, p. 5.

Thai Institute for Rural Development (THIRD). Project Synopsis. 1987, p.5.

__________. *A Way to Development Professionalism: A Concept Paper.* Bangkok: Thai Institute For Rural Development (THIRD), March 1988.

Thai Khadi Research Institute (Thammasat University). Booklet. n.d..

Thailand Development Research Institute (TDRI). *1987 Annual Report.* Booklet.

Thai University Research Association (TURA). *Seminar: Rural Development in Thailand.* Booklet. (October 1985).

REFERENCES

Thai Volunteer Service. *Directory of Non-Government Development Organizations in Thailand 1987*. Bangkok: Information Service Section, TVS, 1987.

__________. Internal Document. April 1980. p. 7.

__________. *Introduction to Thai Volunteer Services*. n.d.

Thaworn Pithirajo. "Villagers' Debt: Case Study of Ban Koo Rang Village," *RUDOC News* Vol. 2, No. 2-3 (April-Sept. 1987), pp. 35-43.

The Asia Foundation. *Annual Report 1985*. San Francisco, CA, 1986.

The Foundation for Education and Development in Rural Areas. *Principles and Administration*. (Report, October 1986).

Thorbek, Suzanne. *Voices from the City: Women of Bangkok*. London: Zed Books, Ltd., 1987.

Tin Prachyapruit. *Thailand's Elite Civil Servants and their Development-Orientedness: An Empirical Test of National Data*. Bangkok: Chulalongkorn University Social Research Institute. n.d.

United Nations Economic and Social Commission for Asia and the Pacific (ESCAP). *Human Resources Development: Its Technological Dimensions*. (March 1986).

Van Beek, Steve, ed. *Kukrit Pramoj: His Wit and Wisdom – Writings, Speeches and Interviews*. Bangkok: Editions Duang Kamol, 1983. Bangkok: Chareon Wit Press Co., Ltd. 1986.

Vanpen Surarerks. *Thai Governmental Rural Development Programs*. Vathit Chansuriyawong. "History and Government Role in developing Tourism in Thailand," *Alternative World*, Vol. 4, No. 1 (April 1987), pp. 15-21.

Virabongse Ramangkura . "Prospects for Thai Economic Development," Paper presented at the TDRI Year-End Conference, November 28-29, 1987 (Regent Cha-Am Beach Hotel, Thailand). Summary report for discussion at the TURA-sponsored meeting, December 21, 1987 (Imperial Hotel, Bangkok), under the title of "The Thai Political Economy is going beautiful in 1988?".

"Voluntary Associations and People's Participation in Development: Report on a Southeast Asian Colloquium," *PRISMA* No. 16 (March 1980), pp. 3-10.

Werachai Narkwiboonwong and Walter E.J.Tips. *Project Identification, Formulation and Start-Up by Non-Government Organizations in Thailand*. Bangkok, Thailand: Asian Institute of Technology, 1986.

White, Louise G. et.al. "Mid-Term Evaluation of the PVO Co-Financing II Project," (493-0342) (June 15, 1987), pp. 122.

Wichit Srisa-an. *Innovations in Higher Education in Education for Development in Thailand*. Singapore: Maruzen Investment, 1982.

World Concern. *New Directions*. Booklet. n.d.

INDEX

INDEX

INDEX

White Lotus Books on Asian Art & Culture

Baker, D. K., *Designs of Bhutan*
Brown, J. M., *From Ancient Thai to Modern Dialects*
Cheesman, P., *Lao Textiles*
Clifford, Hugh, *Further India*
Gervaise, Nicolas, *The Natural and Political History of the Kingdom of Siam*
Fujiwara, Hiroshi, *Khmer Ceramics from the Kamratan Collection*
Gohlert, E., *Power and Culture*
Hallet, H. S., *A Thousand Miles on an Elephant in the Shan States*
Heinze, Ruth-Inge, *Trance and Healing in Southeast Asia Today*
Hesse-Wartegg, E. von, *Siam: Das Reich des Weissen Elefanten*
Htin Aung, *Folk Elements in Burmese Buddhism*
Hutchinson, E. W., *1688 Revolution in Siam*
Itoi, Kenji, *Thai Ceramics from the Sosai Collection*
Labbé, A. J., *Ban Chiang: Art & Prehistory of Northeast Thailand*
La Loubère, De, *A New Historical Relation of The Kingdom of Siam*
Le May, R., *An Asian Arcady*
Lemoine, J., *Yao Ceremonial Paintings*
Lintner, Bertil, *The Land of Jade*
Lintner, Bertil, *Outrage*
MacMakin, Patrick D., *A Field Guide to the Flowering Plants of Thailand*
McKinnon, John, *Hilltribes Today*
Moore, Christopher G., *Enemies of Memory*
Mottin, J., *Allons Faire le Tour du Ciel et de la Terre*
Mouhot, H., *Travels in Indo-China: Siam, Cambodia, Laos*
Neale, F. A., *Narrative of a Residence in Siam*
O'Connor, V. C. Scott, *Mandalay and Other Cities of the Past in Burma*
Ray, Nihar-Ranjan, *Sanskrit, Buddhism in Burma*
Saung, Aye, *Burman in the Back Row*
Sommerville, M., *Siam on the Meinam: From the Gulf to Ayuthaya*
Subhadradis Diskul, M. C., *Hindu Gods of Sukhodaya*
Taik, Aung Aung, *Visions of Shwedagon*
Vincent, Frank, *The Land of the White Elephant: Sights and Scenes in Southeast Asia 1871-1872*

Other Books Available from White Lotus

Adhyatman, S., and Abu Ridho, *Martavans in Indonesia*
Adhyatman, S., *Burmese Ceramics: White Kendi*
Adhyatman, Sumarah, *Kendi*
Braun, R. and L. *Opium Weights*
Briggs, Lawrence Palmer, *The Ancient Khmer Empire*
Brummelhuis, *Merchant, Courtier and Diplomat   A History of the Contacts
    Between the Netherlands and Thailand*
Kartomi, Margaret J., *Musical Instruments of Indonesia*
Piriya Krairiksh, *Khmer Bronzes*
Piriya Krairiksh, *Sculptures From Thailand*
Stock, Diana, *Khmer Ceramics 9th-14th Century*

WHITE LOTUS CO., LTD.
GPO 1141
26 Soi Attakarn Prasit
Bangkok, Thailand 10501
Fax-Tel (662) 213-1175, Tel 286-1100

*Specialists in scholarly books on Asia
rare books, maps, and prints*